CHICAGO PUBLIC LIBRARY
BUSINESS / SCIENCE / TECHNOLOGY
400 S. STATE ST.   60605

D1252123

HC
427.92
.C4654
1994   China's quiet
                     revolution.

$49.95

DATE			

BAKER & TAYLOR BOOKS

China's Quiet Revolution

Studies in Contemporary Asia
Asia Research Centre
on Social, Political and Economic Change

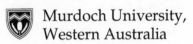 Murdoch University,
Western Australia

China's Quiet Revolution

New Interactions Between State and Society

Edited by
David S.G. Goodman and
Beverley Hooper   1994

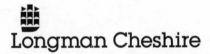

Longman Cheshire

St. Martin's Press
New York

Longman Cheshire Pty Limited
Longman House
Kings Gardens
95 Coventry Street
Melbourne 3205 Australia

Offices in Sydney, Brisbane, Adelaide and Perth and associated companies and
representatives throughout the world.

Copyright © Longman Cheshire 1994
First published 1994

All rights reserved. Except under the conditions described in the Copyright Act 1968 of
Australia and subsequent amendments, no part of this publication may be reproduced,
stored in a retrieval system or transmitted in any form or by any means, electronic,
mechanical, photocopying, recording or otherwise, without the prior permission of the
copyright owner.

Edited by Louisa Ring Rolfe
Produced by Longman Cheshire Pty Ltd
Set in Palatino 10/12
Printed in Singapore

National Library of Australia
Cataloguing-in-Publication data

China's quiet revolution.

   Includes index.

   ISBN 0 582 80164 8.

   1. China - Politics and government - 1976- . 2. China - Social
conditions - 1976- . 3. China - Economic conditions - 1976-
I. Goodman, David S.G., 1948- . II. Hooper, Beverley, 1940-
(Series: Studies in contemporary Asia).

320.951

Library of Congress Cataloging-in-Publication Data

China's quiet revolution / edited by David S.G. Goodman and Beverley Hooper.
   p. cm.
   Includes Index.

   ISBN 0 312 10251 8

   1. China - Economic conditions - 1976- 2. China - Social
conditions - 1976- 3. China - Politics and government - 1976-
I. Goodman, David S.G. II. Hooper, Beverley
HC427.92.C4654 1994

338.951--dc20

First published in the United States of America 1994 by
Scholarly and Reference Division,
ST. MARTIN'S PRESS, INC.,
175 Fifth Avenue,
New York, N.Y. 10010

The
publisher's
policy is to use
paper manufactured
from sustainable forests

Contents

R00966 89193

CHICAGO PUBLIC LIBRARY
BUSINESS / SCIENCE / TECHNOLOGY
400 S. STATE ST.   60605

List of contributors

Anita Chan is an Australian Research Council fellow currently hosted by the China Centre at the Australian National University. She is the author of *Children of Mao* (University of Washington Press) and joint author of *Chen Village Under Mao and Deng* (University of California Press), as well as editor of *The Australian Journal of Chinese Affairs* and *Chinese Sociology and Anthropology*.

David S. G. Goodman is director of the Asia Research Centre on Social, Political and Economic Change at Murdoch University in Perth. His recent books include *Deng Xiaoping* (Cardinal) and *Southern China in Transition* (Australian Government Printing Service).

Hans Hendrischke is executive director of the Centre for Chinese Political Economy at Macquarie University in Sydney. He is the editor of *Access China* and has published a number of articles on Chinese economic matters.

Beverley Hooper is director of the Centre for Asian Studies at the University of Western Australia. Her publications include *Youth in China* (Penguin) and *China Stands Up: Ending the Western Presence, 1948–1950* (Allen & Unwin).

Daniel Kane is senior lecturer in Chinese at the University of Melbourne. He is the author of a number of publications on Chinese culture and is currently completing an ARC funded project on intellectuals in contemporary China.

David Kelly is a senior research fellow in the Contemporary China Centre at the Australian National University. He is joint author, with Bill Brugger, of *Chinese Marxism in the Post-Mao Era* (Stanford University Press).

Ann Kent is with the Department of International Relations at the Australian National University. She is the author of *Between Freedom and Subsistence: China and Human Rights* (Oxford University Press).

Guonan Ma is a research fellow in economics at the Australian National University. He is joint author, with Ross Garnaut, of *Grain in China* (Australian Government Printing Service).

Jean C. Oi is associate professor of government at Harvard University. She is the author of *State and Peasant in Contemporary China* (University of California Press).

Jonathan Unger, a sociologist, is head of the Contemporary China Centre at the Australian National University. His books include *Education Under Mao* (Columbia University Press) and, with Anita Chan and Richard Madsen, *Chen Village Under Mao and Deng* (University of California Press).

Andrew G. Walder is professor of sociology at Harvard University. He is the author of *Chinese Neo-traditionalism: Work and Authority in Chinese Industry* (University of California Press).

Gordon White is a professorial fellow at the Institute of Development Studies at the University of Sussex. He is the editor of *The Chinese State in the Era of Economic Reform* (Macmillan) and author of numerous works on the Chinese economy and politics.

Gu Xin was formerly a research fellow of the Institute for the History of Science at the Academy of Science, Beijing, and is now writing a doctoral dissertation on modern Chinese intellectual history at the Sinologisch Instituut in Leiden. His most recent publication is *Zhongguo Qimeng de Lishi Tujing* (The Historical Prospects of the Chinese Enlightenment), Hong Kong, Oxford University Press, 1992.

Susan Young teaches in the Centre for Asian Studies at the University of Adelaide. Her major writings have been on the development of the private economy in post-Mao China.

List of tables and figures

Introduction:
The political economy of change

David S. G. Goodman

The revolutionary upheavals that have transformed East and increasingly Southeast Asia during the last thirty years stand in great contrast to earlier understandings of the concept of revolution. Previously, greater emphasis was placed on the violent nature of change and the removal of governments or regimes, though, to be sure, fundamental socio-economic transformation was often entailed. Since 1960 the emphasis in modernization has appeared to place economic factors ahead of political change.

With more than a touch of historical irony, the Chinese Communist Party (CCP) appears to have presided over a more considerable, and quieter, social and economic revolution during the era of reform which started at the end of 1978 than in the preceding forty years of its rule. In 1992, China was the fourth largest aggregate economy in the world, and even when measured in terms of Gross Domestic Product (GDP) per capita has long since ceased to be a low-income undeveloped economy (Garnaut & Ma 1992). Unlike any other socialist, or even post-socialist economy, the state sector's share of the economy has been so reduced that in terms of industrial output, for example, the command economy is now only responsible for about half. Exports and savings are high, public sector expenditure low.

Equally as profound, social change has accompanied the economic revolution of the reform era. The development of rural industry has turned many peasants into various kinds of proletariat, created new categories of migrant workers and substantially affected life in suburban China. New professions and types of occupation have emerged or attracted renewed respectability in the wake of reform. Lawyers, accountants and stockbrokers are for the most part no longer regarded as parasites of capitalism. As throughout East and Southeast Asia, categories of new rich have appeared (Goodman 1992).

However, it is far from clear that the political economy of change in China is identical or even similar to developments elsewhere in East and Southeast Asia. Nor for that matter must the emergence of new social forces in China have either dramatic or even predictable consequences. The political future of the People's Republic of China (PRC), in the long as well as in the short term, is clearly uncertain. In addition to the uncertainty about individual leaders, a situation which typifies uninstitutionalized politics when generational change is imminent, there are further and more substantial uncertainties about the form and content of politics resulting from the reform process initiated in 1978. Both indirectly, through the policies implemented by the CCP, and directly, through its encouragement of debate, the role of the state in economics and society has been questioned; the once crystal-clear distinction between capitalism and socialism has been blurred, and 'democracy' has become a legitimate concept of political discussion and not just a 'bourgeois fallacy' (Tsou 1986; Lee 1986, p. 77).

Before the People's Liberation Army (PLA) invaded Tiananmen Square in June 1989 political change was widely regarded outside China as proceeding in a gradual, orderly and incremental manner, albeit lagging somewhat behind the pace and intensity of economic reform. Few would have regarded a multi-party liberal democracy as a likely end-goal, but the state socialism of the Mao-dominated era of Chinese politics was clearly in transition, probably towards some form of reformed CCP-led authoritarianism. For example, Harry Harding (1989, pp. 300–01), without in any way being over-optimistic about the prospects for reform and fully mindful of the problems facing the regime in the 1980s as well as its achievements, predicted the emergence of 'a more relaxed and consultative political system' somewhat like that which existed in Taiwan in the 1970s, but under the leadership of the CCP (instead of the Nationalist Party).

Events since mid-1989 in both China and the former communist party states of Eastern Europe have foregrounded the prospects of more cataclysmic change, including the end of CCP rule. It is now commonly argued that the economic and political reforms implemented since 1978 have effectively undermined the long-term position of the CCP and given rise to social forces which will challenge and replace CCP rule. To meet successfully the challenges posed by reform, the CCP would have to be a more sophisticated and subtle actor than its reaction to the student demonstrations during 1989 would appear to indicate (Hicks 1990).

The argument that the end of CCP rule is inevitable rests heavily on parallels drawn with the experience of the former communist party states of Eastern Europe and the Soviet Union. The implosion of communist parties and the political disintegration of state systems, particularly of the

Soviet Union, are regarded as clear indicators for China's future. The argument also rests on a specific interpretation of the decline in the market share of the state sector and the growth of the more 'capitalist' collective and private sectors. The influence of the CCP-dominated state is said to be in decline as elements of civil society come into their own.

Fashions in explaining systemic political change can and do vary within a relatively short period of time, not least because there can be no simple explanation. The most recent large-scale and comparative attempt, led by O'Donnell and Schmitter (1986), has proved controversial as well as stimulating, particularly since its conclusions appear to contradict much of O'Donnell's earlier work. Previously O'Donnell had taken a more economically deterministic view of political change; now he emphazises the importance of historical accident. However, the contradiction is more apparent than real since there are at least two different types of explanation involved here: the long-term social and economic factors which provide the necessary (but not sufficient) conditions for change, and the more specific short-term political catalysts, which are an essential part of the explanation of specific transitions and transformations.

This volume—which emerged from a conference organized by the Asia Research Centre at Murdoch University held in Fremantle, Western Australia, in January 1992—is concerned with more long-term changes and with general socio-economic conditions, and the consequences of these for political power. The contributors to this book do not see either dramatic change or the end of CCP rule as inevitable. On the contrary, they suggest that, though China may be experiencing a capitalist revolution, a simple dichotomy between state and society may obscure more than it reveals about the dynamics of change.

Socio-economic change since 1978 has created new interactions between state and society, which this volume has begun to describe. Part I outlines the basic parameters of the changing social structure, Part II concentrates on the consequences of rising standards of living and problems of relative deprivation, Part III focuses on the new social forces generated by economic growth and their political consequences. In order to locate the arguments presented in this volume in their appropriate context, the remainder of this Introduction considers the assumptions about China's post–1978 economic development, and its potential consequences, which have been raised elsewhere.

Economic reform and modernization

The process of reform in China during the 1980s, at first sight, certainly seems to suggest the potential for substantial political change. Between 1978 and 1991 the state sector's share of industrial production fell from over three-quarters to little more than half. Government expenditure fell from 41.1 per cent of national income in 1978 to 23 per cent in 1989

(Hussain & Stern 1991). This apparent rolling back of the state has been matched by the growth of what seems to be an independent capitalism in the collective as well as the private sectors.

However, it is far from clear that reform in China during the 1980s resulted in quite the same process of modernization experienced by other countries in the region during the recent past. The socio-economic transformation of China did not start in 1978 alone; though formally the non-state sectors of the economy have grown in importance, the influence of the state has far from declined; and at least partially in consequence there are sound reasons for believing that modernization may not inevitably lead to capitalism and democracy in China.

China's reform era is too easily equated as a period of modernization with those experienced elsewhere in East Asia during the last few decades. That perspective over-states the start of history in 1978, for China had already experienced rapid economic development. Indeed, despite fluctuations and reverses (some of which, such as the consequences of the Great Leap Forward, were severe), the Chinese economy grew overall at an average in excess of 6 per cent a year between 1952 and 1978.

China's reform era initiated at the end of 1978 has led to the restructuring of an inefficiently modernized economy, rather than a transformation from one which was predominantly pre-modern in form. It is thus perhaps better described as a re-industrialization or re-modernization. One obvious measure of economic modernization—the transformation of an economy from agricultural to industrial production—is the point at which the gross value of industrial output surpasses the gross value of agricultural output. An essential part of that process is the growth of white-collar employment and the development of the professional middle classes, the intermediate social classes required to provide support services to both the new modernizing state and the process of industrialization, and whose activism has been seen as crucial to so much of the recent political transformation of East and Southeast Asia.

In China industrial output first exceeded agricultural output during the late 1950s and the Great Leap Forward, though this was more of a statistical than an economic reality, and a distinctly temporary phenomenon. Since 1970, however, industrial output has consistently been greater than agricultural output (Wu 1991). Table 0.1 indicates sectoral shares of GNP for selected years between 1952 and 1990, and indicates quite clearly that in terms of gross data the Chinese economy was well on the way to modernization by 1978, as well as the impact of re-modernization during the first half of the 1980s.

There was also growth in white-collar occupations and the emergence of professional middle classes (although necessarily only within the public sector and albeit of very different kinds to those which existed in liberal democracies and free-market economies) before 1978. The establishment of the communist party state saw a rapid expansion of public-funded positions in education, the state administration, welfare provision and the

Table 0.1: Sectoral shares of GNP, 1952–1990

Year 1952	1957	1960	1970	1978	1980	1982	1984	1986	1988	1990
Sector										
Agriculture										
57.7	46.8	27.2	40.4	32.8	36.0	40.5	39.8	34.6	32.5	34.7
Industry										
19.5	28.3	46.3	41.0	49.4	48.9	45.8	44.5	45.5	46.1	45.8
Construction										
3.2	5.0	6.5	4.2	4.1	5.0	4.9	5.4	6.5	6.7	5.7
Transport										
4.2	4.3	6.9	3.9	3.9	3.4	3.5	3.6	4.1	3.9	4.9
Commerce										
14.9	15.6	13.1	10.6	9.8	6.7	5.4	6.7	9.3	10.7	9.0
GNP per capita			yuan							
104	142	183	235	315	376	422	547	743	1078	1271

Source: State Statistical Bureau 1991 (pp. 32–5).

social services, as well as for various technical personnel. For the most part, it was those in such positions who bore the brunt of the CCP's equivocal attitude to the intelligentsia and associated occupations during the Cultural Revolution. Data on the numbers involved in white-collar work are not readily available. Official employment and income data are aggregated by sector, and not usually presented in terms of any under-standing of socio-economic class. For political reasons, the CCP does not encourage the kinds of data which would facilitate analysis. Nonetheless, from the available evidence it would seem that the proportion of the work-force which might be classified as the new middle classes has not increased significantly since before 1978. For example, a survey of the Shanghai work-force estimated that the professional middle classes (managers, professionals and intellectuals) accounted for 27.5 per cent of the total in that city throughout the 1980s (Pang & Qiu 1989, p. 63).

Capitalism and democracy

Even if the period since 1978 is regarded as one of economic restructuring rather than an initial modernization, there appears to be an almost self-evident argument that leads from the economic reform of state socialism to the eventual establishment of a liberal democracy in China, via the emergence of a free market and a private sector, followed in turn by capitalism and demands for political representation. Ironically, the reform of state socialism is now regarded as containing the seeds of its own destruction: economically, because the free market is regarded as so superior an economic allocator that the state sector cannot compete successfully; and politically, because of the emergence of a civil society.

For many commentators, all that remains to be determined is the length of resistance offered by the CCP, the level of violence accompanying the transformation, and the future form of the Chinese state. In the wake of the events of June 1989, this basic perspective underlies much of what has been written analyzing contemporary China's current trends and political future.

The academic study of China is often criticized for treating the PRC as though it were unique, and without recourse to any wider body of theoretical or comparative knowledge (for example, Harding 1984, p. 297). However, the assumption of future dramatic change in China clearly owes much to the intellectual climate of the 1980s in the Western world. Even before 1989 economic rationalism had predicted and prescribed the withdrawal of the state as an agent of economic development. The end of the Cold War and the collapse of communist party rule in Eastern Europe reinforced long standing arguments about the unilinear political and economic consequences of industrialization. Capitalism and liberal democracy are seen as the goals of economic and political development. Those who have long maintained either that state socialism was pathological (in the China field, for example, Jan Prybyla) or that the CCP was morally degenerate (for example, Franz Michael) have felt vindicated by events during 1989–90, and remain confident that similar forces will impact on the PRC (Prybyla 1990; Michael 1990; Myers 1990).

Arguments about the inevitability of capitalism and democracy in China thus contain statements about their general inevitability, as well as about conditions in the PRC. This is not the appropriate forum for a lengthy examination of the more general justifications of the inevitability of capitalism and democracy, or the more acute definitional problems of either capitalism or democracy which would be central to such a discussion. Both are 'hurrah words' which by now may well be deprived of any real analytical worth by common usage. The definitional debate about democracy is well-rehearsed. There are few political systems which would not describe themselves as a democracy (Held 1987), and it is now widely accepted that even liberal democracy can take many forms: whether it should, is of course, a different matter (Sundhaussen 1991).

Definitions of capitalism would similarly seem to have become less specific—particularly as a result of the emergent 'new world order'—with virtually all economic development described as capitalism. There is a certain logic in this position for those who would choose to argue that development is unilinear. However, such an assumption may also mask aspects of the dynamics of development. The most obvious and relevant example in this particular context is the existence of capitalists as an autonomous (from the state) class of entrepreneurs who lead the process of economic development. As a theoretical construct, capitalism probably entails the existence of this class, or at least of their autonomous economic activity. Description of a system as capitalism usually assumes there are capitalists, often to the extent of requiring their identification. This is undoubtedly the reason why many outside observers place so much emphasis on the emergence in China of the new private sector businessmen as capitalist entrepreneurs. Under such circumstances the observation of capitalism becomes a circular argument. The reform of the PRC's economy clearly has much in common with the development of capitalism. There can also be little doubt that economic growth in the 1980s has profoundly disturbed the social structure (Perry & Wong 1985; Walder 1989a, p. 405). The point at issue, however, is precisely the nature of that transformation and its social and political consequences.

Over and above any general considerations, the claim that fundamental change is inevitable rests basically with three broad China-specific arguments. The first relates to the CCP's loss of legitimacy, and the ungovernability of reform; the second is based on an interpretation of the state's retreat from economic activities; and the third concentrates on the evidence for the emergence of civil society in China.

Legitimacy and reform

The first of these arguments is relatively obvious and, at the same time, a little puzzling. It is obvious because the reform program initiated in the late 1970s was always going to present the CCP with a difficult balancing act. It contained an inherent contradiction in that it was trying to encourage the use of individual and collective initiative in economic production (in a society which had previously often punished such behaviour) but at the same time the CCP tolerated no challenge to its entrenched political position. Economic and political reforms were introduced because the CCP's legitimacy had become so tarnished during the Mao-dominated years. Economic growth and greater responsiveness and accountability in government were seen as necessary for the restoration of popular confidence. However, the limit, as the early (1979) demonstrators of the Democracy Wall period quickly found, was that the CCP was itself to remain subject to different rules (Goodman 1987).

Necessarily, as reform and economic growth have proceeded through the 1980s, other social tensions have overlaid the basic contradiction between reform and control. Not everybody has become wealthier at the same rate, and there has been a fundamental revolution of rising expectations. Because there has been a sudden and substantial improvement in the standard of living (particularly in the urban areas) there is now an expectation that growth will continue. Feelings of relative deprivation have clearly grown exponentially and with them has come an increased sophistication in political activism compared even to 1979, let alone the era of the Cultural Revolution.

The example of striking bus drivers in northern Chinese cities during 1985–86 is particularly illustrative. For the most part bus drivers had learnt to drive when in the PLA, having few other opportunities. By chance, on demobilization, they had been assigned jobs driving buses as opposed to their colleagues assigned to taxis. However, with the introduction of economic reforms, and particularly with substantial deregulation of the local transport industry, taxi drivers had opportunities for improvement in earnings denied to bus drivers. By the start of 1986 a Beijing taxi driver was earning more than twice as much as a bus driver, and with better conditions of work. Though the strike could not turn buses into taxis it could ensure better working conditions for bus drivers, and greater opportunities for bus drivers to change jobs.

These are clearly the problems of a society in transition, as indeed are the economic contradictions emphasized by the 'disaster theorists'. Their essential argument is that plan and market are fundamentally incompatible (Prybyla 1989, p. 1). Here the argument becomes puzzling. 'Dual tracking' clearly has its problems, particularly in a system where managers are being encouraged to use their initiative. For example, if a product is priced considerably lower in the state sector than in the market, the bold manager will exploit the difference as a trader (given the opportunity) to turn an easy profit. No amount of resource supervision can hope to eradicate such practices. However, it is a long way from the identification of those problems to a complete rejection of all mixed economies.

In this view, the events of April–June 1989 are important not least because they demonstrate in high relief the ungovernability of reform and the CCP's loss of legitimacy. The economic problems and social tensions resulting from reform are held to be motivators for the street demonstrations of May 1989. The CCP had succeeded in raising living standards, but had not succeeded in controlling that process, thereby risking its own legitimacy rather than restoring its former glory (Walder 1989b, p. 30). The CCP's inability to handle the demonstrations of May 1989, and its over-reaction in June, when it basically surrendered any attempt to maintain its political balance, further undermined its legitimacy. Saich (1991, p. 34) argues that as a result of 4 June 1989 the CCP must either 'come to terms with implications of its own desire for economic reform' and allow political reform, or it 'risks being swept away by a further round of social unrest'.

The state and society

A second argument that fundamental change is under way rests with the observation that the state is in retreat in the PRC. The gross statistics indicate considerable change in this respect, and there can be no doubt that the CCP consciously attempted to reduce the activities of the state—both the central state and local government—in some respects during the 1980s. In the late 1970s the state sector still produced some 80 per cent of GVIO, and even in 1983 the figure was still 77 per cent. By 1989 the state sector produced only 56 per cent of GVIO, with 36 per cent produced by the collective sector and 5 per cent by the private sector (State Statistical Bureau 1990). In 1991, the state sector's share of industrial production was reduced to 53 per cent of GVIO.

The growth in the collective and private sectors away from agriculture and towards light industry, commerce and the service industry has been substantial. For example, by the end of 1990, some 80 per cent of all light industrial enterprises were collectively owned (Lao 1991), and the private sector employed as many people as the state and collective sectors (NCNA, 1990). The retail trade and services industries are dominated by collective and private enterprises. Although the (central) state only ever played a very small role in such activities (Solinger 1984), even local governments have ceased to be involved in what used to be (before the 1980s) one of their major areas of activity. The transformation has been greatest for restaurants and local transport, almost all of which have become collectivized or privatized (ZTS, 1991). However, perhaps the most remarkable indicator of change relates not directly to economic production but to the provision of welfare. Whereas in 1980 the state provided housing, health care and pensions to some 19 per cent of the working population, by 1990 such provision was available to only 9 per cent.

The prospects for civil society

The consequences for the PRC's political economy from the apparent retreat of the state lead directly to the third portent of fundamental change. The purposive shrinking of the state's interest in economic management may not only reduce its economic base in society, but it also allows for the emergence of other autonomous economic interests. Unsurprisingly (not least because of developments in Eastern Europe), concern with a nascent or re-nascent civil society in China emerged strongly after June 1989.

In part, the discussion of civil society in China examines the period before, sometimes well before, CCP rule in order to determine the applicability of the concept in a Chinese context. Beyond the boundaries of China studies, there has been intense academic debate as to whether civil society is a completely eurocentric and culturally specific term, as certainly its articulators in its 1980s manifestation (as opposed to its original formulation by Locke) would maintain. (Habermas (1969) for example, would certainly deny its existence in China on grounds of cultural specificity.) Nonetheless, and however civil society is defined, there is considerable evidence, in the words of Kelly and He (1991, p. 28), that 'A zone of de facto autonomous social organization had been expanding vigorously through the 1980s'. Reform has of necessity removed the state's absolute monopoly of not only the economy and society, but also politics.

Several commentators have remarked on the role played by private entrepreneurs in the protests and demonstrations of April–May 1989. They have seen considerable significance in the support offered demonstrators from the private sector (Saich 1991, p. 31; Chan & Unger 1991). The evidence of private entrepreneurs being prepared to engage in political activism is by no means straightforward (Gold 1989). Nonetheless, there clearly was involvement in May–June from the private sector. Perhaps the two most famous examples were in Beijing, where the Flying Tiger Motorcycle Brigade provided information to the demonstrators about troop movements and rallied support throughout the city, and the Stone (Computer) Company provided funds and communications systems.

These various arguments, and the perspective of fundamental change they portend, clearly indicate the extent of both the massive social transformation the PRC has experienced in a relatively short time, and the political crisis the CCP now faces. Capitalism and democracy may well result from the resolution of that crisis, but it is clearly somewhat premature to make that judgement at this juncture and on so little evidence. In particular, it is necessary to identify some agents of the predicted systemic change. It is almost as if the motive force for change is to be found solely in the creative tension which binds the state and society. Thus, in a rather crude sense, there is an assumption that if the power of the state declines, it passes to autonomous social organizations, almost regardless of the conditions of their existence.

However, as the contributors to this volume demonstrate, it is far from clear that such a simple distinction between state and society amply describes the transformation under way in the PRC during the 1980s. In the first place, recent research suggests that state sector economic reforms designed to separate the state from enterprise management and to increase the latter's autonomy have been a failure, for the most part, and despite some well-publicized success stories. Rather, the evidence suggests that enterprise management has succeeded in the new 'dual track' marketplace where it has been able to build on the relations and connections previously developed within the state sector and away from the market (Huang 1990; Blecher 1991) .

In the second place, and perhaps of even greater significance, the development of autonomous economic activity is also greatly exaggerated. The decline in the state sector's influence is more apparent than real. The CCP has long differentiated between three ownership systems and sectors in China's economy: state, collective and private. It is easy but misleading to regard the collective and private sectors as independent of the state because they are officially designated as 'the non-state sectors'. However, 'non-state' in this context does not mean either unregulated or independent. The collective sector in particular has always been that part of the state sector outside state economic planning and the command economy.

The collective sector, particularly in urban and suburban areas, is often little more than a second freebooting state sector, and is frequently regarded as a semi-socialist outgrowth of the state sector. In any case, the complexity of management and ownership systems created by economic reform do not always fit into such a simple tripartite characterization as that employed by the CCP. For example, there are collective sector enterprises (that is enterprises officially designated as part of the collective sector) which are owned by their workers and managers, or by a village or locality; those established by enterprises in the state sector, or some that are little more than large private enterprises.

As a State Council report of 1989 makes clear, the categories of state, collective and private sector are not applied consistently across the country, and considerable confusion results. Even categorization itself can become a matter of political debate. It cites the example of Wenzhou where some 22 833 shareholders' co-operatives had been established by 1988. It appears that various (unspecified) central ministries in the fields of industry and commerce wished to treat them as part of the private sector, whilst the local people's government regarded them as semi-socialist, and hence insisted on a collective sector designation (State Council Research Unit 1989).

At the same time, the development of both the collective and private sectors provides ample evidence that the state remains at the centre of economic development. As already noted, many collective sector enterprises are little more than paper companies for state enterprises who prefer to operate in a less trammelled market. Others nominally regarded as rural industry have grown out of the industry bureaux of the former, pre-decollectivization, rural local governments. Still other collective and private sector enterprises are established—with capital, labour and land—from state resources, and many are dependent on state-run systems of supply and distribution.

The economic restructuring of the period since 1978 may thus indicate the expansion and transformation of state influence rather than its diminution. Certainly, as must necessarily be the case at this point in China's development, a substantial proportion of both the new professional classes and the new entrepreneurial classes can be expected to have career and demographic ties with the party–state system. Moreover, the CCP has set itself the task of recruiting amongst those who have not. Given both structural and sociological factors it is not at all surprising to find situations better understood as accommodations between the state and society, rather than the victory of one or the other through confrontation.

References

Blecher, Marc 1991, 'Sounds of Silence and Distant Thunder: The Crisis of Economic and Political Administration', in *China in the Nineties: Crisis Management and Beyond*, eds David S. G. Goodman & Gerald Segal, Clarendon Press, Oxford, pp. 18–41.

Chan, Anita & Jonathan Unger 1991, 'Voices from the Protest Movement in Chongqing: Class Accents and Class Tensions', in *The Pro-Democracy Protests in China*, ed. Jonathan Unger, Allen & Unwin, Sydney, pp. 106–26.

Garnaut, Ross & Guonan Ma 1992, 'How Rich is China: Evidence from the Food Economy', Working Paper in Trade and Development No 92/4,

Department of Economics and National Centre for Development Studies, Australian National University, July.

Gold, Thomas B. 1989, 'Guerrilla Interviewing Among the *Getihu*', in *Unofficial China: Popular Culture and Thought in the People's Republic*, eds Perry Link, Richard Madsen & Paul G. Pickowicz, Westview Press, Boulder, Colorado, pp. 175–92.

Goodman, David S.G. 1987, 'Democracy, Interest, and Virtue: The Search for Legitimacy in the People's Republic of China', in *Foundations and Limits of State Power in China*, ed. Stuart R. Schram, Chinese University Press, Hong Kong, pp. 291–312.

——1992, 'China: the State and Capitalist Revolution', in *The New Rich in Asia*, eds David S.G. Goodman & Richard Robison, *The Pacific Review*, vol. 5, no. 4, pp. 350–9.

Goodman, David S.G. & Gerald Segal 1991, *China in the Nineties: Crisis Management and Beyond*, Clarendon Press, Oxford.

Habermas, Jurgen 1969, *Strukturwandel der Oeffentlichkeit*, Schoeningh, Paderborn.

Harding, Harry 1984, 'The Study of Chinese Politics: Towards a Third Generation of Scholarship', *World Politics*, vol. 36, no. 2, pp. 284–307.

——1989, *China's Second Revolution*, Allen & Unwin, Sydney.

Held, David 1987, *Models of Democracy*, Blackwell, Oxford.

Hicks, George ed. 1990, *The Broken Mirror: China after Tiananmen*, Longman, Harlow, Essex.

Huang Yasheng 1990, 'Web of Interests and Patterns of Behaviour of Chinese Local Economic Bureaucracies and Enterprises During Reforms', *China Quarterly*, no. 123, pp. 432–58.

Hussain, Athar & Nicholas Stern 1991, 'Effective Demand, Enterprise Reforms and Public Finance', *China Paper 10*, March, LSE Development Economics Research Programme.

Kelly, David & He Baogang 1991, 'Emergent Civil Society and the Intellectuals in China', *The Development of Civil Society in Communist Systems* ed. Robert F. Miller, Allen & Unwin, Sydney, pp. 23–39.

Lao Chang 1991, 'Collectives Must Learn Competition', *China Daily*, 3 November, p. 4.

Lee Hong Yung 1986, 'Ideology, State and Society in China', *Journal of International Affairs*, vol. 39, no. 2, pp. 77–89.

Michael, Franz 1990, 'China and the Crisis of Communism', in *The Broken Mirror: China after Tiananmen*, ed. George Hicks, Longman, Harlow, Essex, pp. 445–55.

Myers, Raymond 1990, 'The Next Power Struggle', in *The Broken Mirror: China after Tiananmen*, ed. George Hicks, Longman, Harlow, Essex, pp. 456–65

NCNA—New China News Agency 1990, 24 December.

O'Donnell, Gilliermo & Paul Schmitter eds 1986, *Transitions from Authoritarian Rule*, Johns Hopkins University Press, Baltimore.

Pang Shuqi & Qiu Liping 1989, 'Preliminary Study of the Current Structure of Social Classes and Strata in China', *Shehuixue yanjiu*, vol. 3, pp. 63–75; translated in *Chinese Sociology and Anthropology*, Winter 1989/ 1990, vol. 22, no. 2, pp. 5–20.

Perry, Elizabeth J. & Christine Wong 1985, *The Political Economy of Reform in Post-Mao China*, Harvard University Press, Harvard.

Prybyla, Jan 1989, 'China's Economic Experiment: Back from the Market?', *Problems of Communism*, vol. 38, no. 1, pp. 1–18.

——1990, 'A Broken System', in *The Broken Mirror: China after Tiananmen*, ed. George Hicks, Longman, Harlow, Essex, pp. 180–95.

Saich, Tony 1991, 'The Rise and Fall of the Beijing People's Movement', in *The Pro-Democracy Protests in China*, ed. Jonathan Unger, Allen & Unwin, Sydney, pp. 8–34

Solinger, Dorothy J. 1984, *Chinese Business under Socialism*, University of California, Berkeley.

State Council Research Unit 1989, Supplementary Report on an Investigation of the Question of Wenzhou, Report no. 57, 28 November.

State Statistical Bureau 1990, *Zhongguo tongji nianjian 1990*, Zhongguo tongji nianjian chubanshe, Beijing.

——1991, *Zhongguo tongji nianjian 1991*, Zhongguo tongji nianjian chubanshe, Beijing.

Sundhaussen, Ulf 1991, 'Democracy and the Middle Classes: Reflections on Political Development', *Australian Journal of Politics and History*, vol. 37, no. 1, pp. 100–17

Tsou, Tang 1986, 'Reflections on the Formation and Foundations of the Communist Party-State in China', in *The Cultural Revolution and Post-Mao Reforms: A Historical Perspective*, University of Chicago Press, Chicago, pp. 259–334

Unger, Jonathan ed. 1991, *The Pro-Democracy Protests in China*, Allen & Unwin, Sydney.

Walder, Andrew 1989a, 'Social Change in Post-Revolution China', *Annual Review of Sociology*, vol. 15, pp. 405–26.

——1989b, 'The Political Sociology of the Beijing Upheaval of 1989', *Problems of Communism*, vol. 38, no. 5, pp. 30–40.

Wang Zhonghui 1990, 'Private Enterprise in China', *Journal of Communist Studies*, vol. 6, no. 3, pp. 83–98.

Wu, Harry X. 1991, 'The "Real" Chinese Gross Domestic Product in the Pre-Reform Period', Chinese Economy Research Unit, The University of Adelaide, no. 7.

Yang, Mayfair Mei-hui 1989, 'Between State and Society: The Construction of Corporateness in a Chinese Socialist Factory', *The Australian Journal of Chinese Affairs*, no. 22, pp. 31–62.

Young, Susan 1991, 'Wealth but not Security: Attitudes Towards Private Business in China in the 1980s', *The Australian Journal of Chinese Affairs*, no. 25, pp. 115–138.

ZTS—Zhongguo tongxun she 1991, 22 May, 'Private businesses develop rapidly', translated in SWB FE/1085/B2/4 (Summary of World Broadcasts: The Far East).

嬗 Part I
The changing social structure

1 Evolving property rights and their political consequences

Andrew G. Walder

M any students of China's economic reforms have focused upon their consequences for the country's distribution of income. In the highly redistributive economy of the 1960s and 1970s, in which market allocation played a negligible role, material inequalities were kept to a bare minimum by international standards, especially inequalities within communities.[1] With the spread of market allocation and profit orientations in the 1980s, most observers expected, if not a vast increase in material inequalities, at least major changes in the overall pattern of social stratification. Such changes are of interest because they might lead to a polarization of wealth within communities, or between regions, and bring forth political consequences that range from increased tensions between provinces to the emergence of new social classes, class-based conflicts, or social instability.

In this chapter I examine the changes in patterns of social stratification that have had consequences for the distribution of income and patterns of conflict in Chinese society. When we think of social stratification in relation to politics, I believe that most of us employ tacitly a 'polarization' model, in which the degree of political conflict or normative disapproval of existing institutions rises along with an increase in levels of inequality. Why would we expect this to be true? One possible account is provided by familiar 'moral economy' arguments: if customary subsistence or welfare guarantees come to be threatened or violated, those who suffer from their decline will come to see the new economic arrangements as unjust. Another possible account is provided by familiar 'relative deprivation' arguments, which in turn are based on earlier reference group theories: even if the material situation of a group is improving, that group may grow increasingly dissatisfied if other groups with whom they compare themselves are advancing even more rapidly.

This often-tacit polarization model, which focuses our attention upon income differences, is not the only possible way to think about changes in a system of social stratification or the political consequences of those changes. Social stratification is not simply a static (or even dynamic) pattern of income differences; it is more broadly a social and political process whereby wealth is generated and income distributed. If we are interested in political consequences, it is just as important to know *how* income is earned and distributed as it is to know about the income gaps that result.

The main purpose of this chapter is to offer a different way of thinking about changes in social stratification and their political consequences. It is premised on the idea that widespread changes in property rights have greatly altered the ways in which wealth is earned and income distributed in China. These evolving property rights have certainly altered the distribution of income but they have also created new political conceptions and demands, altered the exercise of political power in grassroots institutions and created new kinds of conflict.

Economic reform and property rights

Reform in a socialist economy proceeds by altering property rights. This statement might appear odd to those who think primarily about the distinction between 'private' and 'public' property in relation to socialism, and who recognize the very limited scope of the private sector in China today, and the near nonexistence of the kinds of 'privatization' processes now associated with the transition to 'post-Communism' in Europe (Stark 1990; Grosfeld 1991). Even in traditional systems of central planning, the fact that property is public rather than private does not mean that there is not a complex if often ill-defined pattern of property rights exercised by government agencies, organizations, households, and individuals, and that these rights may be changed in consequential ways without ever altering the public–private legal distinction (see, e.g., Pryor 1973).

Property rights defined

Property rights may be defined as the sanctioned relationships among people or organizations regarding the use of goods. Sanctioned in norms, customs, and laws, these rights form expectations in dealings with others: an owner of property rights has the consent of others to act in particular ways without interference by the community, provided the actions are not prohibited in the specification of rights (Demsetz 1967). The best known variety of property rights pertain to ownership, which includes (see Furubotn & Pejovich 1974, p. 3):

1 The right to use an asset. This aspect of ownership rights is often referred to as 'control'; it involves the making of decisions about the management of assets. As in a modern corporation in a capitalist economy, the control of assets in a socialist economy is often delegated by owners to agents, or professional managers. Such a separation of ownership from control is in effect a delegation of property rights to management (Demsetz 1967).

2 The right to appropriate the returns from an asset. This aspect of ownership amounts to 'distribution' rights regarding the flow of income. State socialist economies are commonly referred to as 'redistributive' (Szelenyi 1978, following Polanyi 1957), by which is meant a distinctive set of rules regarding the distribution of income flows from productive assets.

3 The right to change the form or substance of an asset by transferring rights to others, and to bear the consequences from changes in value. This aspect might be referred to as 'exchange' rights; it involves both the decision to buy or sell assets as well as the rights to proceeds from the sale (or responsibility for losses).

Ownership, and by extension contract, is the right to exclude others, but this right is always restricted by regulation or law. Ownership rights are rarely unrestricted in any society. This is equally true in market and planned economies. What differs is not the fact of regulation but the entities that are assigned the above rights, and the ways in which these assignments are monitored and enforced. The central insight of the economics of organization is that any type of economic institution is in essence a distinctive configuration of property rights.

Viewed from this perspective, the distinctions commonly drawn between 'market versus plan' or 'public versus private ownership' are not always very meaningful, and are in any event rather blunt tools with which to analyze the organization of an economy. Is the main difference between capitalist and socialist economies the extent of market allocation, or in the methods of economic planning and their effectiveness? One could argue that planning processes within large modern corporations are far more detailed, enforceable, and effective than the crude forms of rationing, inaccurate information, and constant bargaining that characterizes planning in their socialist counterparts: ministries, bureaux and corporations. The main differences are in the methods of planning, how performance is monitored, and what kinds of incentives are provided for agents to comply. Similarly, the distinction between 'private' or 'public' ownership provides limited insight: in capitalist economies assets are held by a wide variety of highly regulated and interdependent private and public institutions (firms, corporations, banks, investment firms, pension funds, households), while in socialist economies assets are held separately (in effect 'privately') by a wide variety of government jurisdictions and agencies (central ministries, provinces, cities, townships, villages). The formal distinction between public and private provides limited insight when ownership rights in each economy are in fact exercised by a wide spectrum of organizations.

The differences between economies and their characteristic forms of economic organization are more fruitfully understood as variations in bundles of property rights regarding the use of assets, the distribution of income derived from them, and their sale or transfer to others. Control over the large firm in both capitalism and socialism is delegated by owners (shareholders or specific government agencies) to professional managers; the main differences are in the regulations and mechanisms that govern the accountability of the latter to the former. Owners of large firms in both capitalism and socialism retain rights to income from their assets; what differs is the ways in which these income flows are calculated and divided with professional managers. Rights to transfer and liquidate assets are probably the greatest contrast between capitalist and socialist economies, since such transfer is much more common in the capitalist. Yet the transfer of assets is nonetheless restricted in capitalist economies by public ownership and regulation (e.g., utilities, railways, port facilities, airport slots, fishing rights), and by-laws designed to avert monopolies and trusts or the transfer of assets to foreign entities. In agriculture, while the contrast between capitalist small-holding and socialist collective farms is more striking, the difference between 'capitalist' sharecropping and 'socialist' household contracting is more subtle.

Reform as a reassignment of property rights

In contemporary economics, especially in the literature on government regulation, 'attenuation' of property rights is a key concept. Attenuation of property rights takes place as restrictions are imposed on uses to which an asset may be put, on the income flows from that asset, and on the freedom of an owner to transfer these rights to others. Attenuation of property rights may occur in two different ways. Many restrictions are established by the state through various legal provisions written into commercial, corporate, and tax law, or in procedural regulations enforced by government agencies. Attenuation may also arise from the inherent unenforceability of laws and regulations, especially due to influence processes within bureaucracies and firms.[2]

While it is natural to think of government regulation in market economies dominated by private sectors as attenuating property rights, the process of economic reform in a socialist economy implies the reverse process: a devolving of property rights downward in political or administrative hierarchies, or reassigning and clarifying property rights among institutions and households. Reform invariably devolves selected property rights over assets (especially those of use and claims to income distributions) from higher to lower levels of government administration, or from government administration to enterprises, households, or individuals. Indeed, an economic reform program may be defined as a specific package of property rights reassignments, and the impact of a reform package will flow directly from the effects of these specific reassignments on incentives for economic behavior, subsequent income flows, and political power and interests. An entire range of phenomena, from economic behavior, economic growth, and changes in income redistribution, to the rise of corruption and changes in the distribution of political power, can therefore be analyzed within a single analytic framework.

The reassignment of use rights. One of the most important latent principles of economic reform in China has been the widespread downward reassignment of use rights within government hierarchies, and at the grass roots, from government agencies to households and individuals. The most dramatic reassignment took place in the dismantling of collective agriculture. Collectively owned village land formerly cultivated under the direction of production team leaders was reassigned to households under long term contracts. While quota-contracts for staple grains were commonly retained, peasant households attained new rights to make cropping, management and marketing decisions on their own. The same principle has been applied widely to collectively held assets in villages, towns, and cities. Agricultural sidelines and small scale industrial and commercial enterprises have commonly been leased to households and individuals under a wide variety of contracts that specify compensating payments to the owners. These payments entitle the leaseholders to a right to manage the assets with considerable autonomy, and in effect remove owners from the direct management of the assets. This principle has also been applied to the larger collective and state enterprises still under the planning authority of rural and urban governments, but here the reassignment of use rights to managers has been far less extensive. Efforts to expand enterprise autonomy within the scope of the plan have been restricted largely to certain areas of staff compensation, sales and supply work, and technical operations. Decisions about investment, technical renovation, changes of product lines, and finance are still closely supervised by government officials.

The reassignment of rights to returns from assets. In all of these downward transfers of use rights, the relationship between principals (owners) and agents (their subordinates) has been altered from one of hierarchical authority, in which the principal specifies in detail the duties and methods of work of the agent, to one of contract, in which the agent gains increased autonomy in carrying out the assigned task, in return for a contractually specified payment to the owner. This means that the widespread downward reassignment of use rights has been accompanied, and given content, by a corresponding downward transfer of rights to returns from assets. Whenever a hierarchy is replaced by a contract, there is a partial reassignment of the owner's right to returns from assets to the contracting agent.

This downward reassignment is most dramatic in the shift from collective to household agriculture. Returns formerly funnelled through production team accounts and redistributed at year's end in the form of work points are reassigned to households, who deliver obligatory crops at low state prices while retaining the right to residual income from their land and other assets. When a village or town leases an enterprise to an individual or household it similarly reassigns part of its rights to income from it. Such contracts typically specify a reassignment that varies from a flat lease payment, which gives complete rights to the agent over all residual income, to various formulae for sharing income over a specified minimum. This principle has been applied, though in a more limited fashion, even in the case of large state enterprises. Various redrawn profit contracting schemes, and the eventual replacement of profit remission by tax payments, has led to the increased retention of profit by firms. While the rights reassigned are still vague and subject to bargaining, it is nonetheless true that state managers now enjoy significantly expanded rights to appropriate and use shares of profit at their discretion.

While the examples cited are fairly self-evident, it is less widely recognized that the reform of China's fiscal system in the 1980s has similarly reassigned downward *within hierarchies of government* these same rights to returns from assets. Keep in mind that the overwhelming majority of productive assets in China are held by *clearly specified government entities*. As far as property rights assignments go, the common categories of 'state' or 'collective' ownership are virtually without meaning. Far more meaningful are the signboards outside Chinese factories, where ownership of the assets is made clear: *Dongguan* Township, *Zouping* County, *Shandong* Province, or the Ministry of Metallurgy. These are the kinds of corporate entities that hold most productive assets in China. Property in China has never been held by 'the State'—it has always been held separately by thousands of separate government jurisdictions, from villages right up to central ministries.

When we say that a government jurisdiction owns an asset, we mean, in part, that it has the right to income from it, and that the asset is part of that government jurisdiction's revenue base. As China's fiscal system has moved from internal transfers of profits and tax payments to new kinds of negotiated tax 'responsibility contracts', the rights of localities to income from their assets is clarified and strengthened. In many areas of the country tax responsibility contracts have been extended down to the level of the village. Responsibility for collecting taxes is delegated to the government jurisdiction (which has also earned new rights to add additional local taxes and levies of its own), and the jurisdiction is obligated to turn over a quota of tax revenues to the level of government above them. Revenues collected above that target level are shared according to a variety of formulae, and in extreme cases are kept entirely by the jurisdiction that collects them. In the same way that household contracting in agriculture reassigns rights to income from assets downward to the peasant family, tax quota contracting reassigns rights to income from assets downward to local governments.

The reassignment of rights to transfer assets. The right to sell productive assets outright remains controversial and highly constrained. Land, factories, and other enterprises are not freely bought and sold, even among local governments, and still generally remain under the *de facto* ownership of territorially defined government agencies. However, the rights to transfer assets have been reassigned in two other areas.

First, enterprises and households have been assigned greatly expanded rights to transfer assets to others in commodity form. The proportion of crops that must be delivered directly to village purchasing stations, and the proportion of industrial products to be delivered to state agencies and enterprises under mandatory plans, has been drastically reduced, and entirely eliminated for much of the small scale rural sector. What we commonly call the 'spread of the market' is in fact founded upon a prior reassignment to households and enterprises of the right to transfer assets in commodity form.[3] These property rights are central to the entire reform process, and despite extensive legal restrictions on sales and prices of various commodities, such rights have become almost unrestricted because of the difficulties of monitoring such a vastly expanded volume of transactions.

Second, there have emerged a number of informal subcontracting and leasing schemes that in effect amount to a *de facto* right to transfer productive assets to others. This has created an extensive 'secondary market' in use rights and rights to income over productive assets. In many parts of the country agricultural land contracted to households is being subcontracted by those households to specialized farmers who amass landholdings within villages and farm on a large scale, while in other areas household land is subleased to poor farmers from mountainous regions who migrate to richer regions. Individuals who lease enterprises from local governments now commonly subcontract those enterprises out to others. And government offices and institutions that had no productive assets before the reforms are now finding that their budgets can be considerably enhanced by transferring use rights over land, buildings, vehicles and meal halls to entrepreneurs who turn them to productive use in return for rents or shares of profits. In all of these cases, there is not a transfer downward of use rights as part of the conception of reform, but a lateral transfer of assets as a secondary effect. Such transfers of rights sometimes have a tenuous legal basis, but the widespread development of such a secondary market in productive assets has had important social and political consequences.

Property rights and political authority

The devolution of property rights downward within government hierarchies, and their reassignment to enterprises and households, has had important implications for the exercise of political authority. Even in China, where such a devolution has been limited, and open 'privatization' rare, political authority is changed in subtle, yet very important, ways. Political changes can occur directly as a result of the reassignment of property rights, or they may occur indirectly through the newly created mechanisms through which incomes are distributed.

For example, two important consequences have flowed directly from the downward reassignment of rights to income flows among levels of government. Fiscal reforms have given local governments, from the provinces down to villages, greater rights over the increased revenues they generate, and the authority to impose new local taxes and extra-tax levies upon enterprises within their jurisdictions. One striking result of this reassignment of rights is the geometric growth during the 1980s of extrabudgetary funds—those funds held by government jurisdictions for discretionary use outside of financial plans sent down from above. They have increased from 31 per cent of national budgetary revenues in 1978 to 90 per cent in 1987 (SSB 1989). This growing fiscal autonomy of regional and local governments is very likely the main foundation for the widely-noted weakening of Beijing over the implementation of policy, especially economic policies, in provinces and localities (Oi 1991; Wang 1991).

A second consequence is the rise of local corporatism and cadre entrepreneurship in China's townships and villages. Fiscal reforms have given these local governments greater rights to retain revenues they generate, and thereby both greater incentive to foster local industrial growth, and the financial means to do so. The rapidly growing rural industrial sector has been centered on enterprises collectively owned by villages and townships. This has drawn rural cadres deeply into the management of local industry, leading to a form of local government that is in effect a territorially defined industrial corporation, in which local officials are leading entrepreneurs (Oi 1990, 1992).

More subtle are the ways in which the reassignment of property rights have altered the exercise of authority by cadres. The change has been most striking in rural areas, where extensive property rights have been delegated to households. There, the decisions of cadres, as either regulators of private economic activity or as custodians of collectively owned property leased to households, now affect family income more directly, and in more dramatic ways than in the past. Within the framework of collective agriculture, cadres had discretion over the assignment of agricultural tasks and work point income, and in assigning people to well-paying factory jobs, but the income differences involved were rather small (Oi 1985). In the new household economy, however, cadre decisions regarding the leasing of collective property (e.g., who shall get the contracts and on what terms), the extension of credit, and the assessment and taxation of income, for example, can have a large impact upon the standard of living of a household. Such cadre discretion is much more limited in urban factories, but even there cadres exercise discretion over the distribution of much larger bonus funds than in the past. In both settings, cadre authority increasingly involves consequential decisions regarding the distribution of income from property. This would appear logically to increase the likelihood of conflict and resistance along with the rise in the economic stakes involved, and there is some evidence of increased contention over cadre exercise of discretion regarding the regulation of household production or the allocation of income (Zweig 1986; Zweig et al. 1987; Walder 1987, 1989, 1991; Nee 1989).

Property rights and cadre incomes

As implied above, local governments in China continue to hold extensive property rights in productive assets, and they also possess considerable regulative powers regarding the exercise of property rights recently delegated to households and individuals. These powers can be converted into sources of income for officials, and have been on a large scale. This is done primarily in two ways: first, by deploying previously unexploited assets of their organization as new sources of income, and second, by converting influence and regulative discretion into sources of income.

China's reforms have provided officials with vast new sources of income by turning their established holdings and authority for the first time into potentially income-producing assets. Several examples will serve to illustrate this principle. In Beijing and undoubtedly in other cities, the control that the Bureau of Public Security exercises over street space in public places has turned into a lucrative source of income. The bureau has subdivided such space and rented it out to agents—often relatives of public security officials—who in turn subdivide and rent out stalls for higher prices.[4] In Wenzhou and undoubtedly also in other regions, private businessmen who seek to grow beyond current limits on private firm size and avoid political difficulties commonly purchase political insurance and favorable treatment from regulative authorities by making payments to local government in return for designating them as a 'collective' enterprise (Liu 1992). In yet another variation of this practice, property not fully utilized by state organizations is turned into revenue-generating assets. Land, for example, can be put up as a capital share in a joint venture, street level offices can be rented out as shop space, or vehicles belonging to a government office or institution can be rented out to individuals who hire themselves out as taxi drivers or truckers.[5] Finally, in what is probably the single most widely analyzed practice, village officials have leased out collective property to themselves and relatives and have entered lucrative careers as 'cadre-entrepreneurs' (Oi 1986, 1989). In all of these cases, powers or properties that in the past had little commercial value are turned into income producing assets by and for officials.

Stratification and popular political perceptions

At the outset of this chapter I referred to a common 'polarization' model widely held by specialists in this field—if often only tacitly—in thinking about the relationship between changes in social stratification and their political consequences. In this manner of thinking, political consequences are seen to flow from the emergence of larger gaps in income, from changing amounts of inequality. I also stated that the main purpose of this chapter is to specify an alternative way of thinking about changes in the stratification order and their consequences. I have reinterpreted the reforms from a property rights perspective, reviewed evidence about changes in income distribution, described some ways in which political authority has been altered by the reforms, and illustrated the new ways in which officials may earn income. In this section I seek to pull together these separate strands and specify the ways in which China's reforms have altered the process of social stratification and brought about changes in popular political attitudes.

That there were decisive changes in popular political attitudes in the 1980s—especially in urban areas—is beyond dispute. Many public opinion polls in China since the middle of the decade reported deep dissatisfaction over official corruption and inflation, a precipitous fall in the prestige of the party, and a widespread perception that the benefits of the reforms had been distributed unfairly (Rosen 1991; Wang 1990; Walder 1991). And of course, the massive popular response in cities throughout China to the student protests of 1989 was an unprecedented sign that the reforms had wrought quiet but massive changes in popular political attitudes during the 1980s. These changes were not the simple result of changes in income differentials, but of two interrelated processes that were a part of the changes described above.

Changes in customary differentials and status orderings

Emerging income differentials may create discontent not so much because of their size, but because they upset custom and the existing status order. Employees of urban state enterprises, both white- and blue-collar, are among those who have felt most left behind by the new income opportunities offered by the reforms. In the Mao period, these state sector people were privileged; they were members of work units with the greatest fringe benefits and status. Now people formerly on the fringes of the state sector are among those receiving the highest money incomes. Petty entrepreneurs, private businessmen, rural construction workers, and workers in small collective factories in the suburbs, all make cash incomes that can vastly exceed that of the fixed state salary (this perception is especially acute in periods of inflation). Even peasant entrepreneurs in the close suburbs are making much higher cash incomes, and building new homes much more spacious and comfortable than those of city dwellers. What is most unsettling about these trends is not the fact that larger income differences are appearing, but that groups formerly secure in their

privileged position are finding that position eroding rapidly, while
formerly marginal groups in despised occupations are newly advantaged
(Walder 1991).

In addition to upsetting the customary status order (and thereby
upsetting those formerly privileged), the new income differentials violate
established conceptions of fairness. State employees in the past have taken
it entirely for granted that they receive massive subsidies to their living
standards and that they have firm job security, and they view these as
legitimate rights. Yet when private entrepreneurs or suburban peasants—
people who enjoy neither the subsidies or the security—come to earn
much higher money incomes, the state employee finds these differentials
illegitimate because this kind of opportunity is distributed unequally. As
suggested in public opinion surveys and my own interviews with recent
emigre workers, state sector employees come to see these high incomes as
the result of a chance distribution of advantages—having a marketable
skill, a knowledgeable or powerful relative, start-up capital, or connections to the proper authorities (Wang 1990; Walder 1991). They are
therefore viewed as unfair because not everyone has an opportunity to
make these large incomes.

Cognitive and normative changes of political consequence

Property rights reassignments have changed the way in which income is
earned and retained in two politically consequential ways. First, in
household agriculture and in the small-scale private and individual
sectors, income earned is now much more clearly due to the independent
efforts of households or individuals. As production has become organized
by households, and as households or small firms have become independent accounting units, the decisions of village officials or various tax,
commerce, or public security officials in cities directly and visibly alter the
income of households and individuals, and the consequences for income
can be quite large. Second, even in those areas of the economy where
property rights have been reassigned only to firms, as in the large-scale
state sector, cadres have greater discretion over much larger amounts of
retained income than at any time in the past. Bonuses now average one-
third of the cash wage, and many state firms now allow the base salary to
deviate from standard state wage scales by considerable amounts. Worker
incomes therefore depend much more so than in the past upon the
discretion of factory officials—how much of retained profit to allocate to
bonuses (and other benefits), and to which workshops and individuals the
highest bonuses shall be allocated.

These changes in the mechanism of income distribution appear to be
having important cognitive consequences: peasants and workers understand that their livelihoods depend considerably upon the decisions of

officials directly above them, and they are able to see more clearly the relationship between cadre decisions and their incomes. Two examples shall illustrate this idea. In collective agriculture, individuals were assigned to various tasks on different plots of land throughout the year. All income was pooled at the team level and redistributed at the end of the year. Households had no conception of the product that was 'theirs' since this was impossible to calculate except through work points, and only team and brigade officials had direct information about collective finances. Under household agriculture, this is radically changed. Any levies or charges placed upon household production impinge directly and visibly upon income that a household now sees as being earned according to their own efforts. In state factories, workers now understand that their incomes depend directly upon their superiors' decisions, and that since factory bonus and welfare funds are fixed, the more that is allocated to investment, or to cadre bonuses and benefits, the less they shall receive. Most important of all, these decisions are not dictated by a distant bureaucracy but are made by officials they deal with every day.

The kind of cognitive changes described above amount to little more than a realistic understanding of a new situation. But I would like to suggest that these changes in understanding may have led to a second-order cognitive change: a clearer recognition of the fact that special privilege and corruption on the part of cadres reduces the standard of living of ordinary citizens. This relationship would be most transparent to peasant households and private entrepreneurs, who understand clearly that the kinds of arbitrary exactions to which they are often subject directly fund a corrupt cadre lifestyle. There is also some evidence that state factory workers are more sensitive than before to distributional issues, particularly to cadre privileges within the firm (Walder 1987, 1989). We can only speculate on this point, but one might readily suspect that a clearer appreciation of the personal costs of cadre privilege and corruption at the grass roots level is readily transferable to special privilege and corruption at higher levels of government. Such a social–psychological mechanism may well be responsible for the vastly heightened sensitivity to the issue of corruption documented in so many opinion surveys in the 1980s, and which erupted so dramatically in 1989.

The final link in this chain of reasoning is that these cognitive changes bring about normative changes as well. New conceptions of citizen, if not individual, rights appear to be growing out of the new property rights assignments and related changes in the production and distribution of income. Cadre decisions now affect household and individual worker income more, and more visibly, and any decisions that appear arbitrary or self-serving are now more likely to be evaluated as unfair, unjust or directly exploitative. This plausibly leads not only to a greater popular sensitivity to, and anger toward, official corruption. It may also be building the cognitive and normative foundations for popular demands for 'democracy', which in this context means fair and clean public administration (see also Nee 1989; Stark 1989). Through this chain of connections between changes in property rights, new patterns of income distribution and resulting cognitive and normative changes, we may begin to grasp the quiet yet profound ways in which economic reform and material progress are generating not only political dissatisfaction, but demands for certain kinds of political reform as well.

Conclusions

Much scholarly discourse about economic reform refers to the market versus the plan, to hard versus soft budget constraints, to unregulated versus administered prices, as if there is some dividing line beyond which economic reform may 'really' be consequential. The property rights approach adapted here from the economics of organization helps us more clearly to understand the momentous changes that have emerged even under 'partial' reform, and even in areas of the economy that have experienced, by common standards, the least change. More importantly, property rights analysis helps us to understand phenomena that are puzzling from the common market versus plan perspective: why and how cadres may continue to hold considerable power even after the spread of commodity markets; why and how local governments become major actors in the economy; and why government has an incentive to subsidize unprofitable firms. And, most of all, property rights analysis offers insight into the cognitive, normative and political processes that can create conflict and political instability.

Viewed purely as a pattern of income distribution, the new stratification order would not appear to have enormous political implications. Income distribution, for example, has been most egalitarian and least altered in cities, where measureable political dissatisfaction (in opinion surveys) and political unrest, has been most pronounced (see Khan et al. 1992). What appears to be much more consequential is the new *process* of social stratification which, when viewed from the perspective of the reassignment of property rights, has a number of interesting implications. First, property rights reassignments have gone farthest in the formerly marginal- and lowest-income sectors of the economy, raising cash incomes in these sectors more rapidly, and upsetting customary differentials—and the social privilege to which urban state employees have long been accustomed. Second, property rights reassignments have altered the ways in which income is earned and distributed—even in state factories—and has caused income to vary more, and more directly, as a visible consequence of cadre decisions. Third, this new situation appears to be having important cognitive consequences: citizens appear to have a clearer understanding of the costs to them of cadre arbitrariness, special privilege, and corruption, an understanding that may be readily transferable from the grass roots to higher levels of officialdom. And fourth, these cognitive changes appear to bring accompanying normative changes: not only heightened disapproval of official corruption, but more positive demands for political change in the direction of fair and clean public administration.

Notes

[1] Indices of income inequality within cities and villages for China in the 1970s were very low by international standards, and near the bottom of the range for socialist economies. The greatest inequalities were between city and countryside, and between different rural regions, where Chinese inequalities were comparatively high (Riskin 1987; Selden 1988).

[2] Problems encountered in the enforcement of property rights are central to the economics of contracts, industrial organization, and bureaucracies, usually focused upon the relationship between principals and agents. The idea is central to transaction cost economics. While the monitoring and enforcement of property rights is a crucial problem in China's reforms, in this chapter I will limit discussion primarily to the government's reassignment of such rights in the process of reform, and their consequences.

[3] In fact, markets in China still are largely restricted to the exchange of finished agricultural and industrial products, precisely because rights regarding the transfer of assets have been widely delegated only with regard to finished commodities. Rights regarding the transfer of assets in all other forms remain highly restricted, and for this reason there are as yet no comparable markets for capital, credit, land, and fixed assets.

[4] This practice was described in an interview with a private clothing vendor interviewed in connection with her activity in the Beijing workers autonomous union (see Walder & Gong 1993). One can imagine the conflict of interest these income flows would create if orders are received from above to crack down on private tradesmen.

[5] Income from such arrangements would properly belong to the unit that owns the assets, but such informally arranged flows of income would appear to be an important source of income for the individual cadres directly involved (who may, in many cases, make the arrangements without formal work unit permission).

References

Demsetz, Harold 1967, 'Toward a Theory of Property Rights', *American Economic Review*, vol. 57, no. 2, pp. 347–59.

Furubotn, Eirik G. & Svetozar Pejovich eds 1974, *The Economics of Property Rights*, Ballinger, Cambridge, Mass.

Grosfeld, Irena 1991, 'Privatization of State Enterprises in Eastern Europe: The Search for a Market Environment', *Eastern European Politics and Societies*, vol. 5, no. 1, pp. 142–61.

Khan, Azizur R., Keith Griffin, Carl Riskin, & Zhao Renwei 1992, 'Household Income and its Distribution in China', *China Quarterly*, no. 132 , pp. 1029–61.

Liu Yialing 1992, 'Reform from Below: The Private Economy and Local Politics in Rural Industrialization of Wenzhou, *China Quarterly*, no. 130, pp. 293–316.

Nee, Victor 1989, 'Peasant Entrepreneurship and the Politics of Regulation in China', in *Remaking the Economic Institutions of Socialism*, eds Victor Nee & David Stark, Stanford University Press, Stanford.

Oi, Jean C. 1985, 'Communism and Clientelism: Rural Politics in China', *World Politics*, vol. 37, no. 2, pp. 238–66.

——1986, 'Commercializing China's Rural Cadres', *Problems of Communism*, vol. 35, no. 5, pp. 1–15.

——1989, 'Market Reforms and Corruption in Rural China', *Studies in Comparative Communism*, vol. 22, no. 2–3, pp. 221–2.

——1990, 'The Fate of the Collective After the Commune', in *Chinese Society on the Eve of Tiananmen: The Impact of Reform*, eds Deborah Davis & Ezra F. Vogel, Harvard Contemporary China Series No. 7, Council on East Asian Studies, Cambridge.

——1991, 'Fiscal Reform and Local Autonomy in Rural China', paper presented to the Annual Meetings of the American Political Science Association, Washington D.C.

——1992, 'Fiscal Reform and the Economic Foundations of Local State Corporatism in China', *World Politics*, vol. 45, no. 1, pp. 99–126.

Polanyi, Karl 1957, 'The Economy as Instituted Process', in *Trade and Market in the Early Empires: Economies in History and Theory*, eds Karl Polanyi, Conrad Arensberg & Harry W. Pearson, The Free Press, Glencoe Illinois, pp. 243–70.

Pryor, Frederick 1973, *Property and Industrial Organization in Capitalist and Communist Countries*, Indiana University Press, Bloomington.

Riskin, Carl 1987, *China's Political Economy: The Quest for Development since 1949*, Oxford University Press, New York.

Rosen, Stanley 1991, 'The Rise (and Fall) of Public Opinion in Post-Mao China', in *Reform and Reaction in Post-Mao China: The Road to Tiananmen*, ed. Richard Baum, Routledge, Boston.

Selden, Mark 1988, *The Political Economy of Chinese Socialism*, Sharpe, Armonk, New York.

Stark, David 1989, 'Coexisting Organizational Forms in Hungary's Emerging Mixed Economy', in *Remaking the Economic Institutions of Socialism*, eds Victor Nee & David Stark, Stanford University Press, Stanford.

——1990, 'Privatization in Hungary: From Plan to Market or From Plan to Clan?', *Eastern European Politics and Society*, vol. 4, no. 3, pp. 351–92.

State Statistical Bureau (SSB) 1989, *Zhongguo tongji nianjian 1989*, Zhongguo tongji nianjian chubanshe, Beijing.

Szelenyi, Ivan 1978, 'Social Inequalities in State Socialist Redistributive Economies: Dilemmas for Social Policy in Contemporary Socialist Societies of Eastern Europe', *International Journal of Comparative Sociology*, vol. 19, nos 1–2, pp. 63–87.

Walder, Andrew G. 1987, 'Wage Reform and the Web of Factory Interests', *The China Quarterly*, no. 109, pp. 22–41.

——1989, 'Factory and Manager in an Era of Reform', *China Quarterly*, no. 118, pp. 242–64.

——1991, 'Workers, Managers and the State: The Reform Era and the Political Crisis of 1989', *China Quarterly*, no. 127, pp. 467–92.

Walder, Andrew G. & Xiaoxia Gong 1993, 'Workers in the Democracy Movement: The Politics of the Beijing Workers' Autonomous Union', *The Australian Journal of Chinese Affairs*, no. 29, pp. 1–29.

Wang, Shaoguang 1990, 'Deng Xiaoping's Reforms and the Chinese Workers' Participation in the Protest Movement of 1989', unpublished paper, Department of Political Science, Yale University.

—— 1991, 'The Rise of the "Second Budget" in Post-Mao China', unpublished paper, Department of Political Science, Yale University.

Zweig, David 1986, 'Prosperity and Conflict in Post-Mao Rural China', *China Quarterly*, no. 105, pp. 1–18.

Zweig, David, Kathy Hartford, James Feinerman & Jianxu Deng 1987, 'Law, Contracts, and Economic Modernization: Lessons from the Recent Chinese Rural Reforms', *Stanford Journal of International Law*, vol. 23, no. 2, pp. 319–64.

2 Income distribution in the 1980s

Guonan Ma

This chapter will review the literature on income distribution in China, systematically examine the broad patterns of personal income distribution in the 1980s and explore some plausible factors influencing these patterns.

Income distribution is a complex issue. It spans questions ranging from the objectives of economic development, proper measurements of distribution, and possible factors affecting this distribution, to the cost and benefits of various policy instruments to achieve greater equality of income distribution both in the short and long run. Needless to say, it is often an emotional issue. Its social and political implications go far beyond pure economics, and are viewed by many as a driving force behind social turmoil.

Attempts by developing economies to attain equitable growth have proven to be difficult and vary considerably from one country to another (Sundrum 1990). China is, of course, a low-income country with a huge population, and has been praised for achieving rapid growth while satisfying basic needs and maintaining egalitarian distribution. It is interesting to evaluate how China copes with the problem of maintaining equality in the context of a market-oriented reform which emphasizes efficiency.

The importance of the income distribution issue is also highlighted in the volatile situation of Eastern Europe which has recently embarked on a path of transformation from a centrally-planned to a market-oriented economy. Even though the social and political contexts are quite different in China and Eastern Europe, China has undergone more than a decade of market-oriented reforms and may provide useful insights and comparisons.

Our effort to understand the development of income distribution is complicated by the vague meaning of equity. There is little consensus in this regard. This chapter focuses largely on the realized outcome of income distribution. There is also great difficulty in assessing the status of income distribution in China, in part because of the complex institutional arrangements and the scarcity of data. For one thing, we do not have sufficient information on household income levels, although family budget surveys are regularly conducted by the State Statistical Bureau. Even the published data at the aggregate level are not comparable for rural and urban households. The reliability of survey procedures and the flawed definitions of survey variables pose another problem. Other scattered evidence contradictory to the official survey data cautions us not to be over-confident about these survey data.

To make matters worse, the distorted price system in China has long been manipulated as a vehicle of income transfer among different sectors. For instance, the 'dual price' system serves as a *de facto* public transfer in the form of implicit tax/subsidy, the economic incidence of which is far from clear. Also, multiple standards of welfare provisions associated with various types of ownership and deliberately established by the Government contradict many China specialists' claim that the Chinese Government considers equitable income distribution as one of its top priorities.

Hence any attempt to use one or two indicators or cases to describe the overall performance of equity in China must be regarded with extreme caution. A more sensible approach is to analyze several major dimensions of the issue based on the published data. In this case: urban–rural inequality, regional variations, and income distribution at the household level.

After examining the above three aspects of income distribution in China during the 1980s, the chapter identifies and analyzes a number of important factors in the determination of income distribution, and later summarizes the main findings of this study, concluding with a brief discussion of policy implications for equitable growth.

Main patterns of income distribution

Urban–rural inequality

One overriding feature of the Chinese economy has been the distinct dichotomy between the rural and urban sectors through strict control over rural–urban migration. Until quite recently, about 20 per cent of the nation's population resided in the urban areas while the remaining majority lived in the rural areas. Most city residents enjoy secure employment and wages, a guaranteed pension upon retirement, rationed supply of the low-priced basic goods, free medical care and subsidized housing.[1] In contrast, peasants have very limited access to state welfare and social security programs, and their income is subject to the vagaries of weather conditions (Rawski 1982; Lardy 1984; Perkins 1988).

The urban–rural income gap in the 1980s is measured in this chapter by the simple ratios of urban to rural income and consumption levels (Table 2.1). The first column lists the income ratio based on the original data from the family budget surveys. It shows that at the start of the 1980s, the urban to rural income ratio was as high as 2.3; it then fell to about 1.7 during 1983–1985, but rose again to more than 2.0 in 1988–1989. A similar pattern is also observed in the urban–rural consumption ratio (column 4): dropping from 2.7 to 2.3, and then rising back to 2.7. This observed U-shaped change in the income gap suggests that the reforms have not yet achieved significant long-term improvements in urban–rural equality.

One possible explanation for this might be that the gap between the costs of living in urban as against rural areas widened so that these ratios exaggerate the recent worsening of the urban–rural disparity. However, urban–rural economic integration has been strengthened in the reform process by price liberalization, expansion of market forces and greater factor mobility. Hence, the law of one price should work to narrow any discrepancy between the costs of living in the urban and rural areas.

Nevertheless, these two ratios may still be biased. An important part of urban incomes and consumption lies in the form of subsidies and collective welfare, which are not included in the official survey definition

Table 2.1: Urban–rural ratios of income and consumption
(Rural = 1.0)

Year	Urban–rural income ratio (original)	Urban–rural income ratio (revised)	Urban–rural consumption ratio
1980	2.29	3.08	2.70
1981	2.05	2.75	2.50
1982	1.83	2.45	2.40
1983	1.70	2.23	2.30
1984	1.71	2.13	2.30
1985	1.72	2.06	2.30
1986	1.95	2.26	2.40
1987	1.98	2.23	2.50
1988	2.05	2.28	2.70
1989	2.10	2.33	2.70

Notes: Figures are expressed at the national average level. The income ratios are calculated from the urban income available for consumption and rural net income in the household survey data. The consumption ratio is derived directly from official national accounts data. The revised income is computed by adding three elements of hidden income to the original figures for urban income: price subsidies, imputed urban rental subsidies, and part of the non-cash collective welfare benefits in the state sector. The detailed derivation procedure and underlying data are available upon request.
Sources: SSB 1985, 1987, 1988, 1989 and 1990.

of personal urban income. Price adjustments and the related direct cash compensation to urban dwellers for higher prices of basic necessities have gradually reduced the relative importance in urban incomes of implicit subsidies and transfers in kind, implying that the 'hidden part' of the urban income is increasingly replaced by additional rises in explicit personal income. As a result, the observed income ratio in the 1980s should have been diminishing in relative terms over time.

We have attempted to take into account part of the implicit subsidies to urban residents, and have recalculated a new series of urban–rural income ratios for the 1980s. The result is shown in the second column of Table 2.1. As expected, the revised ratio is higher than the ratio based on the original data, suggesting that the latter under-estimates urban–rural inequality. The new series also exhibits a U-shaped pattern. However, although the favourable trend in the urban–rural income ratio in the first half of the 1980s was partially reversed in the late 1980s, the reforms as a whole seemed to have somewhat narrowed the income gap.

In sum, our evidence suggests that China's urban–rural disparity in the 1980s can be characterized by an overall but limited decrease in the urban–rural income gap, a partial reversal of this trend in the late 1980s, and a persistently higher urban income nationally.

Regional variations

The issue of regional inequality in China has been a contentious one. The works of Lardy (1978, 1980 and 1983), Donnithorne (1967), Naughton (1988), Tsui (1991) and Kato (1992) suggest that fiscal redistribution and investment strategy were important means for the central government to influence income distribution across regions.

Initially, we examine regional inequality by looking at the rural and urban sectors separately rather than at the overall regional income trends. The justification for doing so is clear from the earlier discussion of urban–rural disparities. Moreover, quite different factors might influence urban as against rural patterns of regional inequality. Finally, we mainly use the published family survey data, providing a useful complement to earlier studies which national accounts data aggregated at the level of the province. Since the survey data of rural and urban households are very difficult to compare, it is desirable to study the regional variations in the rural and urban sectors separately.

The main method of analyzing the regional income differential in personal income levels is the *coefficient of variation*, defined as the ratio of the standard deviation to the mean of the average income levels of the various regions. The higher this ratio is, the larger the variation across regions.

First, the *rural* coefficients of variation across provinces presented in Table 2.2 suggest that there was a general trend towards increasing inter-province income disparities for most of the 1980s. Thus the coefficient rose

Table 2.2: Coefficients of variation for inter-province rural income levels (1978–1989)

Year	Nominal income	Deflated by MP	Deflated by RP
1978	.294	.294	.294
1979	.294	.294	.294
1980	.280	.280	.280
1981	.260	.259	.259
1982	.268	.288	.271
1983	.264	.288	.270
1984	.319	.340	.333
1985	.313	.318	.294
1986	.344	.329	.319
1987	.363	.355	.334
1988	.379	.366	.345
1989	.394	.394	.359

Notes: The *coefficient of variation* is defined as the ratio of the sample standard deviation to the sample mean of the rural income each year and is computed on the basis of the provincial average figures. MP is the free market price index, and RP is the retail price index. Both price indexes are provincial level indexes. Twenty-eight provinces are included. Taiwan and Tibet are not included.
Source: SSB 1981–1989.

from 0.28 to about 0.38 between 1980 and 1989. Two points should be noted. First, the coefficient fell in the period of 1978–1983, suggesting that most of the early rural reform programs might have had equalizing effects on regional distribution in the rural areas. Second, using current price variables tends to raise the value of coefficients of variation as against using constant price variables.

Any analysis of regional inequality in terms of provincial averages is distorted since one province often has the size and population of an average-sized European country. Any measurement of inter-regional inequality may be sensitive to the choice of regional unit. Hence, it is desirable to supplement analysis on the level of the province with that on the county level. This chapter makes a first attempt in this regard by looking at *inter-county* income variations within one province (Anhui) for the period of 1978–1989. Starting with a rather high value of 0.38 in 1978, the coefficient of variation at the county level in Anhui rose slightly in the late 1970s and early 1980s (to 0.41), but fell gradually to about 0.22 in 1989 (Table 2.3).

Notice the sharp contrast between the decreasing trend of regional variations between counties (in one province) and the increasing trend between provinces. One important message is suggested. First, it is often misleading to claim vaguely that the level of 'regional inequality' has changed in one or the other direction solely on the basis of a few case studies. The differing trends at the provincial and county level may reveal diversified patterns of regional variations in personal income during the reform process, which defy simplistic explanations. Depending on the definition of 'region' used, one may reach rather different conclusions.[2]

Table 2.3: Coefficients of variation for inter-county rural income levels in Anhui Province (1978–1989)

Year	1978	1980	1981	1982	1983	1984	1985	1986	1987	1988	1989
	.378	.405	.412	.357	.314	.231	.216	.212	.225	.225	.222

Notes: There are about 85 to 105 counties depending on the year.
Sources: *Anhui Economic Yearbook*, 1984-1990.

Turning to the regional inequality of urban household income as between provinces, the coefficient of variation is computed on the basis of two measures of urban household income (see Table 2.4 for details). A widening of the gap between household incomes in different provinces is confirmed whether the incomes are deflated or not. This may be one main source of the resentment of urban residents towards economic reform in the late 1980s. However, the inter-province differential is much smaller for urban than for rural incomes.

Household-level income distribution

Income disparities between households comprise one of the most basic and direct aspects in the overall pattern of income distribution. Earlier studies of the impact of the reforms on income distribution among households seem to imply a rosy picture for rural China in the early 1980s

Table 2.4: Coefficients of variation for inter-province urban household income levels (1981–1989)

Year	GY	NY	GY deflated by MP	NY deflated by MP	GY deflated by RP	NY deflated by Rp
1981	.106	.118	.106	.118	.106	.118
1982	.110	.113	.123	.124	.106	.108
1983	.118	.121	.131	.141	.113	.117
1984	.126	.129	.156	.159	.130	.133
1985	.146	.150	.167	.171	.154	.158
1986	.135	.143	.143	.151	.120	.128
1987	.143	.153	.141	.152	.124	.134
1988	.164	.170	.159	.168	.137	.144
1989	.184	.192	.171	.180	.134	.143

Notes: GY is 'All Gross Income', while NY is the 'Income Available for Living.' MP is the free market price index, and RP is the general retail price index. Twenty-seven provinces are included. Taiwan, Tibet and Qinghai are not included. Both price indexes are provincial level indexes.
Sources: SSB 1986, 1987b, 1988a, 1988b, 1989b

(Griffin & Griffin 1984; Chai 1985). Our evidence in general does not support this optimistic view.

The two measures used to quantify household income inequality are the Gini coefficient and Lorenz index. The Gini coefficient measures the degree of deviation from a completely equal distribution, and takes on the values between zero and one. The higher the coefficient, the greater the measured inequality. The Lorenz index here is expressed as a ratio of the income share of the top quintile of the sample population to that of the bottom quintile. It is a useful indicator of the gap between the 'rich' and the 'poor'. Again, we inspect the household-level inequality in the urban and rural areas separately. Furthermore, regional differences in household-level income disparities are examined. In doing so, the three important aspects of income distribution are brought together to give a more reliable and balanced picture.

The Gini coefficient for rural China as a whole rose from 0.21 in 1978 to 0.24 in 1980, and further to 0.30 in 1988 (Figure 2.1 and Table 2.5). A similar worsening trend is also observed for the urban Gini coefficient, though the

Table 2.5: Gini coefficients of rural household incomes (1978–1986)

	1978	1980	1981	1983	1985
Total Sample	.2124	.2366	.2388	.2459	.2635
Beijing				.2152	.2400
Tianjin	.1590	.1950	.2240	.2260	.2250
Inner Mongolia	.2292				.2407
Liaoning	.1847	.2315	.2500	.2449	.2929
Jilin			.1943	.2603	.2812
Heilongjiang	.1769	.2353	.2269	.2712	.2760
Jiangsu		.2200			.2500
Zhejiang		.2073	.1885	.2009	.2554
Anhui	.2125		.1742		.1970
Fujian		.1689	.1944	.1865	.2031
Jiangxi	.1680		.1730		.1780
Shandong		.2427	.2255	.2187	.2356
Henan		.1700			.2320
Hubei			.1739	.1895	.2067
Hunan	.1449	.1592		.1724	.1923
Guangdong	.1787	.2105	.2311	.2394	.2918
Sichuan	.1930				.1990
Guizhou	.1560	.1630	.1960	.2090	.2260
Yunnan		.2037	.2151	.2160	.2363
Shaanxi			.1933		.2278
Gansu		.2642	.2674	.2470	.2364
Ningxia			.2905	.2426	.2862
Xinjiang			.2067	.2518	.2877

Notes: Data for the seven provinces not included are unavailable.
Sources: SSB 1987a and 1989a.

Figure 2.1 Rural and urban Gini coefficients (1980–1988)

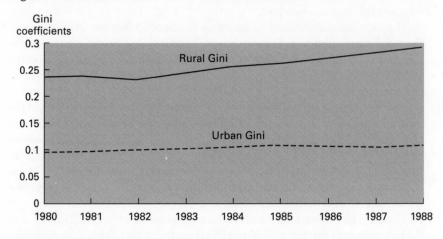

overall level of inequality is much lower (around 0.1). The tendency of the Gini coefficients to rise is also reflected in the rural Gini coefficients in different provinces. Of the 24 listed provinces, 20 provinces show a higher Gini coefficient in 1985 than in 1978–81, depending on which is the earliest figure available. Only those of Anhui, Gansu and Ningxia decreased.

Most of the provincial rural Gini indexes cluster around the range of 0.2 to 0.3. The lowest is Jiangxi (0.178) and the highest Liaoning (0.293). If rural China is divided into three large regions—east, central and west—then an interesting pattern is revealed (see Table 2.6). The more prosperous

Table 2.6: Rural Gini indexes by income group and region (1985)

	Gini index
Total sample	.2635
By region	
Eastern region	.2793
Central region	.2506
Western region	.2400
By income group	
Below Y300	.2267
Y300–Y400	.2389
Y400–Y500	.2616
Y500–Y600	.2402
Above Y600	.2283

Notes: The tripartite division of China's provinces is as follows:
Eastern region: Liaoning, Beijing, Tianjin, Hebei, Shandong, Jiangsu, Shanghai, Zhejiang, Fujian, Guangdong, Hainan and Guangxi.
Central region: Nei Menggu, Shanxi, Henan, Anhui, Hubei, Hunan and Jiangxi.
Western region: Gansu, Shaanxi, Sichuan, Guizhou, Yunnan, Xizang, Qinghai and Xinjiang.
Source: SSB 1989a

eastern region had the highest Gini coefficient (0.279) in 1985, the poorest western region the lowest (0.24). But if we break the whole rural sample into five groups according to income levels, there is no simple relationship between income level and inequality (Table 2.6). This is also confirmed by Figure 2.2.

Table 2.7 presents the income shares of the top and bottom quintiles of the surveyed rural households and their Lorenz indexes in eleven provinces. The income share of the bottom quintile is about 10 per cent and declined between 1978–81 and 1985 by one percentage point for all the listed provinces. The income shares of the richest 20 per cent in the listed provinces rose by between 2 and 8 percentage points, except in Beijing. Their shares ranged between 31 and 38 per cent in 1985. In 1985, Hunan had the lowest Lorenz index (2.5), while Xinjiang had the highest (4.3). Thus, overall the poor became poorer, and the rich richer, as is indicated

Figure 2.2 Provincial income levels (yuan) and Gini coefficients in rural China (1985)

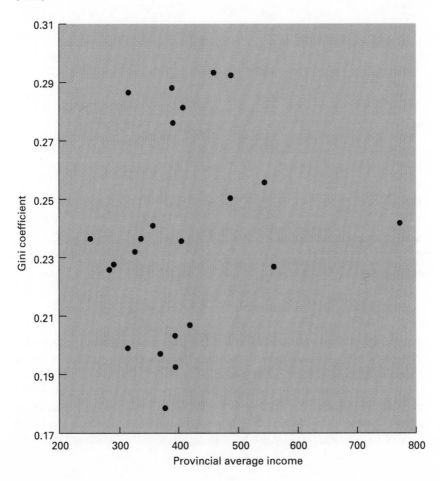

Table 2.7: Income distribution (percentage share of total income) and the Lorenz index of rural households (1980–1985)

Province and Year	Share of top quintile (per cent)	Share of bottom quintile (per cent)	Lorenz index
Beijing			
1980	35.6	10.5	3.39
1985	34.9	9.4	3.71
Tianjin			
1980	31.91	11.2	2.86
1985	33.68	10.2	3.32
Liaoning			
1978	29.0	11.6	2.50
1985	37.4	9.3	4.02
Zhejiang			
1980	32.6	11.2	2.90
1985	35.6	9.5	3.75
Hubei			
1981	31.2	11.4	2.73
1985	32.2	10.9	2.96
Hunan			
1978	26.9	13.5	1.99
1985	31.0	12.4	2.50
Guangdong			
1980	33.7	10.9	3.06
1985	39.2	9.3	4.23
Yunnan			
1980	32.9	10.9	3.06
1985	33.9	9.3	4.23
Guizhou			
1978	31.2	10.1	2.04
1985	36.0	9.9	3.04
Shaanxi			
1981	30.7	12.3	2.49
1985	33.1	10.0	3.31
Xingjiang			
1981	33.1	11.6	2.84
1985	37.8	8.8	4.30

Notes: The Lorenz index is defined as the ratio of the income share of the top quintile to that of the bottom quintile. Quintiles are expressed in terms of sample population.
Sources: SSB 1987a.

by the rising Lorenz indexes for all of the provinces considered between 1978–81 to 1985. This clearly suggests a definite unfavourable trend in income distribution between households in the rural areas.

As to household-level inequality in the cities, the Lorenz indices for urban China which range between 1.6 to 1.8, are much lower than those for rural households (Table 2.8). This is a direct consequence of the larger share of income enjoyed by the bottom quintile in the urban areas (about

Table 2.8: City income shares and the Lorenz index (1981–1989)

Year	Income share of the bottom quintile	Income share of the top quintile	Lorenz index
1981	14.38	24.32	1.69
1982	13.93	23.64	1.70
1983	15.42	25.96	1.68
1984	15.25	25.97	1.70
1985	14.68	26.71	1.82
1986	16.00	26.03	1.63
1987	15.04	26.36	1.75
1988	13.72	24.74	1.80
1989	14.53	26.71	1.84

Notes: Quintile is defined in terms of household numbers rather than population. The income variable is the city per capita 'All Gross Income'.
Sources: SSB 1986a, 1987b, 1988a, 1988b, 1989b.

14 to 15 per cent) and the smaller share by the top quintile (24 to 26 per cent). Greater government controls over the state sector and the high concentration of public servants in the urban areas under a somewhat unified salary scale also help to shape the smaller observed regional variations for urban than for rural income. Moreover, both the Gini coefficient and Lorenz index show only a slight upward trend and are much lower, in contrast with their rural counterparts.

However, income distribution among urban households varies between different regions (Table 2.9). As expected, the Gini coefficients in each of the urban regions are lower than those in the rural areas, and fall between the range of 0.13 to 0.18. While Shanghai, Hunan and Wuhan exhibit a stable or even declining Gini coefficient over time, the Gini coefficients of Guangzhou and Heilongjiang rose from 0.13 to 0.18 during the 1980s.

Table 2.9: Gini coefficient in selected urban areas

Year	Shanghai	Heilongjiang	Hunan	Wuhan	Guangzhou
1979	.1390	.1367			
1980	.1349	.1464			
1981	.1307	.1645		.1600	.1285
1982	.1287	.1534			.1335
1983	.1191	.1604			.1332
1984	.1254	.1631			.1463
1985	.1654	.1679	.1744	.1500	.1558
1986	.1238	.1771	.1709		.1634
1987	.1385	.1811	.1604		.1696
1988		.1825	.1654	.1500	.1754
1989				.1600	

Sources: Consumption Economics, nos 3 and 6, 1989; nos 1, 3 and 5, 1990.

In sum, patterns of household-level income distribution in rural and urban areas differ sharply. The rural disparities are much greater than urban ones and the gap between the incomes of rich and poor households in urban areas is consistently smaller than that in the rural areas. Moreover, this gap widened considerably in most rural areas, but remained quite stable for urban households as a whole.

Key factors shaping income distribution

The review of the above three dimensions of income distribution in the 1980s provides us with a good basis for a further exploration of the underlying causes and policy implications of these changes. However, it is not feasible in such a short paper to cover all of the many potential factors influencing the income distribution. The explanations given below are to some extent selective, to emphasize the point that many of the possible determinants often have different effects on the various dimensions of inequality.

The rural reform programs

The introduction of family farming and the collapse of the commune system may be viewed as one important cause of the greater inequality in rural incomes at the household level. Different demographic features, natural conditions and other endowments of peasant households may result in larger income variations, as compared with those under the 'work point' system of the commune, which pooled individual endowments and efforts. Moreover, rural collective services, which are believed to benefit peasants on an equitable basis, deteriorated (Perkins 1988). Finally, the government policy of tolerating widening income gaps ('To get rich is glorious') is often perceived as the 'cause' of worsening rural inequality.

This interpretation is biased and ignores other dimensions of the issue. First, it is well documented that there was a strong sense of egalitarianism in the elaborate methods of allocating land and other productive assets during the implementation of the 'Household Responsibility System'.[3] Also, self interest and individual efforts to 'get rich' are not the causes of increasing inequality among rural households. Nor is the policy of 'all become rich at the same time' the solution. Figure 2.2 demonstrates no definite relationship between income level and inequality. On the contrary, a better incentive scheme stimulates farm production and improves efficiency which should help reduce the urban–rural gap. This may be one key reason for the decrease in the urban–rural income gap between 1978 and 1984.

Another possible equalizing effect of rural reform is greater factor mobility, at least at the local level. The family farming system gives peasants the fundamental choice of discontinuing farm work and thus enhances regional and sectoral factor mobility. Allowing peasants to reallocate their resources turned out to be one main engine behind the rapid growth of rural industry, which competes strongly with the state sector and reduces urban–rural inequality. Also, it encourages regional crop specialization along the lines of comparative advantage, hence possibly narrowing regional disparities in rural areas for the period of 1978–1983. It appears that since 1985, the tendency towards regional specialization came to a halt (Carter & Zhong 1989) which, in part, explains the growing regional disparities.

Finally, blaming family farming for the decay of the collective welfare services associated with the commune system is rather far-fetched. The provision of public health and education did not have to depend on the commune system. If the financial burden is the problem, then this only suggests that the government discriminates in its provision of public services in favour of the urban and against the rural sector. Thus, at the time the communes were dismantled, the government greatly increased fiscal subsidies in order to keep the retail prices of basic commodities in urban areas low. Between 1980 and 1984, such subsidies almost doubled (SSB 1990).

However, it is also clear that the family farming system might in some way contribute to rising inequality among rural households. The abandoned 'work point' system was in essence a way of pooling different endowments and efforts across local peasant households. Because of the egalitarian methods of distributing the other productive factors in the early 1980s, differences in labour endowment between households could be one most important source of income inequality. Different access to markets is another possible cause of rising income inequality. Rural households in the inner suburbs of large cities will enjoy benefits from the expansion of market forces different from those in remote rural areas (Riskin 1991). But this probably has more to do with the barriers to factor mobility.

Rural industrialization

The spectacular development of rural township and village enterprises (TVEs) is another potentially important factor affecting rural income distribution and urban–rural equality. In 1980, such enterprises employed 22 per cent of the rural labour force and accounted for more than 40 per cent of total industrial output (SSB 1991). The correlation coefficient between average rural income at the province level and the share of non-farm employment in the rural labour force exceeds 0.8, which is consistent with Riskin's finding that off-farm income is a key determinant of the level of rural incomes. One implication is that greater rural industrialization will help relieve the problem of rural poverty, and could be one key reason for the modest reduction in the urban–rural income gap during the 1980s.

On the other hand, it is believed that the development of rural enterprises might have aggravated regional variations and household-level inequality in rural areas because of their uneven regional concentration and because of the practice of raising capital by limiting employment opportunity in these enterprises to those who make initial contributions of capital (Enos 1984; Islam 1991). These factors may to some extent explain the increase in variations in income levels between provinces and the widening gap between rich and poor in rural areas.

Hence there is no clear-cut answer as to the role of rural industrialization. On balance, it seems to be a predominantly positive factor in its influence on the overall pattern of income distribution. Its rapid growth breaks the monopoly of the privileged urban state sector which probably is the most important source of overall inequality in China. Also, these enterprises provide an important source of tax revenues which may be used to finance local infrastructure and public services. Finally, the possible negative effect of uneven regional development has much more to do with distorted price structures and different factor endowments than with rural industrialization *per se*. This factor will be of great significance in influencing the future trend of China's urban–rural equality in the long run.

The bargaining power and reform of the urban state sector

The state sector has always had better capital endowment, easier access to bank credit and the financial backing of the government. Surprisingly, this important source of income inequality is often ignored in studies of China's income distribution. The capital–labour ratio in the state sector is about ten times that in rural enterprises, though this gap narrowed slightly during the 1980s (Table 2.10). Even though it now faces fiercer competition because of lower barriers to market entry, the state sector still receives the lion's share (about 74 per cent) of subsidized credit-financed fixed investment and 95 per cent of budget-financed fixed investment. Meanwhile, its contribution to industrial output fell to about 50 per cent in 1990 (SSB 1981–90).

Table 2.10: Capital endowments of state and rural sectors: average fixed asset differentials

Year	1978	1989
(a) State industry (yuan)	10173	23779
(b) Rural TVEs (yuan)	812	2669
Ratio: (a)/(b)	12.5	8.9

Notes: TVEs refers to 'Township and Village Enterprises'. The average fixed capital in state industry is computed by dividing the fixed assets of the independent accounting state enterprises by the total number of industrial workers in state enterprises. This underestimates the per capita level of capital stock. That of the TVE includes other industries beside manufacturing industry. On the assumption that the capital intensity of manufacturing industry is higher than that of other industries in China, the ratio of (a) to (b) under-states the difference between the capital endowments of the state and rural sectors. On the other hand, the urban collectives probably have a lower capital stock per worker than state enterprises. Hence the figures are a fair proxy for the urban–rural gap in capital endowments. Fixed assets are evaluated at their original value.
Sources: MOA 1991; SSB 1990.

The average wage rate in the state sector has been consistently higher than that in the urban collectives and TVEs (Table 2.11). Despite huge wage gaps, rural labour has been effectively kept out of competition for mainstream employment in the urban state sector (Anderson 1991). To an important extent, these factors perpetuated the sizable urban–rural disparities in the 1980s. Despite some improvements, continuing limitations on factor mobility across the rural and urban sectors appear to be one institutional factor hampering a substantial reduction in urban–rural inequality.

The favourable changes in farm purchase prices in the early 1980s did indeed help reduce urban–rural inequality. However, the politically powerful urban sector was successful in protecting its vested interests. Relatively low urban retail prices for basic food items continued until quite recently and necessitated huge fiscal subsidies. The fact that public finance subsidized richer urban consumers clearly aggravated overall income inequality. Managers and workers in the state sector took full advantage of the newly acquired leeway in wage setting, and the largest wage hikes took place in the state sector (see table 2.11). These developments probably contributed to the reversal in the second half of the 1980s of the earlier trends towards a narrowing in the urban–rural income gap. The political will of the government is critical if a steady lessening of urban–rural disparities is to be achieved.

Price reforms and inflation

Manipulating relative prices has long been one way for the Chinese government to redistribute income among sectors, regions and industries. Hence its role might be potentially important in shaping income distribution in the context of the frequent partial price reforms of the 1980s.

As discussed above, the favourable effect on the urban–rural income gap of raising farm procurement prices is one example. However, this effect has been substantially eroded because of inflation and mounting subsidies to urban workers. Between 1978 and 1985, the overall index of state procurement prices, deflated by the rural retail price index, rose at

Table 2.11: Wage rates in China, by sector (current yuan)

Year	1978	1985	1990
(a) State sector	615	1148	2140
(b) Urban collectives	506	967	1681
(c) TVEs	307	677	1219
Ratio of (b)/(a)	0.82	0.84	0.79
Ratio of (c)/(a)	0.50	0.59	0.57

Notes: The two ratios are likely to understate the actual gap in labour costs between urban and rural areas because numerous non-cash benefits in the urban sector are not included.
Sources: SSB 1991; MOA 1991.

an average compound rate of 5.1 per cent per annum, while in 1985–1989 the increase dropped to 2.1 per cent. If deflated by the free market price index, procurement prices rose by 4.6 per cent during 1978–1985 and minus 1.7 per cent during 1985–1989 (SSB 1990). This phenomenon was one of the causes of the widening in the urban–rural gap in incomes in the second half of the 1980s.

One key feature of the price reforms has been the creation of the 'two-track' or 'dual' system for many prices. The implications of this system for income distribution are far from transparent, and it has obscured the picture of income distribution considerably, frustrating our efforts to evaluate the changes. But one thing is clear: it has provided more lucrative opportunities for rent-seeking behaviour and corruption. Of course, the multiple-price system operates not only in the product markets, but also in the factor markets. The large state-sanctioned wage differentials, mentioned above, certainly affect urban–rural disparities. The louder voice of urban constituents (see above) and the highly distorted factor prices (Rawski & Jefferson 1991) are two key reasons for the wage premium in the state sector and for much of the rampant corruption.

Finally, let us briefly look at two important but rarely explored aspects of the effects of changes in prices on income distribution in China. One relates to the fact that general price inflation might affect people in different income brackets differently. The other point concerns the effect of distorted prices on regional income variations. The much-discussed regional trade wars or barriers (Watson et al. 1989) are in essence a reflection of the price distortions. Greater control by localities over their own financial and real resources certainly motivates them to set up barriers in order not to be net losers in the regional transfer games.

As market forces come to play a greater role, both general inflation and relative price distortions will become more important in influencing the future trend of income distribution in China. The policy implications are simple: stabilize the general price level and get the relative prices right so as to enhance fair competition and discourage rent-seeking and corruption.

Fiscal decentralization

While fiscal decentralization is viewed by some as the main reason for the increase in inequalities in regional income distribution during the reform era (Tsui 1991), the reality is too complicated to justify any sole focus on this issue. Regional disparity might be attributable to a variety of factors, including fiscal revenue transfers, investment strategy, changes in relative prices, inter-regional factor mobility, market access and historical heritage (Kato 1992).

The impact of the reforms on regional inequality goes far beyond the question of the ability of the centre to reshuffle fiscal revenues across regions, though the latter may be potentially important. One possible negative effect of fiscal decentralization might be a lack of resources available to the central government to improve inter-regional transport and other infrastructural facilities, leading to differences in access to markets as between different regions. However, the weakened ability of the centre to influence net transfers across regions might be offset to some extent if greater inter-regional mobility is achieved. There is evidence that, while the control of the central government over fiscal revenues may be diminishing, it is also trying to shift the fiscal obligations for financing health and other public services onto lower levels of government, particularly in the rural areas.

Even though greater flows of fiscal transfers directed by the centre may iron out somewhat the variations in average income levels across provinces, it is doubtful how much of these grants will actually 'trickle down' into the hands of the poor in the receiving regions. In other words, we have little idea about the effect of regional transfers through fiscal redistribution by the centre in improving equality at the household level. Riskin (1991) suggests that two-thirds of the rural poor households are located outside the officially designated poverty areas, which are presumably those regions eligible to receive net fiscal transfers.

Finally, the degree of fiscal decentralization remains an open question. As a share of GNP, consolidated government fiscal revenues have declined sharply, from 31 per cent in 1978 to 19 per cent in 1990 (SSB 1991). But this does not qualify as direct evidence of fiscal decentralization. An alternative measure is the relative importance of the 'extra-budgetary fund', which experienced explosive growth in the 1980s. As a share of GNP, it rose from 10 per cent in 1978 to more than 15 per cent in 1990 (SSB 1991). However, this by no means implies a commensurate degree of fiscal decentralization. A closer look at the distribution of the extra-budgetary fund indicates that the local portion of the total extra-budgetary fund on both the revenue and expenditure sides actually declined from about 67 per cent in 1982 to about 58 per cent in 1985 (Table 2.12).

Table 2.12: Distribution of extra-budgetary funds (per cent)

Year	1982	1983	1984	1985
Local share of extra-budgetary revenue	66.3	62.8	60.4	57.9
Local share of extra-budgetary expenditure	67.8	65.7	62.3	59.1
Local shares of extra-budgetary revenue in different regions				
Coastal	54.1	54.1	54.4	54.9
Central	29.4	29.6	29.1	28.6
Western	16.4	16.3	16.5	16.5
Local shares of extra-budgetary expenditure in different regions				
Coastal	56.0	54.1	54.0	54.3
Central	26.6	29.3	29.5	29.0
Western	17.4	16.6	16.5	16.7

Source: Deng et al. (1990).

Moreover, the local share of the extra-budgetary funds in the three large areas have been remarkably stable (see table 2.12), raising doubts about the validity of using the total extra-budgetary fund as a proxy for fiscal decentralization in explaining the increase in regional inequality (Tsui 1991). A more useful measure might be local government investment, as suggested by Kato (1992) who shows that it was an important force behind the increase in regional inequality.

Conclusion

Our efforts to understand the issues relating to income distribution in post-reform China have been frustrated by the complex institutional arrangements, distorted prices and problematic quality of the data. However, the available data do allow us to draw a number of important conclusions.

Income distribution in China became more unequal over the reform period. One marked feature of China's income distribution has been its multi-dimensional nature. The three important dimensions we have examined are urban–rural inequality, regional variations and income distribution at the household level, all of which show a more or less increasing trend over the last decade.

In particular, although the urban–rural income gap was somewhat reduced in the early 1980s, it increased again after 1984, implying no significant long-term decline in urban–rural inequality. The same trend is also observed in variations in average income levels of rural income across provinces. In urban areas, the provincial differences widened gradually throughout the 1980s. However, the opposite conclusion can be reached in some areas if counties, instead of provinces, are chosen as the relevant unit. There has been a clear trend towards greater household-level inequality in rural China and a slight worsening trend in the urban areas. More seriously, we find the poor getting poorer and the rich richer in a relative sense. Inequality across both provinces and households is much greater in rural areas than in cities.

A number of new factors emerging from the reform process have been examined, and their possible effects evaluated. The effects of any given factor may vary according to the particular aspect of distribution being studied. While the replacement of the communes with family farming ended the earlier tendency to pool incomes, equalizing them as between households, and contributed to greater variations in rural incomes, it also raised the level of rural relative to urban incomes and reduced regional variation through greater specialization and factor mobility. The opposite applies to the different impacts of rural industrial growth on regional variation and urban–rural equality. The state sector might contribute to a more egalitarian income distribution among its members, but at a cost of perpetuating the urban-rural income gap. The effects of the price reforms on various dimensions of income distribution changed over time.

Much of the inequality comes about not because reform has gone too far, but because of its incomplete nature. Extensive subsidies and welfare provisions in urban areas are intended to attain greater urban equality but work only at the expense of urban–rural equality because of restrictions on migration. Collective farming might reduce variations among house-holds within the same village, but could increase variations between different villages and enlarge the urban–rural gap. A partial introduction of the contract system in urban employment discriminated against newcomers and in favour of existing staff members (Davis 1988). The dual price system induces rent-seeking and corruption. Distorted prices and restricted factor mobility lead to unfair competition.

From the point of view of equitable growth, a number of policy implica-tions can be drawn. The government should take greater responsibility for providing basic public services (e.g. health care and education) in rural areas even if it is at the expense of urban welfare. Improvement in infrastructure and factor mobility can enhance equal opportunities. Changes in relative prices to reflect the scarcity of factors and products will reduce regional inequality, discourage corruption and improve efficiency. Finally, the government-sponsored and institutionally-protected advantages of the urban state sector must be removed and fair competition encouraged. The changing pattern of income distribution has shaped the course of past reform, and will determine the pace of the future reform path in China.

Notes

[1] For instance, the average personal outlay on medical care has never exceeded 1 per cent of total city living expenses. Private spending on housing rent accounts for only 1–2 per cent of total urban living expenses (SSB 1981–1990).

[2] This finding is consistent with that of Griffin and Griffin (1984) who argue that their evidence, based on two case studies in Yunnan and Sichuan, fails to confirm the expected rising inequality (in collective income) among the rural households, across teams of the same commune, and across communes in the same county for the period of 1978–1981.

[3] It took place predominantly on a per capita basis with a potentially strong equalizing effect. See Kojima (1988), Chai (1985), Griffin and Griffin (1984), and Central Secretariat (1988).

References

Anderson, Kim 1990, 'Urban Household Subsidies and Rural Out-Migration: the Case of China', *Communist Economies*, vol. 2, no. 4, pp. 525–31.

Carter, Colin A. & Fu-ning Zhong 1989, 'Regional Comparative Advantage in Chinese Agriculture: Some Evidence and Measurement Issues', in *China's Rural Development Miracle*, ed. John Longworth, University of Queensland Press, Brisbane, pp. 226–36.

Central Secretariat 1988, *Zhongguo Nongcun Shehui Jingji Dianxing Diaocha* (National Representative Survey of the Rural Society and Economy, 1985) Social Science Press of China, Beijing.

Chai, Joseph 1985, 'Property Rights and Income Distribution Under China's Agricultural Household Responsibility System', in *Development and Distribution in China*, eds Chi-Keung Leung & Joseph Chai, Center of Asian Studies, University of Hong Kong, Hong Kong.

Davis, Deborah 1988, 'Unequal Chances, Unequal Outcomes: Pension Reform and Urban Inequality', *China Quarterly*, no. 114, pp. 223–42.

Deng Yingtao et al. 1990, *Zhongguo Yusuanwai Zijin Fenxi* (An Analysis of the Extra-Budgetary Fund in China), The Chinese People's University Press, Beijing.

Donnithorne, Audrey 1967, *China's Economic System*, Allen & Unwin, London.

Ghose, Ajit K. 1984, 'Commune- and Brigade-run Industry in Rural China', in *Institutional Reform and Economic Development in the Chinese Countryside*, ed. Keith Griffin, Macmillan, London, pp. 253–302.

Griffin, Keith & Kimberley Griffin 1984, 'Institutional Change and Income Distribution', in *Institutional Reform and Economic Development in the Chinese Countryside*, ed. Keith Griffin, Macmillan, London, pp. 20–75.

Islam, Rizwanul 1991, 'Growth of Rural Industry in Post-Reform China: Patterns, Determinants and Consequences', *ARTEP Working Paper*, International Labor Organization, New Delhi.

Kato, Hiroyuki 1992, 'Regional Development in the Reform Period', in *Economic Reform and Internationalization: China in the Pacific Region*, ed. Ross Garnaut, Allen & Unwin, Sydney, pp. 116–36.

Kojima, Reeitsu 1988, 'Agricultural Organization: New Forms, New Contradictions', *China Quarterly*, no. 116, pp. 706–35.

Lardy, Nicholas 1978, *Economic Growth and Distribution in China*, Cambridge University Press, Cambridge.

——1980, 'Regional Growth and Income Distribution in China', in *China's Development Experience in Comparative Perspective*, ed. Robert Dernberger, Harvard University Press, Cambridge, pp. 153–90.

——1983, *Agriculture in China's Modern Economic Development*, Cambridge University Press, New York.

——1984, 'Consumption and Living Standards in China: 1978–1983', *China Quarterly*, no. 100, pp. 849–65.

Lee, Eddy 1984, 'Employment and Incomes in Rural China: the Impact of the Recent Organizational Changes', in *Institutional Reform and Economic*

Development in the Chinese Countryside, ed. Keith Griffin, Macmillan, London, pp. 132–75.

Lyons, Thomas 1991, 'Inter-provincial Disparity in China: Output and Consumption, 1952–1987', *Economic Development and Cultural Change*, vol. 39, no. 3, pp. 471–506.

MOA (Ministry of Agriculture of China) 1990, *Zhongguo Xiangzhen Qiye Tongji Zhaiyao* (China's Statistical Digest of Township and Village Enterprises), The Reform Press, Beijing.

Naughton, Barry 1988, 'The Third Front: Defense Industrialization in the Chinese Interior', *China Quarterly*, no. 115, pp. 351–86.

Perkins, Dwight 1988, 'Reforming the Chinese Economic System', *Journal of Economic Literature*, vol. 26, no. 2, pp. 628–45.

Rawski, Thomas 1982, 'The Simple Arithmetic of Chinese Income Distribution', *Keizai Kenkyu*, vol. 33, no. 1, pp. 21–36.

Rawski, Thomas & Gary Jefferson 1991, 'Unemployment, Underemployment and Employment in China's Cites as a Constraint on Urban Reform', paper presented at the Conference on China's Reform and Growth, Australian National University, Canberra.

Riskin, Carl 1991, 'Rural Poverty In Post-Reform China', paper presented at the Conference on China's Reform and Growth, Australian National University, Canberra.

Saith, Ashwani 1984, 'China's New Population Policy', in *Institutional Reform and Economic Development in the Chinese Countryside*, ed. Keith Griffin, Macmillan, London, pp. 176–209.

SSB 1981–1990, State Statistical Bureau *Zhongguo Tongji Nianjian* (Statistical Yearbook of China), The Statistical Publishing House, Beijing.

SSB 1986, *A Survey of Income and Expenditure of Urban Households in China*, 1986, University of Hawaii Press, Honolulu.

SSB 1987a, State Statistical Bureau of China *Zhongguo Nongmin Shouru Yanjiu* (A Study of Peasant Income in China), People's Press of Shanxi, Taiyuan.

SSB 1987b, *Woguo Chengzhenjumin Jiating Shouzhi Diaocha Zhiliao—1987* (Urban Family Budget Survey of China—1987), The Statistical Publishing House, Beijing.

SSB 1988a, *Liuwu Qijian Woguo Chengzhenjumin Jiating Shouzhi Diaocha Ziliao 1981–1985* (Urban Family Budget Survey of China, 1981–1985), The Statistical Publishing House, Beijing.

SSB 1988b, *Woguo Chengzhenjumin Jiating Shouzhi Diaocha Ziliao—1988* (Urban Family Budget Survey of China—1988), The Statistical Publishing House, Beijing.

SSB 1989a, *Zhongguo Nongcun Sishinian* (Forty Years of Rural China), The Central Peasant Press, Henan.

SSB 1989b, *Woguo Chengzhenjumin Jiating Shouzhi Diaocha Ziliao—1989* (Urban Family Budget Survey of China—1989), The Statistical Publishing House, Beijing.

SSB 1991, *Zhongguo Tongji Zhaiyao—1991* (China's Statistical Digest—1991), The Statistical Publishing House, Beijing.

Sundrum, R.M. 1990, *Income Distribution in Less Developed Countries*, Routledge, London.

Tsui Kai-yuen 1991, 'China's Regional Inequality, 1952–1985', *Journal of Comparative Economics*, no. 15, pp. 1–21.

Watson, Andrew, Christopher Findlay & Yintang Du 1989, 'Who Won the "Wool War"? A Case Study of Rural Product Marketing in China', *China Quarterly*, no. 118, pp. 213–41.

Yang Dali 1990, 'Patterns of China's Regional Development Strategy', *China Quarterly*, no. 122, pp. 230–57.

Part II
Wealth, status and power

3 'Rich man, poor man': the making of new classes in the countryside

Jonathan Unger

From the ashes of agrarian socialism in China, a new economic system emerged in the early- to mid-1980s, based upon family farming and an increasing flow of private commerce. Some families quickly prospered and some did not. The mechanisms by which this sorting-out process occurred varied. Sometimes demographic factors were at work, sometimes the most important elements involved a bread-winner's level of competence. In yet other cases, official connections spelled the difference between good prospects for success and lack of opportunities. This chapter examines which factors have had the greatest effect upon different types of families in the different regions of China.

Inasmuch as only a decade has passed since the breakup of the collect-ives, there has been scant time for new class structures to have taken full shape. But we can already perceive significant economic stratification in some parts of the country. Indeed, in the wealthier districts we can glimpse the contours of a nascent elite class—one with unusual features.

This discussion will rely almost entirely upon my own interviews with Chinese peasants and local officials during a number of research trips between the mid-1970s and 1991. These included an extended trip to Yunnan Province in 1988, during which research visits were made to thirteen poor and middle-income villages, and a second research trip in 1991 to conduct interviews in nineteen hill-country villages in the three southern provinces of Guangxi, Guizhou and Yunnan. My normal region for interview fieldwork lies in a far richer part of China, Guangdong Province, and interviewing there covered half a dozen villages in the 1970s, two more in the mid-1980s, and seven villages in 1989. My information for the early 1980s, when the collectives were divided into family farms, derives principally from a series of interviews conducted in Hong Kong in 1983 with peasant emigrants from twenty-eight villages spread across China. To supplement this range of personal interviewing, several recent on-the-ground village studies by other researchers will also be cited.

Economic and political stratification under Mao

Interviews with peasants during the 1970s made it clear that before the collectives were disbanded under Deng, the higher levels of the Party had been able to dominate essential parts of village activity. One obvious consequence was that villages were granted little leeway in those activities that were of greatest interest to the government (Unger 1989). In particular, the government was centrally concerned to extract steadily growing agricultural surpluses from the villages in order to develop urban China more rapidly; it was a classic case of forced industrialization based on a primitive accumulation of capital.

To ensure this predictable supply of basic foodstuffs to the cities at depressed prices, the state dictated to the villages precisely what crops should be grown on what fields and precisely how much had to be delivered to the state at artificially depressed prices. Villages were left with little discretion over the constitution of their own production. They were obliged to ignore comparative advantage and to concentrate on the production, in particular, of low-priced grain.

Within most villages, peasants lived lives of poverty, but this poverty was shared on a fairly egalitarian basis. Within the production teams— that is, the ten to twenty-five neighbouring households that worked the land together and shared in the harvest yields—there were group pressures to keep wage differentials quite narrow; in some production teams the differences in remuneration between the weakest and strongest man varied by 10 per cent or less (Unger 1985, p. 131). The main difference in the earnings of neighbouring households, thus, very largely depended upon how many working hands a family had, not on the capability or strength of those hands.

Put briefly, within the peasant villages stratification was not based on wealth. Rather it was grounded almost exclusively on a differential access to power. The peasantry in their daily work—and in almost all other aspects of their daily lives—came under the control of a group of grass roots cadres: the production-team heads who assigned them to work tasks and, above them, the 'brigade' officials who controlled the village's political system. Peasants needed to cultivate good relations with one or more of these low-level officials. A web of patron–client relationships developed, sometimes based upon helpful kinship ties to one of the cadres, as peasants sought to provide themselves with protective niches in the local structure of power-stratification (Oi 1985).

There was also a second important dimension of stratification under the collectives: class background labels that had been appended to each family at the time of land reform. These inherited labels determined who was allowed to become cadres and who was not, which young people were allowed to go on to secondary and higher education, and who would be given the better or more onerous farm tasks. At the top of this caste-like system stood the pre-revolution poor peasantry and their descendants. The middle-status class labels were held by the pre-revolution middle peasants who, by official edict, were only half-trusted and needed to watch their step, especially those unfortunate enough to wear an upper-middle-peasant label. At the bottom huddled the families of the former landlords and rich peasants, discriminated against on a daily basis and subjected to 'struggle sessions' practically every time a political campaign was announced. The cadres, fearful of showing anything but enmity toward these 'bad class' families, almost always excluded them from the patron–client system (Unger 1984). This structure of class-label favouritism and discrimination had been kept in place by the state's sponsorship, and the system crumbled rapidly after 1979, when the state under Deng withdrew its support.

The division of land in the early 1980s

In large parts of China, agricultural production had been stagnating throughout much of the 1970s, and in frustration many of the peasants increasingly had been slackening off in their work. As is well known, the new post-Mao administration under Deng Xiaoping decided to cut this Gordeon's knot by entirely abandoning the system of agricultural collectives. Over the four year period of 1979–82 a top–down decollectivization drive swept through the villages. The peasants had been given no choice in the matter, and almost all villages across China ended up adopting exactly the same new system of family farming (Unger 1986a, p. 587). Some of the village officials were opposed to this breakup of collective agriculture, fearing the loss of power and perquisites, but the orders from on-high to decollectivize needed to be obeyed.

It was the final act of the agricultural command economy. With the changeover to independent smallholdings and the strengthening of market forces, the rural officials—from county headquarters down to brigade Party committees—immediately oversaw and administered far less than they had previously, and thus have had far fewer means at their disposal to impose their will over peasant families. As a peasant interviewee observed to me in 1983: 'If those so-called cadres tell the peasants to do something today, the peasants don't always carry it out. We peasants are practical: if we don't depend on earning collective workpoints that you control, why listen so much to you?'. In short, a beneficial consequence of decollectivization has been that the arbitrary power of the state and rural officials to exact cowed compliance from the peasantry has been weakened.

In most villages, the land was divided among the peasants on a per capita basis—an equal share for every member of the production team, children included. Land was of such key importance to the peasantry that any whiff of favouritism or corruption in this distribution of fields would have discredited the new system of landholding, with bitter recriminations and political repercussions for decades to come. As shall later be discussed, village officials were able to gain undue advantages in the distribution and sale of the production teams' and brigades' other properties—but not in the handing out of agricultural plots. So, too, farm tools and draught animals were distributed free-of-charge among the households. Interviews with peasants from a large number of villages reveal that these land and asset distributions were supervised by county officials, who saw to it that it was done equitably, with a minimum of corruption (Unger 1986a, p. 594). Except in the sense that the fields could not be bought and sold, they effectively were now private property. Families henceforth would have to sink or swim economically on their own.

Technically, the families had been launched into the new system of agriculture on relatively equal terms. The reality was not so simple. Government policies all but assured that some families would reap immediate benefits and prosper and that others would find it more difficult to make ends meet: that economic differentiation among households would grow rapidly. In part this was because the system of enforced cheap grain sales to the state was kept intact by the government. When the fields were divided among households, these grain quotas were apportioned among the families along with the fields. They became the families' personal responsibility, much like a fixed tax.

Families that subsequently became prosperous are currently not obliged to provide any more low-priced grain to the state than the impoverished families of their village.[1] A family that cannot grow enough to fulfil its portion of the quotas after meeting its own consumption needs would have to buy expensive grain on the free market to resell to the state at a loss. In the early 1980s, faced with decollectivization, the families with elderly dependents and a number of small children sometimes foresaw such a dreaded future, as did the households headed by women or by weak, incompetent, or chronically ill men (Unger 1986a, p. 597).

The financial situation of such households was doubly threatened. Before, under the collectives, production team granaries had been required by state decree to lend such families sufficient grain for their dependents' consumption needs even when the families did not have the money on hand to pay for it.[2] But this grain guarantee had been a sore point with most of the other peasants; as one interviewee sourly told me in the early 1980s: 'We others in the team had had to raise those families' kids for them'. He and the majority of his team had been happy to see the collective fields divided, partly because they thought they could be more productive in agriculture on their own but also partly because they saw the return to family farming as a way to get out from under 'raising those other families' kids' at a cost to their own incomes.[3]

Each family, said interviewees, simply looked to its own interests. How decollectivization promised to favour these divergent interests can be seen in the following figures: reports in 1983 from interviewees from twenty-eight villages suggest that cumulatively something like three-quarters of the households in these villages were in favour of the return to family farming and something like a quarter were opposed.

A good number of the households that had opposed decollectivization did not actually end up doing worse. Particularly in districts within striking distance of urban markets, all of the households discovered that they were able to boost their living standards, albeit some families galloped more rapidly into prosperity than others. In such districts, peasants had opportunities to diversify their crop production; so long as they managed to hand in their grain quota, either by cultivating grain on a part of their fields or buying it on the market, they were now free to turn to whatever crops best suited the soil and commanded the highest prices in the urban markets. 'Before,' one of my interviewees from Guangdong Province reported, 'we were forced to grow rice even on swampy land, with miserable results; today we raise water chestnuts there'.

Many of the families with surplus labour found the time to grow animal feed on the hillsides and began raising large numbers of hogs and poultry for the market, or rented the village ponds and raised carp for urban consumption. Other families with labour to spare became heavily involved in cottage industry, even during the growing seasons, or sent a daughter off to work in the new factories that were sprouting in the rural market towns that lie within reach of a city. Some of the men, even from families short of labour, quit their village during the agricultural off-season to work at urban construction sites, where wages are high by Chinese standards, leaving the winter agricultural chores in the hands of wives and children. Through these diverse means, in the rural districts within range of the cities many of the entrepreneurial farming families with labour to spare have more than quadrupled their incomes. They have been competing to build larger homes and are buying colour televisions and video cassette recorders.

Some men, by concentrating almost entirely on entrepreneurial opportunities outside agriculture, have done far better yet. As time goes on, in fact, the main determinants of greater or lesser household income in the more prosperous districts increasingly lies off-the-farm. Extensive field-work in a well-off village in Sichuan province by a group of Danish scholars in 1987 has illustrated this point very clearly (Fenger et al. 1990, p. 78; for a rural site near Nanjing see Christiansen 1990, p. 121; for sites in Henan Province see Zhu 1991, pp. 78, 80). The new class structures that are developing in such villages derive from the households' differential access to non-agricultural opportunities; many peasants are convinced that these opportunities are being cornered illegitimately by families with 'connections' to officials. It is a source of rising political tension.

Class distinctions in the poorest districts: the emergence of a new under-class

An important distinction needs to be made between the more prosperous districts and the impoverished inland districts. I spent almost four months during 1988 and 1991 travelling in jeeps into some three dozen villages in very poor parts of south-west China. In these remote hinterland districts, off-the-farm opportunities remain very limited, and the major gap between the households within each village lies between those who can grow enough on the land to support themselves and those who cannot. Quite unlike the richest districts, a sinking under-class of totally immiserated families has emerged in these villages. The plight of these families has been greatly exacerbated by government policies, and particularly by the continuing program of cheap grain requisitions.[4] Commonly, the households that cannot raise enough grain to feed themselves after their sales of requisitioned grain to the state simply go hungry.

Though the amount of enforced grain deliveries has remained stable, until very recently these poor faced a heavier grain-tax burden than a decade ago, in the sense that until March–April 1992, when the state finally relented and began lifting its procurement price, the government deliberately had not allowed the requisitioned grain price to keep up with inflation. Only on one earlier occasion since 1985 had the price paid for the low-priced levy of grain been permitted to rise—by 35 per cent in 1989. In that year alone, inflation rose by almost the same amount. The falling real price for the requisitioned grain over this half decade had made it all the more difficult for poor peasants to scrape together enough cash to secure the agricultural inputs they need.[5]

The chances of these families producing enough grain are severely damaged by a second deleterious government policy—they are denied access to chemical fertilizers. Such fertilizers are particularly needed by the peasantry of these districts, given the very infertile soils of the inland hill-country. In several dozen such hill villages in 1991, I enquired as to the difference in yields between the families that could afford to apply sufficient fertilizers and those that could not afford to apply any, and almost invariably the figures I obtained showed close to a doubling in production with chemical fertilizers. But to buy fertilizer, impoverished families must seek short-term credit from the local credit association at the beginning of the growing season. A principal function of these state-run credit associations is to provide such loans, but the associations are almost totally controlled and regulated by the central government's Agricultural Bank, and the credit associations' personnel have come under strong pressure from the Bank to be businesslike in their operations. I was told repeatedly that they are rejecting the poorest households' requests for loans on the grounds that such households cannot guarantee repayment, as they do not possess collateral in the form of draught animals or pigs or other movable assets. And these families do not have the wherewithal to raise such animals because, without fertilizers, they cannot grow enough to feed even themselves, let alone livestock. Government policy has ensnared these families in a catch-22 trap. In these inland hill-district villages, a family that falls below a certain threshold can find itself caught helplessly in a downward spiral into slow starvation.

Overall, somewhere between 5–15 per cent of the families in the impoverished villages I have visited in Yunnan, Guangxi and Guizhou provinces have fallen into this abyss, unable to afford any chemical fertilizers whatsoever. In such villages, I have sat on the dirt floors of households which, harnessed to requisitioned grain 'contracts' that they have difficulty meeting, cannot even afford to buy matches or salt.

The nascent class structure in these impoverished inland villages is of a simple order. Some families, perhaps 10–20 per cent, can afford all the fertilizers they want, and are prospering considerably compared to times past. But without external markets within range they cannot readily build up their prosperity further. The majority of families are 'getting by' in circumstances that, on average, are reportedly a bit better than under the collectives, but not by much. They have just enough assets to borrow small sums from the credit association to purchase some fertilizer, just enough to keep their heads above water from year to year. The most noticeable class division in such villages involves the emergence of the desperately immiserated under-class of between 5–15 per cent, a frightening caution to others that no safety net exists to prevent an incompetent or unlucky family's fall into an abyss.

The middle-income districts and the demographics of family change

Though disparities in living standards between neighbours have been growing throughout rural China, the most egalitarian income spread within villages exists today in those districts too remote from urban centres to sustain much off-the-farm opportunities, but sufficiently well off in agriculture not to possess a hungry under-class that must get by without fertilizers. In the villages I have visited in China's south west that were in such circumstances, much of the variation in prosperity stems from the demographics of family cycles and from inheritance patterns. These twin factors influence wealth and poverty in the poorest and richest districts, too, but it is in these remote middle-income districts that the effects stand out most clearly.

It became patently clear during interviews that in this new economy of smallholdings, a peasant family's prosperity tends to rise and fall over time as children are born, grow up and marry: for the household's access to labour varies as mouths are transformed into teenage hands and then, in turn, are lost to the household at marriage.[6] The process of decollectivization in 1982–83 caught different households at different points in this family cycle, and accordingly affected them quite differently. As earlier observed, with land allotted to households largely on a per capita basis, families with several small children often discovered they could not work all of the cropland they had acquired, while families with several teenagers often had enough hands available both to work the allotted croplands efficiently and to handle herding and various economic activities outside agriculture.

In the decade since the breakup of the collectives, however, shifts in the life cycle of families have altered the economic circumstances of these various households. Families that before were struggling to support small children now have strong teenagers to help with the work. In contrast, families that had several teenage boys at the time of decollectivization now sometimes find themselves in financial trouble. The bulk of the money that they had made while their sons were teenagers soon had to be spent to acquire wives for their sons; a son's marriage is an extremely expensive proposition today, often costing more than the annual income of a household. An even more important obstacle to the retention of family capital is that the family invariably divides when the eldest son marries, rather than endure the frictions of an expanding household. The newlyweds move into a new house and the eldest son takes with him his share of the family property, including a portion of the fields that had been allotted to the family. As each succeeding son marries, he too 'divides the household' (fen jia) and takes with him his inheritance. The youngest son stays with the parents after his marriage, and it is he who inherits the ancestral house when the old couple pass away. The daughters take with them a small dowry when they marry, but this is their sole share of family property. They, too, inherit nothing when their parents die.

This is the custom in every one of the several dozen villages in which I have conducted interviews. I had expected to find some families resorting to the traditional extended family as a means to marshal and consolidate economic resources, but I have never come across any such families.[7] The division of family property at so early a point, decades before the older generation's death, poses serious obstacles to the diversification of peasant household endeavours and to long-term investment planning. Problems of land division that would have taken a very long time to be played out in Western societies were already plaguing rural China less than a decade after decollectivization.

A financial crisis now faces a large number of families with several recently grown sons. For as the sons have each brought their new brides from outside into the village, the family has become very seriously strapped for land. A similar problem did not exist under the collectives because the new bride could immediately earn workpoints by working on the collective fields of her husband's entire neighbourhood or village, and could also receive from the collective a new 'private plot'. But the revived system of peasant smallholdings in China today does not readjust land allocations to account for changes in family size.

The young wives, furthermore, have each given birth by now to several children.[8] One Yunnanese peasant whom I have interviewed relates that in 1982, when the collective land was divided among families, he had received five portions of land for himself, his wife and three teenage sons (he had no daughters), but these fields must now support, in addition, the sons' wives and children: eleven people in all (Unger & Xiong 1989, p. 63). With their sons only a couple of years away from marriage at the time of decollectivization, in villages like this, where there is no alternative employment off the land, such families turn out to have been the ones who, most of all, were caught at the wrong time in the family cycle.

Compare this case with that of a middle-aged couple from the same village with three recently grown children—one son and two daughters— who similarly received five portions of land at the time of decollect- ivization. As the daughters married and moved away, the single son and his parents are left with a large five-portion block of property that will be the son's alone to inherit. An initially egalitarian distribution of village land very quickly has been transformed into a land system in which some lucky men (single sons) will hold three or more times as much property as other men. Such households of single sons are, of course, in a far better position to continue to develop economically. Other things being equal, by demographic factors alone, in a purely agricultural village they are in a good position to emerge as the economic elite of the next generation.

In most villages, each of a family's sons receives a relatively equal share of the family property, and then the elder sons contribute some foodstuffs each month to help support the parents. But there are also villages and whole counties where a different system of property division occurs. (By personal knowledge, this alternative system can be found in parts of Guizhou, Hunan, and Yunnan provinces, and doubtless can be found in other provinces as well.) In such districts, each of the elder sons takes with him only a very small individual portion of land when he marries. If a family was initially composed of, for example, a middle-aged couple, three sons and two daughters (that is, the family had received seven portions of land at the time of decollectivization) each of the elder sons ultimately obtains only one portion when he marries and leaves the household, and the remaining five portions all remain with the youngest son. In these villages, inequalities in landholdings are greatly com- pounded by this inheritance practice. The elder brothers and their new households are frequently pauperized; while as a group the youngest sons are on their way to becoming the village squires of the next generation. (This system of inheritance is, of course, entirely at odds with the system of primogeniture that used to prevail among the European nobility, in which the eldest son inherited the bulk of the family property.)

The reason for this system of inheritance, I was repeatedly told, is that rural Chinese parents traditionally dote on their youngest sons: that they are loved more by the parents than the other sons. But this explanation is not entirely satisfactory, since the same inheritance practices are shared by all of the neighbouring households, irrespective of what the various parents' idiosyncratic personal feelings might be toward their children. That is, in the majority of the villages and counties, all of the families grant each one of their sons a relatively equal amount of land; and in these other villages and even whole counties, all of the families grant the lion's share of the land to the youngest son.

Whatever the reasons for this odd distinction between different villages and counties, the effects are obvious. Demographic factors (whether a household has a single son or many sons) and the inheritance practices of the rural Chinese have, within less than a decade, been shaping new divisions of poor and prosperous within each farming community, and have been doing so most distinctly in those communities that grant the bulk of the family lands to the youngest son.

Wealth and entrepreneurship in the middle-income districts

Although disparities in living standards in the middle-income agricultural regions currently are not nearly as graphic as in the richest and poorest districts, the differences even here are growing. And they are not entirely due to the types of demographic factors discussed above. A new class of prosperous peasants is also being generated through personal economic endeavours, especially in those middle-income districts that are accessible to commercial markets.

Success in such endeavours, as expected, appears to be due to a combination of drive, skills, and favourable connections with the authorities. What deserves comment is that these skills and favourable connections seem to adhere to people of particular backgrounds.

In terms of useful entrepreneurial skills, as we would anticipate, an education seems to prove helpful, as does prior experience: a tractor driver or auto mechanic under the collectives holds definite advantages when it comes to earning money privately under the present regime. But in particular, two categories of rural people appear to have had the greatest success since decollectivization—those with prior experience as cadres and those with family traditions of productivity that preceded the revolution.

Again and again in my interview research, in villages both rich and moderately off, it became clear that a disproportionate number of the new entrepreneurs have risen from the ranks of the local cadres. It is not just 'connections' and corrupt practices that have given such men a head start over their neighbours. The socialist era had provided them with a good training in business, unlike the ordinary peasantry: an experience in handling sizeable sums of money, in managing groups of workers, in dealing with the officialdom, and in taking charge of management decisions in a complex agricultural regime. It is ironic that many of the men favoured with leadership positions under the collectives have, for that very reason, benefited subsequently from the demise of agrarian socialism.

That other salient factor—family history—is illustrated nicely by the findings of a recent study in a middle-income north China village on who had become well off and who had not (Yan 1992). 41 per cent of the families of pre-Liberation middle-peasant stock in this village had become prosperous since decollectivization, compared to less than 10 per cent of the families that derived from the pre-Liberation poor peasantry (Yan 1992, pp. 9–10). There appears to be more than one reason for this differential. Among other things, the pre-Liberation middle peasants and their children, unlike the former poor peasants, had had to learn to be particularly conscientious in their work habits under the collectives, lest they be criticized as being politically retrograde. But surely a second and probably more important factor in the recent success of these middle-peasant families lies in the traditional knowledge of economically useful techniques and the cultural skills that have been passed down within these families. (Parallel findings for rural Hungary are found in Szelenyi (1988); Szelenyi very similarly has discovered through surveys that successful rural entrepreneurship clusters in the households that before the socialist era were middle peasant.)

The skills and the drive to succeed that are passed down within families may not be altogether sufficient in China, however, to achieve success outside of agriculture. Any such endeavours will require the acquiescence and co-operation of local authorities; this is usually a *sine qua non*. A recent study of a Sichuan village has concluded that:

> qualifications, defined as technical and management skills, were inadequate. The private entrepreneurs were rather characterized by another requirement: close personal relations (*guanxi*) to the local authorities. This ensured favourable treatment in obtaining rationed goods, official permits, political good-will, etc., which proved of significant importance when developing a profitable business in risky bureaucratic settings (Fenger et al. 1990, p. 84).

Guanxi can give even more direct advantages. A good illustration of this was provided by an interview survey that I conducted in 1991 of the richest homes of a moderately well-off village along the Guizhou–Yunnan border. The economically most successful man in the village has enjoyed a single advantage: a very valuable 'connection' to a minor official in the county town. The two had served together in the People's Liberation Army (PLA), and on their return to civilian life the army buddy had used family connections to get a posting to the county's Foreign Trade Bureau. There, he had garnered for his rural friend a monopoly commission for the purchase from farmers of dried ginger and buckwheat, and had also secured for his friend a low-interest loan from the Foreign Trade Bureau for the purchase of a truck. Whether or not the fortunate man gratefully shares his material gains with his comrade in the Foreign Trade Bureau was not, of course, something that an interviewer could readily ascertain. But given the way such relationships normally seem to operate in rural China today, it would not be at all unlikely.

On the whole, the better-connected and financially better-off households appear to enjoy a distinct edge in getting access to whatever grants or credit become available. As in the above case, a good part of this can be explained as nepotism or corruption; but a 'bet on the strong' bias in government policy is also a significant factor. This is exemplified by the government's special financial backing for so-called 'specialized households' (*zhuanye hu*)—prosperous peasant families that are chosen to receive favoured access to subsidized inputs because they are already generating a higher income than their neighbours (Oi 1986b, pp. 240–1). In 1988, as one pertinent example, I visited a hill village in Yunnan Province where under a provincial government program to sow and fertilize hill pastures, thirty families, less than 10 per cent of the village's households, had been granted near-permanent leases in 1987 to most of that village's common pasturelands. From what could be gathered from interviews with local peasants, corruption or favouritism had not been evident here. But the criteria by which the thirty families had been selected by government officials had stressed their financial soundness: the families needed to have sufficient incomes and assets to ensure that they would be able to repay on time the loans extended to them on special favourable terms to fence and stock the pastures. In short, provincial support and subsidies have gone to an already advantaged minority, with the consequence that a majority of the families in the village have lost access to common grazing lands and thereby have been denied a substantial part of their livelihood. They have ended up on the outside of fences looking in[9] (Unger & Xiong 1990).

When this problem was broached with the provincial official who was in charge of the site, she quoted in response the official slogan that 'some families should be allowed to get rich sooner than others'. Implicit in such a statement was the presumption that other families would later have an opportunity to 'catch up'. But this had, in fact, become out of the question, now that most of the village's pasturelands had been closed off to them. What is occurring, in almost all aspects of the rural economy, is that some advantaged families, often with government assistance, are gaining near-permanent control over local assets, be they ponds, orchards, local industry, or pastures.

In the wake of the Beijing massacre of 1989, the slogan about some getting rich first has been renounced by the central authorities, but policies have not altered much. It is a policy preference, moreover, that for the past decade has served as a convenient pretext and screen for those local officials who have wished to enrich themselves and their own kith and kin.

Entrepreneurship in the well-off districts

Throughout rural China, to greater or lesser degree, the trend is toward wealth becoming increasingly concentrated in the hands of the most prosperous households, due partly to the entrepreneurial initiative of a capable minority, due partly to government policies that favour the already affluent, and in some cases due to corruption and nepotism. But what is evident in a modest way in the middle-income districts is doubly noticeable in the wealthiest districts. There, we are finding the emergence and consolidation of a new upper class of commercially successful entrepreneurs. The liberalization of China's economy, agricultural surpluses, and proximity to urban markets has brought a surge of increased trade and local manufacturing to these wealthier districts, and some of the rural populace have been very quick to grasp the available opportunities.

As a means of focusing on the type of success that can be achieved in such districts, let me resort to one case that strikingly illustrates the phenomenon. In 1986, during four days spent in a rural district of Nanhai County, Guangdong, my host, a peasant turned entrepreneur, took me to breakfast at an ostentatiously elegant teahouse that very recently had been erected by a local businessman at a crossroads between villages. To my surprise, the large teahouse was packed with moneyed entrepreneurs. It transpired that the teahouse served as the local venue for cutting business deals and exchanging news about money-making opportunities. Most of the crowd, I was told, dined here every morning, spending more in one meal than the young women who laboured in the new local textile factories could earn in a day.

My host was the co-owner, along with his brother-in-law and a couple of minor partners, of an artificial silk weaving factory employing eighty women workers. Still in his thirties, he had raised the initial capital for his share in the new factory by buying and selling private motor vehicles, and had supplemented this by successfully borrowing 150 000 yuan from the local branch of a government bank. Though raised as a peasant, he now operated smoothly in a world of complex business deals. Just the previous day, he had returned by jet from Beijing, where he had been negotiating sales of artificial silk to Manchurian wholesalers.[10]

My host largely owed his success, it seems, to the two salient factors identified earlier: first, he had had a number of years of managerial experience as an agricultural production-team head under the system of collectives; and second, he had a commercially advantageous family background. The small rural district in which he lived, some two hours inland from Canton, had been a major centre of rural silk textile production before the 1940s. Starting in the early 1980s, peasant entrepreneurs have revived the industry, to the extent that almost from scratch this small district of a few rural market towns has quickly become one of the three major silk manufacturing areas in China. Vestigial memories of commercial skills had survived the forty-year Maoist interregnum, passed down in households. My host was directly descended from a family once prominent in local silk manufacturing.

Separately, it appears that success in business in the rich districts can often be traced to that third salient factor—official connections. An example taken from Huidong County, Guangdong, illustrates how blatantly the powers of office can be turned to the self-interest of the officials' own families. An interviewee has explained that the sons of the leading officials of his rural township opened motor repair shops, and almost simultaneously a regulation was promulgated that all motor vehicles had to pass safety inspections every year, with these shops the only ones licensed to make the required repairs.

Not surprisingly, peasants declare themselves to be far less resentful about wealth that has been acquired through what they consider legitim-ate means—hard work and skill—than wealth acquired through such official connections (see e.g., Thireau 1991, p. 56). The extent of these latter practices, and their impact on the creation of a new moneyed class, ought not be underestimated. In any account of the concentration of wealth in rural China, the self-enrichment of rural cadres throughout all parts of the countryside deserves attention.

Cadres and the art of making money

As earlier observed, with the return to family farming in the early 1980s the rural officialdom lost control over the daily work of the peasantry, and the cadres' arbitrary power over the peasantry was accordingly weakened. But the state's deliberate pullback from its domination of village life simultaneously weakened the central government's hold over the conduct of rural officials. Increasingly, as the example of motor repair shops suggests, networks of local officials have taken advantage of this pullback to favour their own and their favourites' private interests, unimpeded by fears of anti-corruption campaigns or purges. And they are able to do so not only by positively intervening on behalf of their friends and kin but also by using their power directly to secure payoffs from other families.

The local officials retain more than enough leverage to do so. The peasantry still remains dependent upon the goodwill of village and higher-level rural cadres to get access to fertilizers, credit, new housing sites, and licenses to engage in business, and they frequently need to resort to currying these cadres' favour through gifts and shows of deference (Oi 1986a; Burns 1988).

Corruption most certainly is involved here. But to consider it simply as corruption may miss an important ingredient of what undergirds these transactions. For new types of patronage networks are emerging on this basis. Even where entrepreneurial families do not already have any special *guanxi* relationships in place, through persistent small gifts such families can strategically curry the favour of the various officials who might be helpful to the operation and expansion of family enterprises. Under the collectives, of course, patron–client relationships between cadres and peasants had also existed, but now an already prospering peasant family's wealth provides a distinct advantage in sealing such relationships. 'Oil' now greases the wheels of patronage.

Previously, moreover, the range of potential patrons had been much more restricted. A small group of brigade and team cadres had controlled all of a village's economic and political affairs; all patronage had previously, by necessity, flowed through them. Now a more pluralistic structure of patronage is developing; for different sorts of favours, peasants can go to different patrons. For example, peasants who hope regularly to get preferential access to building materials or to special fertilizers have developed *guanxi* connections on their own account with different particular marketing bureau personnel; such procurements no longer need be funnelled through a single set of village cadres. This recent growth of diffuse patron-client networks provides the peasants with considerably greater freedom to manoeuvre; and their autonomous building of patronage links has further eroded the former rigid structuring of rural power.

Peasant resentments are targeted not so much against all of the cadres who siphon money in this fashion, but rather against those who do so beyond accepted limits. The attitudes of the peasantry in Chen Village, Guangdong Province, provide a good illustration of this (Chan, Madsen & Unger 1992, chapter 10). The village's new Party Secretary has been considered relatively incorrupt despite his marked willingness to accept gifts and cash from his constituents. Villagers reason that a man with the qualifications and connections to be a Party Secretary would, were he to resign, be able to make an excellent living in the private sector. The post of Party Secretary pays only 1 500 yuan a year, far less than the income of the average family, so it is deemed acceptable that he should see to his own interests and make up the difference through private donations. Chen Village is located in one of the richest parts of the Chinese country- side, and a livelihood that is on a par with the village's most successful entrepreneurs—some 15 000 yuan per year—is almost considered his due. Many of the cadres in neighbouring villages and in the local market towns have been far more greedy, reaching well beyond such an income in their demands for bribes and payoffs, and that is sorely resented. Corruption, in short, is defined in the countryside as *overkill* in the taking of payoffs.

The 'take' of Chen Village's Party Secretary is similar in spirit to what the Chinese officialdom of imperial times regularly practised. Underpaid by the imperial court, a county magistrate was half-expected to supple- ment his income in the form of gifts and money from importuning citizens. The Chinese government in the 1980s, caught in budgetary squeezes at all levels, seems tacitly to have reverted to this tradition: setting low salaries for officials and then looking the other way when they augment these as best they can.

The Chen Village peasants tacitly accept this, but as seen, they are angry that so many of the government personnel outside the village 'immorally' take far more than their circumstances should call for, and that their demands keep escalating. In the face of this corruption, the Chens feel that things are amiss in the national government, that it is losing its hold. But one reason why the upper levels of the state permit such overkill in corruption may well be that the national leadership sees it as the needed price to pay in order to win the local officialdom's acquiescence to the economic reform programs. The cadres thus are being allowed to trade off some of their power for wealth, placing their own families into the new monied elite that is in gestation.

In all parts of the countryside, even the poorest districts, such a trend was evident from the very start. At the time of decollectivization, the officials at the grass roots did better out of the distribution of village property than did their neighbours. Even though the distribution of ordinary agricultural land was relatively free of corruption, the leasing or the sale of team and village assets other than farm fields—that is, the orchards, fish ponds, village factories, and equipment—all too frequently enriched the families of the officials involved in their disbursement. Sometimes they improperly sold or leased to themselves the property at very low prices; other times, though the bidding processes were technically open and fair, they were the only villagers with sufficient know-how and market connections, and thus the only ones to make a bid (Unger 1986b, p. 277).

Whatever the particular mechanisms that were at work, the survey previously mentioned of a north China village of average prosperity (Yan 1992) discovered that fully 54 per cent of the village's cadres who have held positions during or since decollectivization are today deemed wealthy by local standards. This compares to only 16 per cent of the villagers as a whole. Interestingly, too, only 17 per cent of those who were once cadres but who no longer were in office at the time of decollectivization are today in the wealthy category. In this particular village, whatever the skills they ought to have acquired during their tenure as cadres, without power over village resources they have done no better economically than the ordinary peasants (Yan 1992, p. 10). Here and elsewhere in rural China, the importance of power and influence in the attainment of wealth becomes obvious.

If this is true of current-day village cadres, their superiors in the market towns and county capitals control yet better opportunities to divert money into their own pockets. This is especially true of the rich coastal and suburban districts: cadres find particularly ample pickings where the rural populace generally is earning more, and where local entrepreneurs are getting into lines of business such as manufacturing that require licenses and frequent interaction with local government offices. In contrast, not one of the six impoverished counties in the interior of China where I conducted research in 1991 contained even a single private factory.

The richer areas not only have spawned a vigorous private industrial and commercial sector that can be soaked. More than this, the most prospering districts have witnessed an extraordinary growth in publicly owned local industry. This has been the single most rapidly growing sector of the Chinese economy, and it comes under the direct control of the local officialdom. It has been relatively easy for well placed officials to turn this growth discreetly to their own advantage.

The rise of a composite monied class

The wealthiest households of rural China today comprise, in short, two types of people: first, some of the cadres and their relatives, who have been converting official positions into sources of revenue; and second, entrepreneurs who have risen through their own skill and resourcefulness, like some of those who crowd that rural teahouse in Nanhai County, Guangdong. Whereas before, under the collectives, there was a single hierarchy that was grounded in differential access to power, now there are two. One is still intimately associated with political and administrative power, but with power increasingly perceived as a means to wealth; and the second originates independently in ownership of economic assets, which in turn is used to buy political co-operation and protection. In certain circumstances these two sets—the Mandarins and the entrepreneurs—have come into conflict, with the officialdom of some districts fitfully moving to suppress or to ruinously milk the latter. But increasingly the two elites have developed a *modus vivendi*, and indeed have begun to coalesce.[11] In some cases, it is through business partnerships. Even more often, as we have noted, the sons of officials have placed themselves among the entrepreneurs, and with the retirement or death of the fathers find themselves entirely associated with the camp of wealth, not power.

A decade is too short a period for a new composite rural elite class to have consolidated itself, or to have established its own distinct mores. But a nascent class structure certainly is becoming discernible. Normally, a class tends to marry most frequently within its own boundaries, and wealth does seem to be marrying wealth. Moreover, I have been told of strategic intermarriages between the offspring of officials and those of wealthy entrepreneurs, bringing such families directly into the same fold.

The development of this new hybrid class does not bode well for the poorer sectors of the village populace. China is going through a wrenching economic and social transformation, and the weaker and poorer members of society sometimes find themselves in vulnerable circumstances *vis à vis* the successful entrepreneurs. As just one example, intervention by local officials sometimes becomes the only available means to ameliorate the harsh Dickensian work regime laid down in some of the private rural industrial enterprises—especially in concerns that employ child labour. Any substantial merging of the local power elite and the new monied elite would seem likely to spell an end to the willingness of an officialdom to play such an interventionary role.

The formation of a hybrid monied class has of course progressed furthest in the more commercialized and more prosperous districts. It might be expected that the developments in these wealthier districts would provide a prototype of what might develop in future in other districts. To a certain extent, that is probably the case, but we can also expect that the class distinctions will never be as well articulated in the less well-off areas. Certainly, some of the local officialdom in the poorer districts participate enthusiastically in graft, but this is not readily transformed into something beyond official corruption. In the poorer districts, after all, there are far fewer opportunities to transfer such ill-gotten gains into ongoing private business activity on any considerable scale. And for that same reason, in such regions the entrepreneurial stratum has few chances of expanding noticeably: indeed, the ranks of the commercialized wealthy may be so small and scattered that any talk of a new hybrid class in such districts may not just be premature, but a moot point.

In terms of social and economic stratification, China today provides us with a 'coat of many colours'. Whereas previously under the collectives the same type of hierarchy had applied almost everywhere in the country-side, based on a state-sponsored structure of differentiated power, nowadays the contours of stratification in rural China increasingly vary between regions of differing prosperity. For the most salient features of grass roots socio-economic differentiation are today grounded very differently, depending upon whether a village is at subsistence level or part of a prosperous market-oriented economy, and depending, too, upon whether the major sources of local wealth are agricultural or commercial. This distinction is clear in the emergence of the desperate under-class of the poor regions, or the importance of demographic factors in the ascend-ancy of new village-level economic elites in the middle-income districts of the hinterlands, or in the gestation of a composite monied class in the wealthier regions. Socio-economic trends in rural China are taking on an increasingly complex and variegated texture, and as China moves forward toward the 21st century these trends can be expected to continue. Even more than at present, the years to come can be expected to highlight the several facets of social differentiation that have been the focus of this chapter, in each type of region holding to a different texture.

Notes

[1] Though the government announced in 1985 that this grain-quota system would be abolished and replaced with a system of contracts between the farmer and state, in most of the villages that I visited in south-west China during 1988 and 1991 the policy change had been in name only. The shift to so-called 'contracts' seems to have been aimed

at regions where grain production had been rising rapidly and where the state wanted to free itself from an obligation to buy more grain than it needed. In the regions which did not see such sharp rises in·grain production, the state has chosen to continue to extract grain from the villages on the same terms as previously.

2   Such families went into long-term debt to their team. This accumulated debt gradually would be deducted from the family's wages when the children grew old enough to begin earning incomes in the team. But for the families with a number of small children such repayments were set so far in the future that other team members tended to consider the grain more as a gift from team coffers than as a loan.

3   This interviewee noted that, as a means of clearing off the longstanding grain debts, when the agricultural implements were distributed, the households with debts did not receive a full share. Another interviewee remarked that under the new system of family farming, 'there's little relief grain available … if someone suddenly falls sick in your family it's your own tough luck'.

4   Some villages that are desperately poor are excused from their grain sales to the state, but this relief usually applies only to whole villages, not to individual families. Thus, a family that is financially at its wits' end in a village where most households are 'getting by' normally is forced to hand over its grain levy to the state.

5   Zweig (1989, p. 640) reports that in the summer of 1988 local officials in Yunnan Province forcibly had to extract grain from an angry peasantry.

6   This peasant family cycle of increasing and decreasing prosperity is quite similar to what Chayanov discovered in his famous study of the pre-revolution Russian peasantry (Chayanov 1966).

7   A village that does contain such extended families is analysed in Huang (1992).

8   China's countryside follows a two-child population-control policy, not the urban areas' one-child program.

9   One disgruntled peasant from this village, interviewed while tending sheep as a hired hand on his more fortunate neighbour's fenced pastures, defiantly claimed that he would somehow build his own large flock anyway, even without access to good pasturage. From his tone of voice, it was obvious that he did not genuinely see this as a viable plan; rather, he seems to have been trying to express his own angry refusal to accept that, in one fell swoop, a new economic/social structure in the village had been erected upon unequal access to property.

10 Despite his success, he was obviously worried as of 1986 that government policies might change. He purposely had not reinvested much in the factory's premises—the buildings were ramshackle temporary structures—and his wife, rather than stay home or work in his firm, was bicycling off every morning to work on the production-line of a county-owned textile factory. She did so not for the pay, which they did not

really need; it was to retain a secure job with pension benefits just in case the national regime shifted course dramatically, as had occurred so often before in socialist China's history.

[11] Based on research in Sichuan, Odgaard (1992) separately has come to similar conclusions.

References

Burns, John 1988, *Political Participation in Rural China*, University of California Press, Berkeley.

Chan, Anita, Richard Madsen & Jonathan Unger 1992, *Chen Village under Mao and Deng*, University of California Press, Berkeley.

Chayanov, Alexander V. 1966, *The Theory of Peasant Economy*, R.D. Irwin, Homewood, Illinois.

Christiansen, Flemming 1990, 'The De-rustication of the Chinese Peasant? Peasant Household Reactions to the Rural Reforms in China since 1978', PhD dissertation, University of Leiden, Netherlands.

Fenger, Peter, Steen Folke, Allan Jorgensen, Peter Milthers & Ole Odgaard 1990, 'Occupational Patterns and Income Inequality in a Sichuan Village', *Copenhagen Papers in East and Southeast Asian Studies*, no. 5, pp. 73–90.

Huang Shu-min 1992, 'Re-examining the Extended Family in Chinese Peasant Society: Findings from a Fujian Village', *The Australian Journal of Chinese Affairs*, no. 27, pp. 25–38.

Odgaard, Ole 1992, 'Entrepreneurs and Elite Formation in Rural China', *The Australian Journal of Chinese Affairs*, no. 28, pp. 89–108.

Oi, Jean 1985, 'Communism and Clientelism: Rural Politics in China' *World Politics*, vol. 37, no. 2, pp. 238–66.

——1986a, 'Commercializing China's Rural Cadres', *Problems of Communism*, vol. 35, no. 5, pp. 1–15.

——1986b, 'Peasant Households Between Plan and Market,' *Modern China*, vol. 12, no. 2, pp. 230–51.

Szelenyi, Ivan 1988, *Socialist Entrepreneurs: Embourgeoisement in Rural Hungary*, University of Wisconsin Press, Madison.

Thireau, Isabelle 1991, 'From Equality to Equity: An Exploration of Changing Norms of Distribution in Rural China', *China Information*, vol. 5, no. 4, pp. 42–57.

Unger, Jonathan 1984, 'The Class System in Rural China: A Case Study', in *Class and Social Stratification in Post-Revolution China*, ed. James L. Watson, Cambridge University Press, Cambridge, pp. 121–41.

——1985, 'Remuneration, Ideology, and Personal Interests in a Chinese Village, 1960-1980', in *Chinese Rural Development: The Great Transformation*, ed. William Parish, M.E. Sharpe, Armonk, New York, pp. 117–40.

——1986a, 'The Decollectivization of the Chinese Countryside: A Survey of Twenty-Eight Villages', *Pacific Affairs*, vol. 58, no. 4, pp. 585–606.

——1986b, 'Decollectivization in a Guangdong Village: An Interview', in *Policy Conflicts in Post-Mao China: A Documentary Survey, with Analysis*, eds John P. Burns & Stanley Rosen, M.E. Sharpe, Armonk New York, pp. 274–79.

——1989, 'State and Peasant in Post-Revolution China', *The Journal of Peasant Studies*, vol. 17, no. 1, pp. 114–36.

Unger, Jonathan & Jean Xiong 1989, '*Zou fang Yunnan shancun ting xinsuan de gushi*' (Bitter tales heard during a visit to a Yunnan mountain village), *Chaoliu* (Hong Kong), no. 31, pp. 61–4.

——1990, 'Life in the Chinese Hinterlands under the Rural Economic Reforms', *Bulletin of Concerned Asian Scholars*, vol. 22, no. 2, pp. 4–17.

Yan Yunxiang 1992, 'The Impact of Rural Reform on Economic and Social Stratification in a Chinese Village', *The Australian Journal of Chinese Affairs*, no. 27, pp. 1–23.

Zhu Ling 1991, *Rural Reform and Peasant Income in China*, MacMillan, London.

Zweig, David 1989, 'Peasants and Politics', *World Policy Journal*, vol. 6, no. 4, pp. 633–45.

4 Rational choices and attainment of wealth and power in the countryside

Jean C. Oi

A number of different studies have documented the spread of markets in China (Watson 1988; White 1987; Skinner 1978). Such findings tell us that the monopoly of state power has ended—there is now the ability to buy and sell goods on a free market. The existence of markets, however, tells us little about the degree to which the markets allocate resources, the degree to which peasants use markets, or whether cadres may still be able to influence distribution within a market context. The existence of markets is an insufficient indication of a market economy in a classic economics sense.

A decade or more after the market reforms were instituted in China's countryside a consensus exists that cadres still are powerful. This stands in contrast to the predictions made early in the reforms that markets would break the honeycomb nature of Chinese society and erode the power of local officials, allowing central authorities for the first time to exercise effective central control (Shue 1988). Likewise, it contrasts sharply with Victor Nee's theory of market transition, which argues that 'in reforming socialist economies, the transition from redistributive to market coordination shifts sources of power and privilege to favour direct producers relative to redistributors. The shift ... provides entrepreneurs an alternative path for socioeconomic mobility.' (Nee 1989, p. 663).[1] Nee asserts that '... within a span of seven years, China's rural economy experienced a rapid transition from a redistributive/collective economy to a market like economy' (Nee 1989, p. 664) and criticizes those such as Zweig (1986) and Oi (1986), for failing 'to take into account the changes in the underlying processes that determine socioeconomic attainment accompanying a shift from redistributive to market coordination' (Nee 1989, p. 671).

In recent years, however, even the more optimistic observers have come to realize that the impact of markets is less than was originally thought. Nee (1991) no longer refers to the 'rapid transition from a redistributive/collective economy to a market like economy' (Nee 1989, p. 664), but instead refers to the partial reforms in China. In a 1991 restatement of his theory of market transition, Nee stresses the continued importance of the redistributive mechanisms that 'interact with market forces in a manner that subordinates market institutions' (Nee 1991, p. 268). Most recently, Nee adopts the position that cadres not only still have power, but in fact are running local economies as corporations (Nee 1992).

While it is significant that there is now substantial agreement that the market reforms have had only a limited effect on the distribution of power in China's partially reformed economy, there is still need for a more detailed understanding of the markets that do exist and how those markets relate to cadre power. How should we understand the concurrent spread of markets and the continued (and, in some cases, an increase in) cadre control? Is it only a matter of time before the market transition will be accomplished? Or might it be the case that a market economy, in the classic economic sense, may not be the end result of market reform in China?

In this chapter I examine various responses to markets in the Chinese countryside. I examine different instances where those in rural areas have consciously chosen to avoid direct market participation. Such descriptions are consistent with much of the literature on peasant societies and peasants' reported hesitancy to participate in markets (Scott 1976; Migdal 1974). Although China is more developed economically than most peasant societies referred to in the general social science literature, we should remember that the context is similar. Markets are a recent and alien phenomena for many in China. The peasants' reluctance to participate in markets questions whether the partial nature of the reforms in China is more than a matter of incompleteness, but the result of rational choices made by peasants and cadres. It questions whether markets, even when legal, are always the option of first choice.

Risk minimizing and utility maximizing strategies: the existence of markets and the non-market allocation of goods and resources

Why would the market not be pursued when such an alternative is present? Classic economic theory says that markets will be pursued because it is the most efficient form of distribution. While it may seem irrational to some, avoiding markets is a practice that is found in both traditional and developed Western economies. In developed market economies, the avoidance of markets and the adoption of non-standard or non-market behavior is most pronounced in the operation of cartels, such as in the sale of diamonds. Milgrom and Roberts (1990) show that the 'bargaining costs' of market transactions sometimes make it in the interest of buyers to enter into set arrangements that on the surface put the buyer at a great disadvantage.[2] For example, De Beers, the famous diamond company, forces all those who wish to buy diamonds to become a member of a cartel. Members of the cartel are not allowed to select the individual diamonds they buy; the diamonds must be bought in complete boxes that are presorted. Bargaining costs make this more centralized allocation system more cost effective for all concerned.

A more familiar example for the purposes of this discussion is peasants shying away from markets in traditional societies. Anthropological research has long shown that in more traditional market settings smaller traders often forgo the uncertainty of the market and rely on well-established trading partners, even at the cost of less advantageous prices for any particular transaction (Mintz 1967). In China the rural population seems similarly careful in its calculations about participation in the market. It is by no means clear that markets are preferred.

The peculiarity of the Chinese case, which sets it apart from more traditional peasant societies, is the availability of marketing alternatives, ranging from trading with the state to engaging in intermediate activities such as contracting. This offers the benefits of a market system but entails fewer risks and greater security. My point is not that peasants want to retain the old system and stay within the confines of the plan. Quite the contrary. My point is simply that peasants and cadres alike are constantly trying to maximize their positions by utilizing and manipulating the alternatives that are available when there is both plan and market.

Utility maximizing strategies

The preference of individual peasants and enterprises to buy state supplied goods, particularly when it involves production inputs (given that freshness or quality are not relevant here as they are in the case of food products like fruit or fish), is one of the simplest examples of utility maximization. If the state supply system works properly, goods can be procured at the lowest price with the least effort spent in transaction costs. There is no need to bargain and supply is assured. Even when the system is distorted as it has become in China, where ration coupons do not assure access, it still makes sense first to try to procure goods through the central planning system. The existence of the hierarchy of prices (Oi 1986), or what the Chinese refer to as the dual track price system, continues to provide less expensive alternatives to free market goods. Many of the same goods can be obtained through the official supply system rather than the market, and usually at prices lower than those of the market. Consequently, it is only when one cannot buy through the official system that one goes to the market (Oi 1986).[3]

The problem with the above strategy is that the ability to buy from the plan is increasingly difficult, especially in the rural areas. Individual peasants are forced to buy on the market. But as the reforms have progressed, enterprises have developed additional strategies to avoid the high costs of the open market. One such system is through barter. This uses state supplied goods as a currency of exchange, but the circulation of goods is not planned by the state or based on production needs. The inputs purchased or traded do not necessarily have direct productive value for the consumer. Factories use state supplied goods, which the factories themselves produce or acquire through trade, to secure other goods. In some cases factories accept goods for which they have no production use, but can use in the procurement of needed production goods in later barter arrangements. For example, a factory which itself has no use for steel, but through various exchanges or special connections obtains a load of steel, has a powerful currency to secure materials that it actually will use in production.

A second example of utility maximizing strategies that uses non-standard market alternatives is factories investing in enterprises such as mines or small steel mills that in return will provide a guaranteed supply of key inputs at set prices. This saves larger factories the trouble of having to seek out scarce materials. It usually also means that they pay a lower than market price for the materials.

These preferences are indicative of broader trends practiced by rural enterprises, including private enterprises, which want to maximize profits and minimize risks. Whether open markets are preferred depends on considerations of comparative advantage and security. There is no reason to assume that peasants will opt for the market just because they now have that option. As I will show, some of what is generally thought of as market activity is to a significant degree transactions that are conducted as part of the plan. This is not to minimize the importance of the re-emergence of the market. It has introduced competition and has provided alternatives to the state's monopoly on resources. Selling to the state, selling on the open market, buying on the open market, or buying from the state are simply different marketing options. There is no inherent preference for one over the other.

Since the reforms began, individual peasants have shown that they will sell to whomever offers the better overall price.[4] For example, during 1983–4, in spite of the existence of free markets, peasants queued for days to try to sell grain to the state at state set prices (Oi 1989). The overly abundant harvest caused a drop in the free market grain prices that made the state the better marketing option. After the next harvest, however, as soon as market prices became higher, peasants again turned to the open market leaving the state procurement system short of grain. Peasants more recently seem to want again to sell to the state under a new state incentive scheme designed to maintain peasant enthusiasm for grain production. Starting in 1991 the state established a special category of above quota sales known as 'grain reserves' (*chubei liang*) sales. The amount peasants can sell is limited, but the price for each jin of grain is much higher than the quota prices, and, in places like Shandong, is higher than the market prices.

Individual entrepreneurs and risk minimization

It is commonly assumed that private entrepreneurs are the most active participants in the market. They are often thought of as embodying the spirit of a 'market economy,' seen by some as the seeds of a 'civil society' that will emerge in China as a result of the market reforms (Gold 1990; Chan & Unger 1990). Some see them as the driving force of the market, generating the growth that has taken place in the decade of reform. It is also often assumed that such private entrepreneurs have become rich because of the market. To a certain degree that is obviously true; without the market there would be no entrepreneurs. However, evidence suggests that the routes that private entrepreneurs travel to get rich involve substantial dealings with the state and collective sectors.

Some of the most successful, larger private entrepreneurs seldom venture into the open market, either for the procurement of production materials or in the sale of their products, to deal directly with the public. Instead they produce as individuals, but sell their products to large collective or state enterprises on contract.[5] These enterprises to whom they sell their goods often supply them with the basic raw materials and design options. The role of the individual entrepreneur is processing. For example, a sofa frame maker in a village in Shandong did not have to worry about supplies, designs, or the retailing of his products.[6] He simply produced the sofa frames and delivered them to the large collective enterprise with whom he had contracted to make the frames. The price, the provision of materials, and the amount to be produced were determined beforehand by contract. Interestingly, as the sofa maker became more successful he also became a middleman and subcontracted to smaller producers in his village. He provided them with a 'market', the expertise and the experience needed to break into what appears to be a rather profitable profession.[7] He collected the sofa frames made by his neighbours and sold them along with his own sofa frames to the large collective in the nearby large city.[8] A private shoe maker who operated a smaller operation than the sofa maker was also quite successful by engaging in market production with minimal risks. He produced on orders for the large local department stores in the area. The materials, styles, etc., were provided by the collective or state stores; the entrepreneur merely produced according to specification.[9]

The above discussion also describes another example of contracting, the crosswise linkages (*hengxiang lianhe*) between larger state or collective factories and rural collective enterprises. Minimal risk is involved; materials and designs are supplied by the larger and better connected state or collective enterprise. And because of the limited size of most of these enterprises and the fact that peasant workers have land to fall back on, there is built-in flexibility and security if business orders are not forthcoming.

Even in places like Wenzhou, which is noted for its private enterprises, individual entrepreneurs are often part of an assembly line operation, where an entire village contracts to make certain items, and individual households do specialized tasks necessary for the final finished product. Somewhat like the sofa maker and the shoe maker described above, instead of directly participating in the 'market' as individuals, these individual entrepreneurs contract with a larger corporate organization, in this case either the village or smaller subgroup within the village that handles the marketing. The various trade associations (*xiehui*) is another mechanism by which small producers reduce some of the difficulties of having to operate in a market context with limited information and skills. The associations find markets and sometimes help with the procurement of materials.

This is not to suggest that all individual entrepreneurs must have a collective or state link,[10] but the importance of such contracting arrangements should be noted. Even private entrepreneurs have become part of, and in some cases dependent on, the state and collective sectors, to reduce risks while pursuing, if not maximizing, economic interests. This type of market activity has very different implications for the distribution of power than that predicted by the theory of market transition.

Up to now I have tried to make clear how some in the countryside have chosen to pursue alternatives to direct market participation. The political actors with whom I have been concerned have been either individual peasants or enterprises, either private or collective. I now wish to examine the decision by local governments to allocate resources through hybrid market mechanisms.

The marriage of plan and market: fiscal reform and the emergence of guided markets

Political economist Robert Bates, looking at Africa, has warned that one cannot assume that just because markets in the long run are more efficient in allocating resources, and markets are a legitimate means to allocate goods, markets will in fact be allowed to allocate goods. One must look carefully at political factors that may prevent the allocation of resources through the market (Bates 1990). This caveat is especially appropriate in China's reform context.

It is often assumed that the reforms introduced after the Third Plenum in 1978 promote the development of a market economy so that the market will eventually replace the plan in China. The decollectivization of agricultural production and the reopening of markets would certainly seem to fall into that category. But a third set of reforms, fiscal reforms, has had unintended consequences that work at cross purposes with the aims of the decollectivization of agriculture—disengaging government from the economy—and has skewed the operation of markets.

As I have detailed elsewhere, the fiscal reforms decentralized fiscal control and created a revenue-sharing system between the central government and different levels of local government (Oi 1990, 1992). The purpose was to provide incentives for local economic development and to foster fiscal self-sufficiency. But because local governments are dependent on local revenues for their expenditures, the reforms have prompted local officials to take a more, rather than less, active role in the management of the rural economy to ensure that sufficient revenues are generated. Officials have become entrepreneurs to ensure maximum revenues. Local governments have intervened heavily in the development of revenue generating activities, most noticeably in the operation of rural enterprises (*xiangzhen qiye*) (Oi 1992, 1991).

Simply put, the fiscal reforms have made revenues too important to risk relying on the market. The fiscal reforms have produced incentives for officials to guide the operation of markets. Instead of the upper levels funding local expenditures, local governments, down to the township level, are assigned responsibility for their own expenditures. To accomplish this local governments have taken on the role of managers, similar to those of a corporation. The rural economy is treated as a diversified corporation with different divisions, some in agriculture, some in industry, all of which should contribute to the collective need, but some of which are more profitable than others. In an attempt to maximize local revenues, officials have taken a very activist role and have intervened directly in the management and development of the most lucrative sources of local income, which in most cases are rural collective enterprises. Local officials would like to ensure that these enterprises do well, but because of resource constraints they must make strategic choices to foster the development of those enterprises deemed to have the best chances of producing the most income for local coffers. Key to this strategy is the manipulation of market mechanisms to allocate production inputs (Oi 1992).

The prices of these goods are market prices—rural areas have few inputs to distribute from the plan and even fewer at the lowest subsidized prices. However, access or opportunity to buy is not allocated according to market forces. The principle of first come, first serve does not necessarily determine access. Nor are goods and resources necessarily given to those willing to pay the highest price. Goods are secured at market prices and sold at market prices, but allocation is influenced by official intervention. Enterprises are rated and services provided accordingly. The distribution of some key resources is determined on the basis of official estimations of how limited resources can best be utilized to maximize local fiscal interests. This does not affect the distribution of all inputs; it depends on the supply and demand, but it includes the allocation of credit and inputs known to be in short supply, such as steel and electricity. There is a hierarchy of enterprises and the favoured customers are designated 'key point units (households)' (*zhongdian hu*). A link exists between wealth and access; the key point units are likely to be wealthy. But designation by local officials that the unit should get first access to the scarce input is more important than wealth. Among those which are designated to get priority access, the larger and wealthier the operation, the more likely is access to key inputs such as credit and service from the local banks.

Contracts for the lease of collectively owned enterprises, particularly for the larger more lucrative ones, are similarly allocated in a non-market fashion (Oi 1990). Bids are taken; the contracts do not always go to the highest bidder but to the individual whom the local cadres trust and consider capable of managing the enterprise in question. Officials have explained this in terms that reflect concern for risk minimization. They say that even though a household is willing to put in the highest bid, it can not necessarily be trusted to best manage a business or actually to pay the agreed rent to the local government. This provides some insights into why, even when markets exist, the situation Nee describes where '... the transition from redistributive to market coordination shifts sources of power and privilege to favour direct producers relative to redistributors' (Nee 1989) is not always the case. Wealth is important but not sufficient for power.

The position of private entrepreneurs in these guided markets depends on local officials. Judging from the phenomena of the 'fake collectives' and private enterprises seeking the protection of the 'red umbrella' that have been reported by various observers (Young 1991; Wank 1992), private entrepreneurs deem it prudent to get official status. In the context of fiscal austerity officials seem to be taking an increasingly interest maximizing attitude toward the development of private enterprises. Much seems to depend on the political costs, as well as the financial benefit such assistance would bring to the local coffers.

We should also realize that different types of marketing arrangements allow different access. Most discussions about markets seem to assume that the sellers are individual entrepreneurs, but in fact, an increasing number of official government bureaux have started competing with the material supply bureau in selling inputs. Should this type of 'market' activity be equated with that run by private individuals? It is when the supplier is a bureaucratic agency that there is most likely to be a hierarchy of customers, who have to pay market prices but whose access is not determined by ability to pay, but rather by relationship to the bureau.

The strategy that local officials have taken to maximize fiscal interests is not unique. The combination of plan and market is a very crude and elementary form of the administrative guidance practiced in Japan, where government agencies co-ordinate development, selecting certain industries for growth, and then encouraging their development by offering privileged access for goods and markets (Johnson 1982). In such a framework, there can be markets, but the markets are manipulated by government intervention or bureaucratic allocation that guides the allocation of goods. Plan and market are not exclusive in the current Chinese context.

The importance of contracts and the crude form of administrative guidance are what undergird the continued power of some cadres. One could argue that, in a number of respects, cadres decide which entrepreneurs will be successful. Cadres are the king makers, as it were. Cadres can decide who will get the scarce supplies and the protection, and they can influence who gets the contracts. The relationship between cadres and entrepreneurs is one of mutual dependence. Moreover, it should be highlighted that cadres not only receive gifts and perks from the entrepreneurs, but in the new fiscal context, an equal, if not more important consideration is the revenues for local coffers—the realization of which may determine whether a cadre can keep his position. But can all cadres wield such influence?

The entrepreneurial basis of cadre power

Markets may have only limited ability to allocate goods and resources, but they have had a significant effect on cadre power. It is misleading to think that cadre power is simply based on the continued ability to allocate resources, as Nee (1991) seems to imply.

During the Maoist period, power also involved control over resources, but the resources needed for an effective power base came with office. Included was the right of local officials to allocate people and their labour under the system of collectivized agricultural production. This power was most evident at the level of production and accounting, in the production teams, and in the hands of team leaders who decided when, how, and for how much the individual peasants would work. The ability of local officials to exercise power was made possible and premised on the lack of alternatives. Jobs were allocated and food was rationed. The closure of markets meant that the state allocation system was the only source for securing a livelihood (Oi 1989).

With the reforms, official position still carries with it control over some resources. Local officials at different levels of government are still in a position to allocate important goods and services. There is a crucial difference, however. With the reforms, the resources that come with official position are not necessarily sufficient as a power base. Consequently, not all officials have the ability to exercise effective power. Because markets have been reintroduced, there are alternatives to the state's supply system, and thus official power, by definition will be less complete than in the Maoist period. Moreover, the amount of goods allocated through the plan is limited and is likely to decrease. This, however, does not mean the end of cadre power, only that the power of local officials now depends on their own initiative and local conditions. The question, therefore, is not whether market reforms have eliminated cadre power, but how the market reforms have altered cadre power.

The partial nature of the reforms allows officials who have entrepreneurial ability to amass resources, through both the market and the plan. Effective patrons are those who are effective entrepreneurs. They themselves may not have wealth, but they must control the resources that are necessary to generate wealth, including market information and access to credit and scarce inputs. The relationship is not a linear one. Power in one area does not necessarily translate to another area. More often than not, the reforms may have undermined and ended power in certain spheres of the economy, but this should not automatically be assumed to extend to other sectors of the economy. The removal of local officials from day to day control over agriculture does not mean that they have similarly withdrawn from control over the direction of rural industry.

No simple correlation exists between the reforms and cadre power. Rather, the key variable is the resources local officials have to distribute after the reforms. Conflicting findings in the literature on cadre power can be reconciled in these terms. It is not surprising that in some areas local government offices are almost deserted, officials almost powerless, and no one wants to be an official (Nee 1989; Nee & Su 1990); this is perfectly compatible with the findings in other areas that cadres are very powerful (Oi 1990, 1991).

Which cadres are likely to have power? This is a difficult question to answer conclusively. However, it seems that where agriculture is the only source of income and where local governments have little or no legal access to the income derived, officials have little power because they have nothing much to allocate once land was contracted to households. Aside from the informal surcharges that local officials squeeze out of their population, these officials have little or no legitimate access to any of the peasants' income and control few resources that determine how well peasants will fare under the reforms. There are exceptions, but overall, the dependency of peasants on officials has been substantially reduced by the household responsibility system in land.[11] As recent research has shown, the greatest variability in peasant income is not from market activity but from wage labour (Khan et al. 1992).

In richer areas, where local officials have succeeded in developing substantial non-agricultural sources of income, such as rural industry, especially collectively owned enterprises, officials are strong.[12] Cadres in such areas, by developing non-agricultural enterprises, can control highly desired opportunities ranging from jobs for the average peasant to leasing contracts and subsidizing the more entrepreneurial members of the village who want to manage the collectively owned enterprises on a profit basis (Oi 1989).[13]

Mediating the effects of increasing income inequality

Finally, let me consider the status and behavior of those who have become rich in China's reform economy. Substantial income inequalities obviously exist in China; the question is how these differences are manifested on a day to day basis. Is there blatant flaunting of income inequalities or is some effort made to maintain traditional equalization rituals, such as inviting one's neighbours to feasts, giving donations, gifts, etc.? The answers to such questions are obviously complex and need further research. Let me just note some impressionistic findings based on limited fieldwork and interviews.

I have been struck by the similarity of the contemporary situation to much of the behavior anthropologists and others have described for traditional communities. In today's villages the rich seem similarly to make a big effort to ingratiate themselves with their neighbours, to be as helpful as possible, by giving them information on how to do certain types of trade, such as the example of the sofa maker described earlier, or how to raise rabbits or cultivate oysters. They are very conscious of doing good deeds and letting others know of their goodwill, such as raising the child of a poor relative, giving loans, taking care of a sick relative. Such acts still carry great significance and are cited as evidence of a 'good' person and solid member of the community. For example, when I asked why there were such negative feelings toward a certain entrepreneur, I was told that he was no longer filial; he did not properly take care of his mother—the implication seemed to be that wealth had corrupted his family values.

Why should the rich peasants be so concerned and cater to local feelings? Like traditional peasant societies, in contemporary China, (even though there is now increased opportunity) peasants essentially still live in closed corporate villages. They still must maintain cordial face-to-face relations with their neighbours, a situation where rumour still is an effective control against socially unsanctioned behavior. Peasants can still get rich, but they generally must still live in their own village. They do not yet have the option of moving to another community where they can freely spend their wealth without having to endure directly the negative comments of their disapproving neighbours.[14]

As a result, like traditional peasants, the newly rich peasants are taking rational actions to minimize the risk of alienation and jealousy, including engaging in philanthropic deeds.

Is there reason for such worry by the rich? How are the rich treated in China's reform society? It is difficult to generalize about attitudes without survey data, but based on limited field work and interviews, there is reason to believe that there exists considerable suspicion and, in some cases, hostility toward rich private entrepreneurs. As others have reported, I also found significant amounts of negative feeling toward the individual entrepreneurs. Susan Young (1991) suggests that it is greatest toward those in the commercial sector. That may well be, but I have also found similarly negative feelings toward those in industry. The following example illustrates the degree to which such animosity can be carried.

In a village in Shandong a very successful private entrepreneur who was in the oil-pressing business had been treated poorly by his neighbours. This was in spite of the various large donations he made to the village. He even went so far as to give gifts to his neighbours in a veiled attempt to buy their friendship. Nothing seemed to change their attitude. Finally, he took the drastic and unusual step of leaving the village and asking to be admitted to another in the nearby township, which is technically almost impossible. In large part because of the trouble that his business had caused, he sold his business to the village into which he was moving. The sale of his business was the price he had to pay to gain a new residence. He remained the manager of his business, but it was now a collectively owned enterprise rather than a private business.

The sale of a private business to a collective, as described here, is not an isolated incident. I was told of a number of such transactions. I was unable to get the details of all the sales, but there are indications that part of the motive for the sales was due to indirect pressure and discrimination against wealthy entrepreneurs. This negative attitude, moreover, is not restricted to the countryside. Even well educated urban residents of China's largest cities have expressed similar distrust of *getihu*.

These examples strongly suggest that wealth in China, while important and desired, is not sufficient to ensure happiness and high status. The exception to this is wealth held by collectives. Those village heads who have developed successful enterprises, who have access to substantial capital and who employ large numbers of peasants, are clearly important, even outside of township boundaries. A village party secretary, for example, can command great respect even from county and prefectural level officials when he oversees a wealth of resources, employs substantial numbers of the local population, and generates sufficient revenues for local coffers.

But regardless of whether the wealth is held by an individual or by a village, there is still in China considerable ideological and social pressure to redistribute one's wealth. This extends to communities as well as to individuals. Those who have become rich are expected to help their poorer neighbours, to teach them to learn their trade, to give them loans, to throw feasts. One village, for example, was the source of loans for numerous township projects.

The pressure to redistribute is one of the reasons why peasants have been so hesitant to make public their financial worth, for fear that others will come to their door with hands outstretched. Especially early in the reforms, peasants tried to keep it as quiet as possible that they were becoming rich. Now, the situation is more complex. The rich are less secretive about their wealth, perhaps because their wealth can no longer be hidden. Consequently, there is, on the one hand, ostentatious spending by the rich entrepreneurs. Restaurants are catering to people who spend small fortunes for banquets that are only sampled and left, ordering only the best liquors and most expensive dishes. At the same time, however, great effort is made to include key individuals in this banqueting, implementing the more traditional strategies I described earlier. For example, after an interview with a successful entrepreneur, he insisted on inviting me to lunch at one of the best restaurants in town. When I protested, it was explained that I should let the entrepreneur play host so that he could invite the local township officials and the county official accompanying me to a banquet. The explicit implication was that I would be doing him a favour by giving him an excuse to treat the local notables.

Conclusion

In this chapter I have assumed that peasants and cadres are rational actors who make their choices about participation in the market as actors who seek to maximize their interests, while minimizing risks. The pursuit of non-standard market behavior is rational action that allows the satisfaction of economic interests with minimal risks. My findings suggest that much more research needs to be done on the precise nature of the markets that are developing. Who are the participants? Are they primarily wholesale markets? Are the participants bureaucratic agencies or are they private traders?

Wealth by non-cadres can be achieved through official intervention and manipulation of market mechanisms. Markets have provided 'entrepreneurs with an alternative path for socioeconomic mobility', as Nee has argued, but much of this wealth is achieved via the plan or some variation of it. Markets and hierarchies are not mutually exclusive in China's reform context. Instead of displacing the plan, in practice, even after ten years markets still must operate alongside centralized distribution and rationing for key inputs and commodities. What has emerged is a variety of alternatives to both plan and market. One is contracting, which offers greater security and fewer risks. The other is a hybrid market system where goods and services are allocated according to a guided market directed by official estimations of the most effective use of limited resources.

The complex operation of market with plan in China allows for the expansion of markets, continued cadre power, and the attainment of substantial wealth by entrepreneurs. Contracting, for example, allows both non-cadres and cadres to gain. The relationship between wealth and power, as I have tried to show, is a complex one where wealth may be a component of power but not sufficient for power. Intervention by and connections to officials still seems to be an important filter. The relationship between cadres and entrepreneurs is ambivalent, but it is one of mutual dependence and exchange.

Finally, my findings suggest that the effects of wealth in such a context still seem to be kept within certain prescribed limits. Those who do get rich in China pay a price. Evidence suggests that existing social and ideological factors are still sufficient to force rich non-cadre entrepreneurs, not only to use their wealth to buy privileged access, but to redistribute some of their wealth to the community. In this sense, entrepreneurs only have limited rights over their new wealth. Property rights are still very much a fluid concept in China, dictated in some respects by traditional notions of the moral right of one's neighbours to share in one's wealth. The continued presence of such ideas and the redistribution of income that takes place through the collection of local taxes may, at least in the medium term, mediate possible class conflicts that might otherwise develop amidst the increasing stratification in China's countryside.

Notes

1 Andrew Walder (1991, p. 355) characterizes such views as examples of the markets as 'political solvent' school.
2 Milgrom and Roberts (1990, p. 65) define bargaining costs as 'all the costs associated with multilateral bargaining, competitive bidding, and other volutary mechanisms for determining a mutually acceptable agreement'.
3 In addition to the issue of price, for some food products there also seems to be some suspicion about free market goods, for which there are no inspection standards.
4 As I have detailed elsewhere, part of this preference for the plan involves calculations that the lower price of state sales is more than compensated for by the security and the bonus allotments of fertilizer or other hard-to-get inputs supplied by the state (Oi 1989).
5 Young (1991) similarly finds that the *siying qiye* sell to collective or state enterprises. Larger enterprises with more than 7 employees are given the title *siying qiye* (private enterprises).
6 As he progressed in his business and became more secure and accumulated more capital he has found it more profitable to procure some of his own materials. China Interviews 11 August 1991.
7 This entrepreneur also happens to be a village official.
8 China Interviews 11 August 1991.
9 China Interviews 15 August 1991.
10 As Young (1991) and others have shown.
11 The exception to this appears to be in extremely poor areas where peasant dependence still is substantial because of the importance of such basics as fertilizer and reliance on welfare which is still distributed by local officials. Personal communication with Jonathan Unger based on his research in poor regions of Yunnan. See also Unger and Xiong (1990).

[12] Even in these areas, peasants are not as highly dependent as during the Maoist period.

[13] Nee, in a later article, modifies his earlier position to account for the continuing power of cadres by examining the non-agricultural sectors (Nee 1991).

[14] The example of the oil press factory owner moving his residence is an exception. It illustrates the degree to which negative feelings exist toward rich entrepreneurs and the steps these people are willing to take to escape the discrimination against them.

References

Bates, Robert 1990, 'Macropolitical Economy in the Field of Development', in *Perspectives on Positive Political Economy*, eds James E. Alt & Kenneth A. Shepsle, Cambridge University Press, Cambridge, pp. 31–56.

Chan, Anita & Jonathan Unger 1990, 'Voices from the Protest Movement, Chongqing, Sichuan', *The Australian Journal of Chinese Affairs*, no. 24, pp. 259–80.

Gold, Thomas 1990, 'Urban Private Business and Social Change', in *Chinese Society on the Eve of Tiananmen: The Impact of Reform*, eds Deborah Davis & Ezra Vogel, Harvard University Press, Council on East Asian Studies, Contemporary China Series no. 7, Cambridge, pp. 157–80.

Johnson, Chalmers 1982, *MITI and the Japanese Miracle: The Growth of Industrial Policy*, 1925–1975, Stanford University Press, Stanford.

Khan, Azizur R., Keith Griffin, Carl Riskin & Zhao Renwei 1992, 'Household Income and its Distribution in China', *China Quarterly*, no. 132, pp. 1029–61.

Migdal, Joel 1974, *Peasants, Politics, and Revolution: Pressures Toward Political and Social Change in the Third World*, Princeton University Press, Princeton.

Milgrom, Paul & John Roberts 1990, 'Bargaining Costs, Influence Costs, and the Organization of Economic Activity', in *Perspectives on Positive Political Economy*, eds James E. Alt & Kenneth A. Shepsle, Cambridge University Press, Cambridge, pp. 57–89.

Mintz, Sidney 1967, 'Pratik: Haitian Personal Economic Relationships', in *Peasant Society: A Reader*, eds Jack Potter, Ma M. Diaz & George M. Foster, Little, Brown, Boston, pp. 98–110.

Nee, Victor 1989, 'A Theory of Market Transition: From Redistribution to Markets in State Socialism', *American Sociological Review*, vol. 54, no. 5, pp. 663–81.

——1991, 'Social Inequalities in Reforming State Socialism: Between Redistribution and Markets in China', *American Sociological Review*, vol. 56, no. 3, pp. 267–82.

——1992, 'Organizational Dynamics of Market Transition: Hybrid Forms, Property Rights, and Mixed Economy in China', *Administrative Science Quarterly*, vol. 37, no. 1, pp. 1–27.

Nee, Victor & Su Sijin 1990, 'Institutional Change and Economic Growth: The View from the Villages', *Journal of Asian Studies*, vol. 49, no. 1, pp. 3–25.

Oi, Jean 1986, 'Commercializing China's Rural Cadres', *Problems of Communism*, vol. 35, no. 5, pp. 1–15.

——1989, *State and Peasant in Contemporary China: The Political Economy of Village Government*, University of California Press, Berkeley.

——1990, 'The Fate of the Collective After the Commune', in *Chinese Society on the Eve of Tiananmen: The Impact of Reform*, eds Deborah Davis & Ezra Vogel, Harvard University Press, Council on East Asian Studies, Contemporary China Series no. 7, Cambridge, pp. 15–36.

——1991, 'Fiscal Reform and Local Autonomy in Rural China', Paper presented to the Annual Meeting of the American Political Science Association, Washington, D. C.

——1992, 'Fiscal Reform and the Economic Consequences of Local State Corporatism in China', *World Politics*, vol. 45, no. 1, pp. 99–126.

Scott, James 1976, *The Moral Economy of the Peasant: Rebellion and Subsistence in Southeast Asia*, Yale University Press, New Haven.

Shue, Vivienne 1988, *The Reach of the State: Sketches of the Chinese Body Politic*, Stanford University Press, Stanford.

Skinner, William 1978, 'Vegetable Supply and Marketing in Chinese Cities', *China Quarterly*, no. 76, pp. 733–93.

Unger, Jonathan & Jean Xiong 1990, 'Life in the Chinese Hinterlands under the Rural Economic Reforms', *Bulletin of Concerned Asian Scholars*, vol. 22, no. 2, pp. 4–17.

Walder, Andrew 1991, 'Social Structure and Political Authority: China's Evolving Polity', in *Two Societies in Opposition: The Republic of China and the People's Republic of China After Forty Years*, ed. Ramon Meyers, Hoover Institution Press, Stanford.

Wank, David 1992, 'Entrepreneurship, Social Structure and Politics in Post-Mao China: The Reemergence of the Commercial Middle Class in a South Coast City', unpublished PhD dissertation, Department of Sociology, Harvard University.

Watson, Andrew 1988, 'The Reform of Agricultural Marketing in China Since 1978', *China Quarterly*, no. 113, pp. 1–28.

White, Gordon 1987, 'The Impact of Economic Reforms in the Chinese Countryside: Towards the Politics of Social Capitalism?', *Modern China*, vol. 13, no. 4, pp. 411–40.

Young, Susan 1991, 'Wealth But Not Security: Attitudes Towards Private Business in China in the 1980s', *The Australian Journal of Chinese Affairs*, no. 25, pp. 115–38.

Zweig, David 1986, 'Prosperity and Conflict in Post-Mao Rural China', *China Quarterly*, no. 105, pp. 1–18.

5 Standards of living, relative deprivation and political change

Ann Kent

S tudents of revolution are often required to account for the fact that radical popular uprisings in a state frequently coincide with a period in which the general standard of living is improving and the political climate liberalizing. In China's case, scholars must explain the reasons why in 1989, after ten years of rising living standards, interrupted by a brief bout of high inflation, and after considerable relaxation in the political environment, a demonstration of students and intellectuals in Beijing calling for civil and political rights expanded into a nation-wide movement joined by workers and ordinary citizens, who protested against not only the lack of civil and political freedoms but economic and social injustice. This explanation is necessary not only to throw light on the Democracy Movement but also to facilitate reasonable projections of political developments into the 1990s.

As earlier chapters have shown, economic reform in China has had a positive effect on living standards. In absolute terms, the overall standard of living, if measured in terms of average per capita income and consumption patterns, has risen perceptibly. Thus, in a report on economic and social progress of the 1980s, the State Statistical Bureau (1991) estimated that during the 1980s the real level of consumption increased on an average of 5.9 per cent annually, compared with an average rate of 2.6 per cent over the previous twenty-eight years. In 1990, the per capita income of city and town residents averaged 1 387 yuan while the average per capita net income of farmers was 630 yuan; allowing for price rises, these figures represented a 68.1 and 124 per cent increase respectively over the figures for ten years before.

Such average per capita net income increases, however, should not disguise the changes which have occurred in relative standards of living in the modernization era. In China under Mao, and particularly by the mid-to-late 1970s, there was a lack of correlation between measured income and welfare outcomes. This divergence was due to the existence of a substantial network of state and collectively supported basic health care, education, hygiene and welfare relief services which protected both urban, and to a lesser extent, rural consumers. The actual income coefficients of important welfare outcomes such as longevity (measured at the end of this period by Chinese sources as over sixty-eight years) were small. Therefore, income measures of poverty, and indeed living standards, needed to be supplemented by consideration of access to welfare and other services (Riskin 1991).

During the modernization period since 1978, Chinese statisticians have measured the standard of living by the per capita cash incomes of urban and rural residents that can be used for living expenses, by consumption patterns, and by state outlays on housing construction, education, social welfare, social relief and social security. In this era, however, the sharp increase in per capita cash incomes, the erosion of collective welfare systems, and the privatization of some welfare services have combined to place increased focus on per capita incomes. Apart from the special cases of the officially designated 'poor' areas of China, and of destitute and disabled people, the economic and social benefits to Chinese citizens resulting from economic reform have been seen more in the light of an improved standard of living resulting from the trickle down effect of increased overall economic prosperity than, as in the past, one of the goals of socialist economic development to be achieved through redistributive mechanisms. The formal reordering of the state's priorities to the achievement of economic prosperity through combined market and planning mechanisms has meant that the stress is on direct rather than indirect gainsharing, and on the improvement of real income and consumption levels, rather than on the right to work and the provision of social services *per se*.

In other words, while the average living standard has risen in the modernization era, the more equal distribution of goods and income which was a priority of the Mao era has not been, with the exception of a brief period after June 1989, a goal of the reform leadership. The short term policy, in fact, has been to encourage differentials in living standards. Thus in 1987 Liu Guoguang and Liang Wensen referred to 'our long term task to raise efficiency by widening income gaps' (p. 365). The resulting discrepancy between average and relative standards of living in China raises two important questions. The first is the contentious question of the relationship between successful economic reform and more equitable distribution policies. The second, less controversial issue, the subject of this chapter, is the relationship between living standards and the political environment.

The assumption here is that, although economists may debate whether poverty is best treated as an absolute or a relative condition (Riskin 1991), for political purposes living standards should be treated as a relative phenomenon. On the basis of this premise, an attempt is made to examine the complex and maverick role which living standards have played in the dynamic relationship between economic reform and political stability in China during the modernization era, and in particular during the decade leading up to the 1989 Democracy Movement.

Theorists of revolution or popular uprisings include Samuel Huntington who, in his *Political Order in Changing Societies* has identified the main source of political disorder as the high rate of social mobilization and political participation against the low rate of political organization (Huntington 1969, p. 5). Another theorist, Chalmers Johnson, has analysed revolution as 'one form of social change in response to the presence of dysfunction in the social system' (Johnson 1964, p. 10). Both these theories of political change are posited on extensive and dramatic social change which defies the ability of the political system to absorb it. A third theorist, Ted Gurr, basing himself on the same premise, has extended the analysis from the political emphasis of Huntington, through the social emphasis of Johnson, to the realms of social psychology (Girling 1980, p. 99). In the light of the unanticipated popular uprisings in China, the Soviet Union and Eastern Europe, Gurr's theory in particular warrants reconsideration, and provides an alternative to particularistic or convergence theory models of social mobilization.[1]

The theory of relative deprivation

Relative deprivation is a concept of psychology which was first given a collective social dimension by W. G. Runciman.[2] It is defined by Runciman (1966) as a sense of deprivation borne of perceptions of inequality in class, status or power when compared with a 'comparative' or 'normative' reference group. While Runciman uses the theory as it pertains to feelings of inequality in inter-personal or inter-group relations, Gurr (1970) utilizes it to explain revolutions or popular uprisings. For Gurr, relative deprivation is a condition of disequilibrium resulting from the gap between collective value expectations and collective value capabilities. It exhibits three main patterns: 'decremental' deprivation, where value expectations are constant but capabilities are seen to decline; 'aspirational' deprivation, where capabilities remain static and expectations intensify; and 'progressive' deprivation, marked by a substantial and simultaneous increase in expectations and a decrease in capabilities. Although not utilizing the precise Weberian terminology adopted by Runciman, that is, of class, status and power, Gurr nevertheless utilizes the same category of value distinctions, between 'welfare' values (physical well-being and self-realization), 'interpersonal' values (status, communality and ideational values), and 'power' (participation and security) (Gurr 1970, p. 25).

Relative deprivation only brings revolutionary change when there is a confluence of a number of factors—the existence of objective sources of deprivation, a subjective sense of grievance, and a perception of the realistic possibility of political change.

'Relative deprivation' is both a vertical and a horizontal concept. That is, it occurs with reference to time, felt in relation to the loss of some value or values enjoyed in the past or to some disequilibrium between expectations and present capabilities, and to space, or 'reference groups', with whom the deprived group compares itself. While normally this reference group is close to the condition of the class, status and power of the referring group, in situations characterized by a loss of societal norms— the condition of *anomie* referred to by Durkheim—there is a 'danger of confusion and violence precisely because people do not know where to look for their reference groups, whether comparative or normative, and thereby become prone to exaggerated hopes or fears' (Runciman 1966, p. 22). Relative deprivation has led to collective violence, or collective action, in cases where 'citizens felt sharply deprived with respect to their most deeply valued goals, had individually and collectively exhausted the constructive means open to them to attain those goals, and lacked any nonviolent opportunity to act on their anger' (Gurr 1970, p. 92).

The theory of relative deprivation is not without its critics. Some have reservations about the application of concepts of individual psychology to the social arena; others have objected that the theory is too all-inclusive (Girling 1980, pp. 93–5). Still others could complain that it is just another way of describing what it was intended to explain. What the theory does offer in terms of explanation, however, is located in the word 'relative'; expectations or disappointments are not necessarily objectively based, but relative to time and to space. Explanatory power also lies in the idea that deprivation is as much a function of hope as it is of disappointment, that is, it is as much the result of a reasonable expectation of change as of verifiable, empirical circumstances. As such, it is based as much on perceptions of reality as on the reality itself.

For China, the main relevance of the theory of relative deprivation is that it allows a view of popular uprisings as rooted in the combined outcome of objective sources of deprivation and of perceptions of deprivation, in living standards, in access to political power, and in social status. It also allows protest movements to be understood as the result of heightened expectations of political change. In terms of living standards, it explains what can happen in a period of rapid economic and social change when a clash of value systems produces a condition of *anomie* or normlessness in which people compare their material condition not only, as is normally the case, with the closest reference group, but with a variety of distant and elite 'normative' and 'comparative' reference groups. Finally, it explains not only the sense of popular deprivation derived from inequality of access to goods, but the sense of grievance based on relatively equal access to goods. Both are the result of 'aspirational deprivation', felt when capabilities remain static but expectations intensify. This is what is meant by the 'maverick' role played by living standards in the political environment of a transitional socialist economy. Because the theory views popular perceptions of grievance as being more significant indicators of political change than objective sources of grievance, and is therefore based in value systems rather than solely in empirical reality, it helps explain the apparent anomaly that it was precisely urban areas in China (where income differentials and inequality of access to economic and social rights were least a problem) which were the locus of popular protest in 1989.

To apply the theory of relative deprivation to China, one must isolate not only the objective circumstances of deprivation but chart popular perceptions in China about these developments, and about the possibility of political change. In addition, abstracting from the Chalmers Johnson theory of revolution, this chapter identifies 'accelerators of dysfunction', such as the sharp increase in inflation in 1988 and the approaching seventieth anniversary of the May 4 Movement, which acted as precipitants of the 1989 movement and determined the precise timing of the demonstrations.

Living standards and relative deprivation in the modernization decade: 1979–1989

Objective sources of deprivation

The objective sources of deprivation which will be emphasized here relate to the standard of living. They include income disparities, themselves related to unequal opportunities to profit from the modernization process, the existence of corruption, and unequal access to social services and social security. Associated and relevant changes, such as alterations in social status, in shared community norms and in access to power, will be referred to only parenthetically.

Income disparities in this decade exhibited themselves in differentials between urban and rural China, between provinces and regions, between agricultural and enterprise based occupations within the countryside, and between public and private enterprises. As Guonan Ma has shown, in the late 1980s there was a partial reversal of the narrowing of the urban–rural income gap which had occurred in the early 1980s; in the first half of the 1980s there was also a growing inequality of income distribution at the household level in the rural areas, whereas such inequality in the cities was much smaller. The World Bank (1985a) also noted in the mid-1980s that while the policy of national uniform wages had resulted in extremely small income differentials among urban areas, large differentials in average incomes remained between urban and rural areas, especially in poorer regions.

Chinese awareness of these differentials was reflected in the admission by Xue Muqiao (1986, p. 92) of the 'shortcoming' in Chinese studies on the question of distribution, which 'concentrated on distribution within the ranks of the workers and staff in state-owned enterprises and state organization, paying little attention to distribution between the working class and the peasants and still less to distribution among the peasants'. In particular, Xue singled out for concern the differentials in living standards between the working class and the peasants and the differentials in living standards among peasants which, he observed, were 'even more pronounced' (pp. 89, 91). A further widening of these disparities could only be prevented 'by helping the poor collectives increase their income and not by forcing down the income of the rich ones' (p. 92). In comparison, he saw the main problem within the ranks of the workers as 'egalitarianism rather than extreme differences'. In general, however, Xue defended the maintenance of the current differentials in living standards because of the 'extremely low level of productive forces which cannot be developed properly if a premature attempt is made to minimize the differences' (p. 89).

Similar findings on differentials in living standards are revealed in the World Bank report *China: Agriculture to the Year 2000* (1985b). The World Bank found that recent rural reforms had significantly narrowed the average urban/rural income differential, although 'in real terms it remains large, partially because the government pays for as much as one half the cost of non-commodity expenditures in urban areas (rent, water and power, schooling, child care, transportation, etc.) and urban residents receive additional consumption benefits through their employers' (pp. 109–10). However, during the same period, interpersonal income differentials in the rural areas 'almost certainly increased, with official support' (p. 110). While taxation offered an instrument to control interpersonal income differentials, the Bank stated that the Chinese government had paid less attention to geographical and interregional income disparities. Relative poverty remained characteristic of much of the north-west and parts of the north and south-west. Similar geographic income differentials existed within provinces. In addition to the Bank findings, it has been argued that in terms of absolute poverty, estimated as a poverty threshhold of 333 yuan per annum, the rural poverty rate, after declining sharply in the early 1980s, rose again after 1984 or 1985; in 1988 the rural poverty rate was an estimated 13 per cent, or 107 million people (Riskin 1991). In terms of distribution, it was estimated that in 1980 the average net per capita income of ten poor counties supported by the state was 127 yuan less than the country's average: but in 1988 the difference had reached 289 yuan (Thireau 1991).

In rural areas, from the mid-to-late 1980s, millions of peasants 'took leave of the soil though not of the countryside' (*li tu wei li xiang*), or left rural areas altogether: the incomes of those who found, or created, employment in manual labour, transportation, shipping, construction businesses and food services were much higher than those of peasants engaged in farming. In one village in Hunan, for instance, peasants who went into business producing ointment earned an average per capita yearly income of over 10 000 yuan compared to the average annual income of agricultural workers of 600–700 yuan or less (Liu 1991, p. 78). Within one village, four different kinds of households were identifiable. Thus in Hebei province, with a per capita peasant income of 589.4 yuan, 6.7 per cent were poor households with per capita income of less than 200 yuan, 38.8 per cent were households with sufficient food and clothing and a per capita income of between 200 and 500 yuan, 43.1 per cent were well to do households with per capita incomes of between 500 yuan and 1000, and 11.4 per cent were households with an annual income per capita of more than 1000 yuan (Thireau 1991, p. 42). There were also large disparities between incomes of wage dependent state employees and the incomes of self-employed entrepreneurs and operators of private businesses. The latter might earn average real annual incomes of between 3.8 and 6 times higher than the average annual wage of the former (Liu 1991, p. 77). And there were some disparities between mental and manual labour, as well as 'unreasonable' income differences between mental labourers working in different institutions (ibid.).

After the beginning of the 1980s, inequalities of income distribution were the chief source of grievance about unfair distribution in China. A secondary source, however, suggested in the citation from Xue Muqiao, was 'egalitarianism', or the 'iron rice bowl' which still existed in urban China. The unfairness of 'egalitarianism' was seen as similar to income inequalities in that both represented (1) unrepaid appropriation by one group of the fruits of labour of another group; or (2) the unrepaid appropriation by a person contributing less or inferior labour from another contributing more or superior labour (ibid.). This 'egalitarianism' had become even more marked in the late 1980s. Thus a comparative survey in forty-eight cities between 1985 and early 1988 showed that differentials in income between senior and junior or between skilled and less skilled workers, both manual and mental, in different parts of the public sector had diminished from as high as 1:3.1 to as low as 1:1.6 (Chen 1991, p. 14). Moreover, although egalitarianism was the chief manifestation of 'unfair' income distribution in the public sector of the urban economy, there was substantial inequality between the public and non-public urban sectors. This was manifested in huge differentials in income between state workers and the *getihu*, private enterprise workers, contracted or hired labour, workers in SEZs (Special Economic Zones) and workers in high technology companies like Sitong and staff of high class hotels (ibid., p. 15). Thus, while the yearly income of state workers in Shanghai was more than 2000 yuan, over 20 per cent of workers in private enterprises in industry and commerce made more than 10 000 yuan and over 11 per cent made 30 000–50 000 yuan (ibid.).

Closely related to the problem of inequitable income was the existence of inequality of opportunity and the related problem of corruption. Official and non-official corruption in the modernization decade basically represented the expansion into economic channels of the political and administrative clientelism of the Mao era. This expansion was encouraged by numerous developments—the new support for profit making and competition and consumer spending, the removal of central controls, and the new emphasis on the expansion of the economy at the expense of other goals. In urban China this economic corruption took a predominantly 'disintegrative form', resembling what has been termed 'crisis corruption'. This form of corruption was characterized by a situation in which 'private parties ... so thoroughly penetrated the public realm that most public goods and services (were) up for sale', and in which there was 'an extraordinary influx of illicit resources from without' (Meaney 1991, p. 129). In urban areas, economic corruption was encouraged by the freedom given state enterprises to contract among themselves, set prices and engage in profit-making activities. Individual cadres or entire state organizations bought scarce commodities at low state prices and resold them at inflated prices; power abuse for personal gain, excessive price hikes, bribery, graft and nepotism were rife. In rural areas, apart from such problems as nepotism and cronyism, the key administrative and decision-making role of cadres made them open to bribery in matters of specialised households, the determination of contracts, the securing of loans, foreign currency, technology and scarce raw materials (Oi 1991, pp. 149–56). Jean Oi has concluded that: 'The reforms clearly have made peasants more vulnerable as *individuals* to a *wider variety* of arbitrary or discriminatory behaviour by officials and petty clerks than during the Maoist period' (ibid., p. 154).

The fourth objective source of deprivation in relation to living standards was inequality of access to economic and social rights—the right to work, the right to social welfare and to social security (Kent 1992). Inequality of access to economic and social rights in the 1980s was the product of four main developments: (1) the commodification of social welfare (Davis 1989); (2) the increase of the rural/urban gap in the provision of social services (Davis 1989; Taylor 1988); (3) the devolution of responsibility for social welfare and social security from the state and the collective to lower administrative levels and to the family; and (4) the lack of an effective and comprehensive unemployment insurance system (Kent 1991a, 1991b).

The proliferation of different forms of ownership and the near-collapse of the collective sector of the economy meant the creation of two classes of citizens in terms of access to social welfare and social security—the ever more privileged workers in state enterprises and collectives employed before 1986 who enjoyed differing degrees of wages, bonuses and welfare protection from the state—and the rest. The latter comprised contract workers, or workers employed after 1986, who were vulnerable to dismissal and who, in many cases, lacked social security and welfare benefits, workers in the SEZs who enjoyed higher wages, social security benefits but no employment tenure, workers in private enterprises who had no old age pensions or medical insurance, and peasants, temporary migrant workers and the unemployed who were equally unprotected (Leung 1988). In the countryside, by 1989, the loss of collective services for social security funding had not been replaced by any universal social services scheme. Thus, in terms of social welfare and social security access, two classes of peasants were created, those from wealthy villages who could afford to finance their own services and those from poor villages who could not (Unger & Xiong 1990, p. 14).

More important than the schism between citizens in terms of access to social services was, however, the social and economic polarization which occurred in this decade between the employed and the unemployed. Chinese unemployment statistics suggested the realization of the World Bank's warning about the changing pattern of poverty in East Asia:

> Rising incomes and strong employment growth ... have meant that the poor are increasingly confined to those groups that are unable to benefit from employment opportunities and rising real wages— notably the elderly and the infirm. Demographic and social forces are also increasing the need for state provision of health care and safety nets for these groups (World Bank 1990, p. 140).

In China's case, demographic and social forces joined economic forces, which included the rationalization of labour in the rural and, to a lesser extent, urban sectors of the economy. In July 1988 twenty million or twenty per cent of the total state employed workforce were estimated redundant (*RMRB*, 29 July 1988). In addition were those declared redundant in private enterprises and six million young people joining the workforce every year. Finally, rural migrants in search of a job helped comprise some fifty million Chinese on the move—one in twenty of China's population, subject to no-one's jurisdiction, and ineligible for social welfare and social security benefits (*RMRB*, 26 February 1989). In March 1989 it was estimated that 'since the adoption of the responsibility system and the leasing out of land to individuals', 180 million farm labourers had become redundant and another 200 million would probably be out of work in the coming decade (*SWB*, FE/0402/B2/3).

Popular perceptions of deprivation

Objective sources of deprivation are a necessary but not sufficient condition for popular political protest. Perceptions of deprivation are more important: although they bear a relation to objective sources, it is not always a direct one. Thus, for instance, while inequality of access to employment, social welfare and social security in China were objective realities, perceptions of popular deprivation were often directed at precisely those socio-economic groups who enjoyed high incomes but who had little access to social welfare and social security, like the *getihu* (Chan 1991, p. 107). This was partly because access to social benefits had in the Maoist era been built into the socio-economic system and was part of the 'implicit social contract' (Hartford 1990, p. 77); welfare benefits were therefore assumed, rather than consciously valued, commodities. On the other hand, the loss of these rights, especially in view of spiralling medical costs, placed a priority on the size of disposable income and thus exacerbated popular perceptions of grievance, whether in relation to the unfairness of the egalitarian state wage structure or the unfairness of inegalitarian incomes.

That Chinese society in the modernization decade experienced the most profound convulsions is not in doubt (Baum 1991). That these changes were changes in 'kind' rather than 'degree' has been well substantiated by a book published in 1989 which was entirely devoted to listing and explaining the new concepts and attitudes that were a product of the economic reforms. These included a new concept of value, of time and space; the concepts of efficiency, the market, competition; equality before the law, separation of Party and state; new concepts of marriage, divorce, of care for the aged, and new life-styles; and they involved the rejection of old concepts, such as the idea that power prevailed over the law, and the notion of personal dependency (Liu & Zheng 1989; Huang 1990). However, the new ideas, together with expectations of increased personal prosperity encouraged by the reform leadership, did not replace, but co-existed with, egalitarian assumptions from the Maoist era. These contradictory assumptions were in turn reflected in the evolving public perceptions of the empirical results, both positive and negative, of the economic modernization process.

In the pre-June 1989 decade, popular perceptions of deprivation in urban areas could be gleaned from numerous opinion polls.[3] The double-edged nature of these polls has been pointed out by Stanley Rosen (1991) who observed that, once the polling process was established as an import-ant part of policy making, 'the public pulse required constant monitoring, and public demand for the tangible benefits of reform grew faster than the available supply' (ibid., p. 60). During the 1980s, polls were carried out by official, private and semi-private organizations. Findings suggested that a focal point of popular resentment was the unequal distribution of new wealth, a fact particularly disturbing for pensioners and urban fixed-salary earners, including academics, whose salaries were low and who did not enjoy bonuses. The widespread perception that the children of top officials and their children, Party members and local cadres were, through various corrupt practices, receiving a disproportionate share of new wealth, only exacerbated the sense of inequality produced by inflation. For instance, a poll conducted among 12 000 workers (36 per cent manual, 64 per cent non-manual) in sixteen cities in August 1988 by the Institute of Sociology of the Chinese Academy of Social Sciences and the State Statistical Bureau, revealed that 94 per cent of the interviewees felt that prices were rising too rapidly; 64.1 per cent believed that further price rises would be more likely to lead to social unrest, and 35.3 per cent that the ever widening income gaps would be the precipitant of social unrest. 46 per cent of the respondents claimed that embezzlement and bribe-taking by government employees were the biggest social problems and 61 per cent felt that officials often took advantage of their position and power by disregarding the law (do Rosario 1989).

The most relevant findings came from the Chinese Economic System Reform Research Institute (CESRRI) polls, which suggested that while most people understood the need for price reform, popular support for such reform depended on whether respondents felt their standard of living was rising, stagnant or falling (Reynolds 1987, p. 34.) The CESRRI polls were important, not only because they were followed up over time, but because they revealed a simultaneous sense of popular discontent and of rising expectations. Fourteen longitudinal surveys conducted by CESRRI between 1984 and 1986 suggested three stages in the evolution of popular attitudes (Reynolds 1987; Rosen 1991). The first stage followed the adoption of urban reforms by the October 1984 Party plenum, which met an enthusiastic popular response. The second stage, which focused on the issue of price reform in 1985, was marked by increasing popular dissatisfaction, particularly over commodity price rises, coupled with widespread optimism that popular aspirations for higher income were justified. The third stage was similarly marked by both dissatisfaction and expectations. Sources of dissatisfaction in the last two stages included rising prices, nepotism, wage inequities, and abuse of official power for personal gain, while hopes extended not only to rising income but to a variety of political, social, and economic issues (Rosen 1991, p. 67). The problem of 'upward emulation', constantly referred to as a social problem in the 1985 CESRRI report, was reflected in the finding that although enterprise cadres regarded their work as important, fully 78 per cent of those interviewed would prefer to leave their management work, mainly to join government bureaucracy. They felt squeezed between the demands of the workers and the demands of the state, a dilemma that had sharpened as reform increased managerial power and, thus, the workers' expectations of what the managers could provide (Reynolds 1987, p. 43; and Walder 1989).

The most potent source of discontent, however, was inequality of opportunity, most clearly reflected in a February 1986 survey which indicated that only 29.3 per cent of the people felt that reform offered opportunities to all (Rosen 1991 p. 67). On the other hand, a July 1985 poll revealed that 79.8 per cent of respondents preferred 'living a stable life at the expense of earning less', while only 18.6 per cent would choose 'living a life full of challenge, but with a bigger opportunity to earn more' (Reynolds 1987, p. 21). The polls thus demonstrated that not only was there excessive concern about what had been lost as a result of the reforms, both in relation to time and to other groups, but that there were excessive expectations of, and anxieties about, the future. These excessive responses, coupled with the wide range of 'reference groups' to which the discontented compared their lot, reflected a profound sense of *anomie*. Although there was increasing disparity between groups as regards aspirations and attitude to reform, the tendency was to compare one's lot not just with the closest 'reference group', but even with the elite stratum of Party officials, at least in the sense that this stratum was seen as a 'normative' reference group (for instance Oi 1991, pp. 156, 161 f. 50). In this sense, socialism was still used as a yardstick by which citizens measured their conditions. On the other hand, the 'comparative' reference groups to which citizens compared their lot, the *getihu* and popstars, were a reflection of the extent to which modernization had changed Chinese values (Goodman 1991b, p. 7). Because of this dual value system, the issue of corruption, which was the one issue uniting all social groups in the 1989 Democracy Movement, was of crucial concern.

The public issue of corruption was particularly powerful because it was at once a symptom of deprivation and of public expectations: it represented the clash of old and new values. Popular resistance to the many forms of corruption which emerged at the interface between the command economy and the market economy in the modernization decade only achieves perspective when seen against earlier Maoist norms of equality and personal abstinence. Corruption within the Party itself was the greatest source of resentment, as it symbolized the abuse of power by an elite whose status and claim to rule was vested in the very norms it was in the process of dissolving. On the other hand, the new values of the modernization decade were reflected in the fact that the main popular objection to rampant official corruption was not that it represented a denial of the values of equal distribution, but that it represented a denial of equal opportunity—the equal opportunity to taste the benefits of the fruits of economic reform.

Using relative deprivation theory in relation to living standards, the grievances of China's urban population in the modernization decade may be understood as having originated in two main sources. The first source was the narrow income differentials existing within the state-owned sector, and the relative equality in incomes of mental and manual workers at a time when the market was supposed to be determining values, that is, when both mental and manual workers believed that their own enhanced value in the new era should be reflected in higher wages relative to the other. The objection on both sides was thus to the 'unrepaid appropriation by a person contributing less or inferior labour from another contributing more or superior labour' (Liu 1991, p. 77). This sense of a disequilibrium between value expectations and value capabilities reflected the new value system of the market economy. The second source of urban grievance was the disequilibrium in living standards which developed between those employed in the more egalitarian state sector and the small percentage of *getihu* and top Party officials making large incomes outside this system, out of all proportion to the average urban per capita income. This discontent reflected the old egalitarian value system. In the case of the *getihu*, intellectuals in particular felt the deprivation characteristic of the perceptions of a high social status group resenting the improved material circumstances of a previously low status group.

Perceptions of grievance in the rural community, although equally strong, fell more into the category of opposition to 'unfair' disequilibrium in living standards, rather than of 'unfair' equality. This was because structural change in the countryside had already advanced beyond the egalitarian structures, such as the state wage system, still in place in the cities. Peasants' reactions were gauged not from polls but from letters from peasants listing grievances to the press, and from individual research conducted in villages (Oi 1991; Zweig 1986; Thireau 1991; Delman 1989). Of a list of seventeen commonly cited grievances, the majority of issues involved charges of arbitrary official interference with legal rights of the peasants, or self-enrichment by officials at the peasants' expense. Some of the income inequalities were regarded by the peasants as fair if they were related to the size of the family labour force, or if they derived from family cohesion, educational level, technical expertise or managerial experience; the legitimacy of prosperity also depended on whether it was perceived that the well-being of the community as a whole was thereby being served. On the other hand, behaviour which went against either traditional or pre-reform communist morality was regarded as illegitimate, *even if legal*, that is, even if it conformed to new legal regulations (Thireau pp. 45–9). Particular sources of grievance were preferential treatment in the allocation of collectively owned means of production which could not be equally distributed, the issue of hiring labour which was proscribed in pre-reform China, and, as in the cities, personal enrichment on the basis of *guanxi* (personal connections). Thus, a strong sense of pre-reform egalitarian values persisted in the countryside, despite the fact that rural values were also seen to have changed (Li 1990; Huang 1990).

By the beginning of 1989, the sense of a loss of societal norms, of *anomie*, reflected in popular attitudes to corruption, was manifested in the general urban political environment. A widespread feeling of crisis was suggested in the nationwide debate as to whether China's political system should incline towards 'democracy' or towards 'new authoritarianism', a concept derived essentially from the politico-economic systems of the Capitalist Development States (CDS) in Asia, or the 'four little dragons'.[4] The sense of crisis, as many have observed, was reflected in the powerful and emotive six-part documentary, *River Elegy* (*Heshang*) televized throughout China in the last quarter of 1988. Using the history and character of China's Yellow River as a metaphor for the history and fate of China, the documentary concluded that China was approaching an historical crossroads, where the traditional culture was giving way before the forces of modernization. In the face of this crisis, China's people had the opportunity to create a new society based on new principles and institutions. The problem, however, was that neither China's leaders nor its intellectuals were able to project a coherent and realistic vision for the future of this society. Intellectuals adopted and then rejected a panoply of ideas, ranging from systems theory, cybernetics, econometrics, existentialism and Jungian psychology, to a contagious iconoclasm: in this 'floundering eclecticism' there was no consensual or consistent political vision (Madsen 1990, p. 252). The *embarras de richesse* in ideas became, paradoxically, a source of intellectual immobility.

Expectations of political change

Despite the apparent lack of intellectual coherence, a reasonable expectation of the possibility of political change was exhibited in urban areas both in China's polls and in the political behaviour of its intellectuals and workers. A July 1987 poll prepared by a private research organization in China asked the question, 'Do you think that China needs to carry out a reform of the political system?'. A positive response was received from cadres (80.4 per cent), intellectuals (78.89 per cent), workers (57.39 per cent), farmers (53.17 per cent), and hired labour (44.82 per cent positive, 28.45 per cent negative) (*Inside China Mainland* 1989). A more detailed survey on political reform was carried out by the Public Opinion Research Institute at the Chinese People's University in the summer of 1987; it involved a random selection of 1240 Beijing residents (Zhu, Zhao & Li 1990). The sample differentiated itself into five groups of political attitudes, notably the 'emulators', 'optimists', 'spectators', 'radicals' and 'outliers': the 'emulators' and 'optimists' (comprising 47 per cent of those interviewed) had a strong feeling of political efficacy (defined as the citizen's feeling of capacity and desire to influence political life), and the 'spectators' (or 29 per cent of the sample) had a lesser sense of political efficacy. In addition, while the 'emulators' (or 34 per cent of the sample) supported the official agenda for political reform (separating Party and government functions and simplifying the administration), others chose as the most urgent political issues the ensuring of socialist press freedom, the reform of the electoral system and the guarantee of citizens' civil liberties.

An expectation of change was also reflected in the behaviour of intellectuals who, particularly in the year leading up to June 1989, demanded greater political powers, greater mobility, more information, and higher wages. Even their action in calling for an amnesty for prisoners of conscience was an indication of intellectuals' confidence in the reality and prospect of greater freedom of speech. Political confidence was also indicated by the number of strikes held by workers in the modernization decade, despite the fact that the right to strike was no longer guaranteed by the constitution (Kent 1991, p. 193, f.83). The result of these expectations, at least in the cities, was 'a profound shift in the traditional relationship between strong Leninist states and their weak, captive societies' (McCormick 1990, p. 185).

China's peasantry, in contrast, appeared to lack a perception of the realistic possibility of political change. Although the objectively based and perceived grievances of peasants, and their changing value system, were in many ways similar to those of the urban population, their political life was inhibited by a relatively weak class consciousness and by the lack of an institutionalized base from which to press their claims. One is reminded of Marx's half despairing description of the mass of peasants in mid-19th century France as 'formed by the simple addition of isomorphous magnitudes, much as potatoes in a sack form a sack of potatoes' (Marx 1852). Although the situation of the Chinese peasants in the 1980s differed from that of the French peasant, in that post-1949 events had politicized them to some extent at least, in the absence of institutional mechanisms or of urban centres facilitating peasant mobilization, peasant grievances before 1989 were expressed mainly in sporadic and diffuse acts of violence, and in physical conflict between and within villages (Zweig 1986; Thireau 1991). This political condition of Chinese peasants, in fact, had strong resonances with the situation in the 1930s and 1940s described by Lucien Bianco (1983):

> Almost without exception, the peasant rebels of Republican China— their leaders included—do not seem to have followed any overall strategy, nor to have been inspired by any global vision of society: they did not challenge the bases of social organization, they wanted only to obtain the righting of a wrong or a return to an idealized earlier state of affairs. The only implicit ideology which one might, if one had to, infer from their actions is that of a backward-looking utopianism, a protest against the hardships of the time accompanied on occasion by a nostalgia for the good old days.

In addition, the existence within a single village of the four different types of wealth (Thireau 1991) meant that, unlike the city, rural comparative reference groups tended to be local ones. Reports of internecine rural conflict emphasized the loss of community norms, the confusion of pre-modernization norms with current norms, uncertainty about what constituted illegal entrepreneurial activity, loss of cadre authority, and the inability of the legal system to substitute for the loss of consensual norms or official authority within rural areas. Finally, the new mobility of redundant peasant labour meant that much of the negative impact of economic and social change in the countryside was being transferred from rural to urban areas.

If, before 1989, all the revolutionary pre-conditions of the theory of relative deprivation were not met in rural China, they were more than satisfied by the conditions in urban China. In the cities, relative economic deprivation was acutely felt both in relation to the past and to the ideal future; at the same time, both the opinion polls and observable behaviour suggested rising expectations (or what Gurr (1970) would call 'aspirational' deprivation) about economic and political values as well as optimism about the likelihood of political change. This overall condition of simultaneous expectation and dissatisfaction, moreover, corresponded to Gurr's notion of 'progressive' deprivation.

The theory of relative deprivation does not, however, provide a sufficient explanation of why an uprising or a revolution occurs at a particular point in time. The Chalmers Johnson (1964) theory of revolution, which is not inconsistent with the Gurr model, serves to bridge the gap. It sees revolution as the combined product of 'multiple (social, political and economic) dysfunction', of elite intransigence and of 'accelerators of dysfunction' (pp. 12–13). 'Accelerators of dysfunction' are seen as the immediate factors which bring to a head underlying unrest. The preceding section has documented objective sources of dysfunction. The 'accelerators' of dysfunction in China in 1989 included circumstantial factors such as price reform which, in helping to produce inflation rates of an unacceptable level, acted as precipitants of mass protest. In 1988, the sharp price rises, estimated officially at 18.5 per cent but by other sources as fluctuating between 20–30 per cent, effectively undermined the improved living standards which, until 1987, had served to cushion and disguise the slow erosion of economic and social rights.

Even in the two previous years of moderate price rises, Chu-yuan Cheng (1990, p. 29) has argued that the real effects were severe, because of the high food component of the price index. Thus, when in the first quarter of 1988 the national retail price index rose another 11 per cent over the 7.2 per cent increase in 1987, the price of nonstaple foods went up by 24.2 per cent, with a rise of 48.7 per cent in the price of fresh vegetables (Cheng 1990). The high inflation rate in 1988 thereby exacerbated an already serious situation by transforming the 22.2 per cent increase in nominal per capita income over the previous year to an actual rate of increase in real income of 1.2 per cent. More significantly, it led inevitably to a redistribution of income, so that a sampling survey in thirteen cities revealed that the real income of 34.9 per cent of all families had actually decreased simply because of price rises (State Statistical Bureau, March 1989, SWB/FE/0401/C1/5–6). Aside from inflation, the more immediate 'accelerators of dysfunction' which sparked off the Democracy Movement were the approaching seventieth anniversary of the May 4 Movement and the death of the political moderate and ousted Party leader, Hu Yaobang, on 15 April. A potent influence on the course of the movement proved to be the arrival of Soviet President Gorbachev in Peking one month later for talks with Chinese leaders. By that date, the Democracy Movement had taken off in Beijing and was igniting the sparks throughout China's cities.

Implications for China's political future

In the aftermath of the Democracy Movement and its brutal suppression by the Chinese government in June 1989, it is possible to draw certain conclusions about the implications of the theory of relative deprivation for China. The theory suggests that in a period of rapid economic and social change, the popular perceptions of grievance which fuel revolutionary change are exacerbated by conflicting value systems and by the extension of the normally narrow range of 'normative' and 'comparative' reference groups. In what superficially appears as a paradox, it also determines that, contrary to popular belief, radical political action is made more likely not as a result of government oppression, but as the result of popular perceptions of a realistic possibility of political change.

For these reasons, the unequivocal nature of the June action, which in the short term severely undermined public confidence in the possibility of political change, served to switch the focus of political attention from the people's perceptions to the behaviour of the government. After June, the government's pre-1989 emphasis on economic reform changed to a more overt and complex effort to balance the often conflicting requirements of economic reform and political stability. At the same time as it publicized its intention not to allow meaningful political change, the government began an attempt to alter the objective conditions of popular grievance and to respond to popular perceptions. At first, the goods offered or promised by the leadership were remedies to the problems of 'relative deprivation' through 'inequality substitution'[5]: the attack on corruption, attempts to improve the relative standard of living and to control inflation, the expansion of economic and social rights, and moves to close 'unfair' income gaps.[6] Government recognition of the problem of disequilibrium in living standards was exemplified by Jiang Zemin's statement on National Day 1990 that 'unfair social distribution is not only an economic problem but a social and political problem to which we must give a high priority and work hard to find solutions' (cited Chen Qingji 1991, p. 18).

In exchange for popular recognition that acquiescence to the government's will was less harmful than continued resistance, the government found it expedient not only to stress performance goals, but gradually to develop more acceptable negative means to induce popular compliance to its will through resort to the law. However, precisely because of the regime's need to continue economic reform, that is, to continue the process of rapid economic and social change, political stability was perpetually at risk. For this reason, the 'implicit social contract' between the government and its people had to be continually renegotiated.[7] This subterranean process of 'renegotiation' became the effective source of an informal 'democratic' process in China, as compared to the ritualism and rhetoric of 'political reform', which served mainly to enhance the legitimacy and efficiency of the Party and government. Thus, not only have popular perceptions of the likelihood of political change altered, but leadership resistance to structural political change, combined with an implicit acknowledgement of leadership accountability, has resulted in the diminution of pressures for public participation in the political process. At the same time, the government's basic recognition of its accountability has opened its performance to critical assessment by the people. Thus, in the future, should government performance not be perceived to be adequate or effective, or should any 'accelerator of dysfunction' such as high inflation or the death of a powerful political leader occur, pressure for popular political participation could increase.

In addition, the dual value system, reflected in popular attachment to both the old egalitarian norms and the new market values, may well continue in the forseeable future as a threat to political order. This conflicting system of values, which makes the question of living standards such a maverick issue, is, as has been argued, responsible for increasing popular dissatisfaction not only with unequal living standards but also with an egalitarian state wage system. All things being equal, the effluxion of time would attenuate the grip of Maoist values: but the reassertion of more egalitarian values in official rhetoric, if not in official policies, since June 1989, has meant renewed emphasis on Maoist norms and has thus given an official imprimatur to the continuation of the dual value system. Since the present leaders still derive a measure of legitimacy from the values of the socialist system, it would in any case be difficult for them to place sole emphasis on those of the market economy. Equally, it is impossible for them to abandon market values. It is thus likely that popular perceptions of relative deprivation in living standards will continue to be a powerful political force, along with the tendency to choose distant as well as close reference groups with which to compare the individual's material lot. The grievances which fester, however, are unlikely to fuel popular protest unless sparked off by accelerators of dysfunction or fed by perceptions of a reasonable likelihood of political change. In other words, a number of the factors of relative deprivation are still dormant in the Chinese political system. But it will take the intervention of other factors before they re-emerge as significant forces for change.

In the meantime, the Chinese leadership continues to struggle with new and seemingly insoluble difficulties. As it faces the problem of widening gaps in living standards, it is handicapped by its decreasing share of total revenues and the loss of control over distributional decisions. It is also confronted with the rise of the middle class, and the burgeoning of small towns and small town enterprises which will change the social and political character of rural areas. The urbanization of China may well result in the spread of entrepôts in which rural grievances can be expressed and organized. It may also provide focal points of relative deprivation, with peasants, often immigrants, working on the land and watching with envy their more prosperous neighbours working in local enterprises. In addition, plans to close down unprofitable state enterprises, and to extend the contract system to all state enterprise workers, if implemented, will give rise to increased inequities in urban living standards and to industrial unrest. This unrest will be exacerbated by the corruption permeating elite and grass roots levels of leadership. Finally, the government must contend with the unsettling impact of the communications revolution, which, by alerting Chinese citizens to the political and economic conditions obtaining in the outside world, will further extend the range of comparative reference groups. Thus, in the next decade, although the problem of relative deprivation in living standards may not provoke another protest movement, it is likely to persist as a dynamic force within the Chinese political system, and, together with the related threat of inflation, to present a major obstacle to the government's attempt to balance the simultaneous requirements of reform and stability.

Notes

[1]   For the latter models, see Halpern (1991) and Dittmer (1991).

[2]   See also chapter 7 of Kent (1993) which incorporates some of the following argument.

[3]   For instance, the *Beijing Review*, 29 June 1987, p. 22, cited 14 surveys on popular attitudes to reform. Other surveys included an August 1989 poll co-sponsored by the Institute of Sociology, Chinese Academy of Social Sciences (CASS), and the State Statistical Bureau, reported in *Liaowang* and *China Daily*, 11 February; '1987 Survey of the Political Psychology of Citizens in China', *Inside China Mainland* May 1989, vol. 11, no. 125, pp. 1–3; and public opinion polls reported in Reynolds (1987). See also surveys of political opinion in Min Qi (1989) and Chan (1991, p. 106).

[4]   This debate is synthesized in a collection of writings edited by Liu and Lin (1989). For a perceptive analysis of the CDSs, see Johnson (1989).

[5]   The term 'equality substitution' was coined by Guonan Ma and is taken here to suggest attempts to compensate for the inequalities created by the workings of the market economy, in the liberal 'welfare state' sense, rather than to reinstitute mechanisms of egalitarian redistribution.

[6]   For detailed analysis of the three different phases of Chinese government policies from 1989–1991, see Kent (1993, chapter 8).

[7]   Before 1976 there was an 'implicit social contract' between leaders and led, whereby citizens were guaranteed the rights of subsistence, the right to work and the gradual raising of living standards (Hartford 1991). Between 1976 and 1989 there was an *explicit* government undertaking to raise living standards via improved income and direct gainsharing. What was different about the bond established after June 1989 between government and people was that it became another *implicit* social contract, but one which was being frequently renegotiated. Moreover, the parameters of renegotiation had expanded from the pre-1976 emphasis on economic and social rights alone to include formal political, and to a lesser extent, civil rights.

References

Baum, Richard 1991, 'Epilogue: Communism, Convergence, and China's Political Convulsion', in *Reform and Reaction in Post-Mao China: The Road to Tiananmen*, ed. Richard Baum, Routledge, London, pp. 183–99.

Bianco, Lucien 1983, 'Mobilisation in the Fields', *Times Literary Supplement*, September, p. 1060.

Chan, Anita 1991 'The Social Origins and Consequences of the Tiananmen Crisis', in *China in the Nineties : Crisis Management and Beyond*, eds David S.G. Goodman & Gerald Segal, Clarendon Press, Oxford, pp. 105–30.

Chen Qingji 1991, 'Lun shouru fenpei bu gong de biaoxian, yuanyin ji duice' ('On the Manifestation and Causes of Unfair Income Distribution and Its Solutions'), *Fudan xuebao*, no. 6, pp. 13–19.

Cheng Chu-yuan 1990, *Behind the Tiananmen Massacre: Social, Political, and Economic Ferment in China*, Westview Press, Boulder.

Cheng, Joseph, ed. 1989, *China: Modernization in the 1980s*, The Chinese University Press, Hong Kong, and Allen & Unwin, Sydney.

Davis, Deborah 1989, 'Chinese Social Welfare: Policies and Outcomes', *The China Quarterly*, no. 119, pp. 577–97.

Delman, Jorgen 1989, 'Current Peasant Discontent in China: Background and Political Implications', *China Information*, vol. 4, no. 2, pp. 42–64.

Diao Xinshen 1987, 'The Role of the Two-Tier Price System', in *Reforms in China: Challenges and Choices*, ed. Bruce Reynolds, M.E. Sharpe, New York, pp. 35-46.

Dittmer, Lowell 1991, 'Socialist Reform and Sino-Soviet Convergence', *Reform and Reaction in Post-Mao China: The Road to Tiananmen*, ed. Richard Baum, Routledge, London, pp. 18–37.

do Rosario, Louise 1989, *Far Eastern Economic Review*, 2 March, p. 62.

Girling, John 1980, *America and the Third World: Revolution and Intervention*, Routledge & Kegan Paul, London, pp. 93–5.

Goodman, David S.G. 1991a, 'Introduction: The Authoritarian Outlook', in *China in the Nineties: Crisis Management and Beyond*, eds David S.G. Goodman & Gerald Segal, Clarendon Press, Oxford, pp. 1–18.

——1991b, 'Leadership, Social Change, and Foreign Influence: The Prospects for Political Stability and Reform', paper presented to Conference on China's Reforms and Economic Growth, Australian National University, Canberra, November.

Gurr, Ted R. 1970, *Why Men Rebel*, Princeton University Press, Princeton.

Halpern, Nina 1991 'Economic Reform, Social Mobilisation, and Demo-cratization in Post-Mao China', in *Reform and Reaction in Post-Mao China: The Road to Tiananmen*, ed. Richard Baum, Routledge, London, pp. 38–59.

Hartford, Kathleen 1990, 'The Political Economy Behind Beijing Spring', in *The Chinese People's Movement: Perspectives on Spring 89*, ed. Tony Saich, M.E. Sharpe, New York, pp. 50–82.

Huang Chunsheng 1990, 'Cong Guangdong jingji fazhan kan shehuizhuyi shangpin jingji yu jiazhiguan de guanxi'('The Relationship between the Socialist Commodity Economy and Values in the Light of Guangdong's Economic Development'), *Zhongshan daxue xuebao*, no. 4, pp. 36–44.

Huntington, Samuel 1969, *Political Order in Changing Societies*, Yale University Press, New Haven.

Inside China Mainland 1989, May.

Johnson, Chalmers 1964, *Revolution and the Social System*, The Hoover Institution, Stanford.

——1989, 'South Korean Democratisation: The Role of Economic Develop-ment', *The Pacific Review*, vol. 2, no. 1, pp. 1–10.

Kent, Ann 1991a, 'Waiting for Rights: China's Human Rights and China's Constitutions, 1949–1989', *Human Rights Quarterly*, vol. 13, no. 2, pp. 170–201.

——1991b, 'Human Rights: The Changing Balance-Sheet', in *China in the Nineties: Crisis Management and Beyond*, eds David S.G. Goodman & Gerald Segal, Clarendon Press, Oxford, pp. 64–86.

——1993, *Between Freedom and Subsistence: China and Human Rights*, Oxford University Press, Hong Kong.

Leung Wing-yue 1988, *Smashing the Iron Rice Pot: Workers and Unions in China's Market Socialism*, Asia Monitor Resource Centre, Hong Kong.

Li Zubao 1990, 'Nongmin qunti yishi nibei xianxiang ji qi chengyin', ('The Adverse Phenomenon in Peasant Collective Consciousness and its Consequences'), *Beijing shehui kexue*, no. 4, pp. 149–51.

Liu Guoguang, Liang Wensen et al. 1987, *China's Economy in 2000*, New World Press, Beijing.

Liu Jianxing 1991, 'Luelun "shehui fenpei bu gong de wenti"' (On the Question of Unequal Social Distribution), *Beijing shifan xueyuan xuebao*, no. 1, pp. 76–82.

Liu Jun and Lin Li eds 1989, *Xin quanwei zhuyi: dui gaige lilun gangling* (New Authoritarianism: Towards a Theoretical Programme of Reform), Beijing jingji xueyan chubanshe, Beijing.

Liu Peng and Zheng Lansun 1989, *Xin guannian—guannian biange mianmian guan* (New Concepts—Every Aspect of the Change in Concepts), Zhongguo xinqiao chubanshe gongsi, Beijing.

Madsen, Richard 1990, 'The Spiritual Crisis of China's Intellectuals', in *Chinese Society on the Eve of Tiananmen: The Impact of Reform*, eds Deborah Davis & Ezra Vogel, Harvard University Press, Cambridge, pp. 243–60.

Marx, Karl 1852, 'The Eighteenth Brumaire of Louis Bonaparte', in *Marx: Surveys from Exile*, part 2, ed. David Fernbach, Penguin Books, Harmondsworth.

McCormick, Barrett L. 1990, *Political Reform in Post-Mao China: Democracy and Bureaucracy in a Leninist State*, University of California Press, Berkeley.

Meaney, Connie S. 1991, 'Market Reform and Disintegrative Corruption in Urban China', in *Reform and Reaction in Post-Mao China: The Road to Tiananmen*, ed. Richard Baum, Routledge, London, pp. 124–42.

Min Qi 1989, *Zhongguo zhengzhi wenhua: minzhu zhengzhi nanchan de shehui xinli yinsu* (Chinese Political Culture: Social Psychology and the Birthpangs of Democratic Politics), Yunnan renmin chubanshe, Yunnan.

Oi, Jean 1991, 'Partial Market Reform and Corruption in Rural China', in *Reform and Reaction in Post-Mao China: The Road to Tiananmen*, ed. Richard Baum, Routledge, London, pp. 143–61.

Reynolds, Bruce ed. 1987, *Reform in China: Challenges and Choices*, a Summary and Analysis of the CESRRI Survey Prepared by the Staff of the Chinese Economic System Reform Research Institute, M.E. Sharpe, New York.

Riskin, Carl 1991, 'Rural Poverty in Post-Reform China', paper presented at the Conference on the Chinese Economy in the Reform Period, Australian National University, Canberra, November.

RMRB—*Renmin ribao* (People's Daily).

Rosen, Stanley 1991, 'The Rise (and Fall) of Public Opinion in China', in *Reform and Reaction in Post-Mao China: The Road to Tiananmen*, ed. Richard Baum, Routledge, London, pp. 60–83.

Runciman, Walter G. 1966, *Relative Deprivation and Social Justice: A Study of Attitudes to Social Inequality in Twentieth Century England*, Routledge & Kegan Paul, London.

State Statistical Bureau 1989, SWB/FE–BBC *Summary of World Broadcasts— Part 3: The Far East*, 0401/C1/5–6.

——1990, 'Statistics for China's National Socio-Economic Development in 1989', Documents, *Beijing Review*, 26 February, pp. i–viii.

——1991, 'China's Economic and Social Progress of the 1980s', *Beijing Review*, 15–21 April, pp. 14–18.

Taylor, Jeffrey 1988, 'Rural Employment Trends and the Legacy of Surplus Labour, 1978–86', *China Quarterly*, no. 116, pp. 736–66.

Thireau, Isabelle 1991, 'From Equality to Equity: An Exploration of Changing Norms of Distribution in Rural China', *China Information*, vol. 5, no. 4, pp. 42–57.

Unger, Jonathan & Jean Xiong 1990, 'Life in the Chinese Hinterlands under the Rural Economic Reforms', *Bulletin of Concerned Asian Scholars*, vol. 22, no. 2, pp. 4–17.

Walder, Andrew G. 1989, 'Factory and Manager in an Era of Reform', *China Quarterly*, no. 118, pp. 242–64.

——1990, 'Economic Reform and Income Distribution in Tianjin, 1976-1986', in *Chinese Society on the Eve of Tiananmen: The Impact of Reform*, eds Deborah Davis & Ezra Vogel, Harvard University Press, Cambridge, pp. 135–56.

World Bank 1985a, *China: Long Term Development Issues and Options*, Johns Hopkins University Press, Washington D.C.

——1985b, *China: Agriculture to the Year 2000*, International Bank for Reconstruction and Development, Washington, D.C.

——1990, *Poverty: World Development Report 1990*, Oxford University Press, Oxford.

Xue Muqiao 1986, *China's Socialist Economy*, Foreign Languages Press, Beijing.

Zhu, Jianhua, Xinshu Zhao & Hairong Li 1990, 'Public Political Consciousness in China: An Empirical Profile', *Asian Survey*, vol. 30, no. 10, pp. 992–1006.

Zweig, David 1986, 'Prosperity and Conflict in Post-Mao Rural China', *China Quarterly*, no. 105, pp. 1–18.

崛 Part III
New social forces

6 Private entrepreneurs and evolutionary change in China

Susan Young

During the 1980s, the private sector in China grew from tiny beginnings to play an important role in providing employment, developing the market economy, and delivering an acceptable standard of goods distribution. In the course of this development, the private sector became much more than just a fringe dweller on the edge of the socialist economy, and private entrepreneurs formed close and complex relationships with enterprises and individuals both in other ownership sectors and in government. It is now clear that the private business sector is an important source of power and economic benefits to state cadres, to other enterprises and individuals within them, and to consumers. It is also a very complex sector, with wide variation in the role of private entrepreneurs in different localities and according to the type and scope of their enterprises. The data available is still far from satisfactory, and it is difficult to make an accurate and comprehensive assessment of the nature of private business in China. It is clear, however, that the Chinese private sector is developing in its own distinctive way. It is not the marginal, precarious private sector described by observers of reforming Eastern Europe under socialism, but neither is it part of a free market economy with a sound legal basis. Instead, it is closely intertwined with other ownership sectors and with local government, and is an example of how, in China under the reforms, the established definitions of both Chinese Communist and Western economics are becoming inadequate.

A number of studies of the private sector in Eastern Europe before the collapse of communist rule have explored similar questions concerning the role and behaviour of private entrepreneurs in state-socialist systems (e.g. Grossman 1977, 1990; O'Hearn 1980; Sampson 1987; Aslund 1985). These shed light on the Chinese situation, not only for the similarities between Chinese private entrepreneurs and their Eastern European counterparts, but for the differences. Most studies associate the sector of full-time, acknowledged businesses with the more shadowy, informal realm of moonlighting, pilfering from the state sector, farmers selling a few private-plot vegetables on the side—that is, any private profit-seeking activity. The impression gained from this literature is that openly operating private businesses did indeed have a lot in common with other private business pursuits, remaining extremely peripheral, surviving only through extensive reliance on connections and bribery, operating on the margins of legality, and in fact having close economic links with the less open types of 'informal economy'.[1]

Not surprisingly, therefore, the private business sector in socialist countries has generally not been seen as a very cohesive force politically, at least not in an obvious way. Private entrepreneurs have been too marginal, too reliant on the goodwill of their connections in the state sector, and too busy making a quick profit. In addition, many have had no long-term commitment to developing their enterprises. Some entrepreneurs gave up private business once they had provided for their own and their children's future; indeed in some countries discrimination against private businesspeople meant that their children's chances would be better if they did so. It has also been pointed out that the high stress level of private business under socialism is not something everyone wants to put up with for very long (Hegedüs & Markus 1979). This lack of a long-term interest in developing private business is also a result of the constraints placed upon private business by regulations and political uncertainty, which made operators either unwilling or unable to invest their income in further expansion. Instead, they have used it for consumption at a level well above that of their non-enterpreneurial neighbours, often building large and well-equipped houses or apartments. Given the unstable history and uncertain future of private enterprise in socialist countries, this was a rational investment decision to make.

In China, too, private business was initially revived only as a supplement to the state and collective sectors. The early arguments in its favour emphasized its smallness, its subordination to the socialist economy, and the ability of the government to limit its activities to 'the trades, the state and collective economies don't do or don't do enough' (He 1981, p. 15). It was argued that the private sector would be easily controlled because 'in the scope of management, in the supply of raw materials, price and taxation, it is subject to control and restriction by the public economy and by the state organs concerned' (BR 18 August 1980, p. 4).

In fact, the private sector has grown to become a major new force in the Chinese economy and in society. Given that a large and vigorous private sector is quite new and is almost totally antithetical to both the pre-reform economic system and to pre-reform ideology, it seems inevitable that it will be a force for change. Yet it is not the private entrepreneurs who have led the demands for political change. Although a few were involved in the protest movement of 1989, especially by donating funds, most have so far been keeping their heads well down.[2] In this chapter, I shall argue that some of the reasons for this can be found in the type of person who becomes an entrepreneur, and in the course that private sector growth in China has taken, suggesting that there are institutionalized features of the reform process which militate against private entrepreneurs becoming an independent political force.

The focus of this chapter is not all forms of private economic activity in China (of which there are many), but the sector of private industry and commerce which is clearly acknowledged, namely, the *getihu* (small family or individual businesses) and the *siying qiye* (privately owned businesses employing over seven people, officially regulated since 1988). The chapter also touches upon other enterprises, indistinguishable in form and nature from *getihu* and *siying qiye*, which for a number of reasons have been included in other categories, for example rural joint enterprises (*lianheti* or *lianhu*) and specialized households (*zhuanyehu*) or collective enterprises. These categories are officially described as part of the collective economy, but the people running them are really private entrepreneurs, and in practice, if not in theory, are often recognized as such.

This gap between theory and practice is becoming increasingly wide, and, as Andrew Walder argues in this collection, the old ownership categories simply no longer match the complexity of ownership relations in China. However, it should be remembered that, despite appearances sometimes, China is still led by a communist party, and the division of state, collective and private ownership still retains great political significance. This has important consequences for the strategies adopted by entrepreneurs and the development of private enterprises in China. Therefore, even though I refer to the 'private' sector, I am actually arguing that it is not as private as the name suggests.

The Chinese private sector

In China under the reforms, the private sector has not been successfully constrained. Even the *acknowledged* private sector can no longer be described as peripheral. In official statistics, which are widely held to be vastly understating the true situation, registered private businesses (*getihu* and *siying qiye*) made up over 80 per cent of retail, food and service outlets and around 18 per cent of national social retail sales value in 1989 (*ZGTJNJ* 1990, p. 416). In 1988, they made up 85 per cent of rural township enterprises, producing 27 per cent of their gross income and 24 per cent of their gross industrial output value, and employing 38 per cent of the township enterprise labour force (*ZGXZQYNJ* 1989, pp. 75–7). In some localities, private enterprises actually dominate their local economies in terms of output value, income, and contribution to local revenue. Estimates of the private share of gross output value in some of the more developed regions range from 40 per cent to as high as 74 per cent in one example from Fujian Province (Zhang 1988; Chen Jianhua 1988, p. 42). Furthermore, in addition to enterprises which are acknowledged as being privately owned, there are also a large number of enterprises which either are privately owned, but are registered under other ownership categories, or which are nominally collectively owned, but are leased and independently run by private individuals for profit.[3]

Private business has also developed to include a wide range of trades and industries, moving well beyond the original emphasis on retailing, repairs and food service aimed at improving services to consumers. The figures used by the State Statistical Bureau show that these fields still dominate, with nearly 80 per cent of registered individual businesses involved in retail, service, catering or repairs in 1989 (ZGTJNJ 1990, p. 17). These figures have an urban bias, however, as the number of private businesses they recognize is much smaller than the number the Ministry of Agriculture's statistics give for rural private enterprises alone. Among rural private businesses, there is a much larger proportion (37.6 per cent in 1988) in industry, with 21.8 per cent in transport and only 19.9 per cent in commerce (ZGXZQYNJ 1989, p. 77). In particular, over 70 per cent of the siying qiye are involved mainly in industry (predominantly processing and light manufacturing), construction, and transport, with very few in pure commerce (ZGGSB 29 April 1991, p. 1). In some areas, many of these larger enterprises are doing business with overseas companies; for example a large proportion of those in the lists of registered siying qiye published by the Shanghai ICB (Bureau of Industry and Commerce) in 1991 are processing for foreign firms, and the same is true of many private enterprises in Guangdong.[4]

Private entrepreneurs

The rapid growth of the private sector, and especially the appearance within it of a number of reasonably large, capitalist enterprises which are able to have a considerable impact on their local economies, naturally raises the question of whether these entrepreneurs will form some sort of social elite. This question is difficult to answer, but the evidence available suggests that a more likely outcome is their integration with, or subordination to, the existing elite, as cadres co-operate with them to manipulate the reforms to their advantage.

The majority of private businesses in China are very small, and not particularly glamorous or powerful. In urban areas, attitudes towards private businesspeople have been a combination of disdain for the moneygrubbing, dishonest, uncultured popular image of getihu, and envy of the high incomes they are generally supposed to earn. The demanding workload, high risks, difficulty of establishment, and the political uncertainty surrounding private business have meant that a state or collective job is still the preferred option for many people, and young school-leavers will often remain unemployed for years rather than go into business for themselves. People who do venture into private business are usually the ones with the least to lose: those who for reasons such as poor education, criminal background, or age have little chance of a good public-sector job; those who for financial or personal reasons find a state or collective job unsatisfactory, or those with other family members able to provide the benefits and security of a state job (Bruun 1989). Thus, on the whole, the people who engage in private business are not seen as potential leaders in society, nor do they see themselves in this way. Like their counterparts in the former communist countries of Eastern Europe, many *getihu* aim to make money, spend it, and, if possible, prepare the way for their children to find a niche in the state system, for example by going to university.[5]

There is, of course, a difference between the average *getihu*—for example, a small shop or repair stall—and some of the larger enterprises, although there is no sharp division between the two and many *getihu* develop into large enterprises from very small beginnings. But it is the smaller concerns which are the most visible in the urban setting, and the two types are often lumped together when private business comes up in conversation. Obviously the wealthy entrepreneurs are envied and grudgingly admired for their success, but there is a widely held belief that this success is somehow undeservedly or dishonestly gained.

In rural areas, the situation appears to be quite different. Here, there has been the same level of risk and political insecurity, but the opportunity cost of going into private business has been much lower, and the other options less appealing, than in the cities. Rural residents, too, are people who have little to lose by going into private business. They are not giving up the chance of security and welfare benefits by doing so: on the contrary, the income so gained should enhance their future security. Most rural entrepreneurs still retain their land allocation as security, so that if private business were again to be suppressed they would be no worse off than before. They might even be better off: private enterprise in rural areas has not generally been associated with low status. It is mostly in rural towns that the large private businesses, the *siying qiye*, have emerged. According to the State Council's Bureau of Industry and Commerce (ICB), over 70 per cent of *siying qiye* are located in rural areas (*GMRB* 16 March 1988, p. 1), and it is in rural collective enterprises that the practice of leasing to private entrepreneurs is most common. In a village setting, these owners or leaseholders of enterprises which are able to provide jobs and income to their local communities are highly visible, and their position is one to which many people aspire. Jobs in private enterprises are often actively sought after by rural residents, who see them as a way of obtaining not only a higher income and often more pleasant work than agriculture, but also the skills, contacts and capital needed to start up their own enterprise.

In one enterprise in Renshou county, Sichuan, over 100 employees of a certain private enterprise left to start their own businesses during the period 1983–1988 (Odgaard 1991, p. 179).

The first wave of people to take up private business in the late 1970s and early 1980s was made up largely of people who had not managed to find a place in the public economy. Early surveys show a large proportion of people with little education among private operators (Zhang et al. 1982; Yudkin 1986; Ren 1987). This first wave also included people who had been engaged in private business, on and off, for many years; these were often craftspeople with a high level of pride in their work, glad of the opportunity to exercise their skills independently again. Then, as the reform program continued, the composition of the private entrepreneurs began to change. As the commune system was dismantled in the early to mid-1980s, the number of rural cadres was reduced and many turned to private business. From the mid-1980s the size of the army, too, was reduced, and many returned soldiers also went into private business, often using acquired skills such as driving or mechanical knowledge to run very profitable enterprises in the growing field of transport. This influx of former cadres and army personnel helped raise the level of skills, contacts and education among rural private entrepreneurs (Odgaard 1991, pp. 185–6). The educational level of both rural and urban private entrepreneurs also rose as the comparison between private enterprise and other choices became more favourable. From 1984 to 1988, as more and more limitations on private business were being removed, the increasingly open theoretical debates on ownership reform suggested a rosy future for private business. Rising prices and increasing consumerism made the higher incomes of private business more important. Meanwhile, further reforms meant that even state enterprises were often offering less security to employees, while many collective enterprises were just like private ones but offered lower pay.

On a less material level, one effect of the rise of private business in China has been to widen dramatically the life choices open to individuals, and this may have important consequences for the nature of Chinese society. In the late 1980s, there was an increase in the number of highly skilled people leaving or foregoing good jobs in the state sector for the greater independence and freedom of a career in private enterprise (*SWB* FE/0279 B2/9, 11 October 1988; *SWB* FE/0523 B2/8, 1 August 1989; *JJXZB* 27 March 1988, p. 5). Some of the more successful private entrepreneurs I have interviewed had this background, for example, a state-employed forestry engineer who left to establish a plastic container factory, both to make money and because he felt he was wasting his time in the forestry job; or the technician who left his cadre job to start an electronics factory and by 1988 had also persuaded four university researchers to join its research and development section. People can have more personal reasons, too, for joining the private sector: like the Sichuan Medical College graduate (the daughter of a friend of mine) who ran away to

Hainan Island after a difficult broken engagement, got a job in a private taxi and car import firm, and ended up helping run the business (and, if readers will forgive the Mills & Boon touch, marrying the owner). By providing alternatives, the private sector also reduces the state's ability to control people's lives. With most of the necessities of life now available on the open market, the former high degree of control over people's work, residence, and even marriage and reproduction is seriously compromised.

A question much debated both within and outside China is the proportion of cadres in private enterprise and its significance. A number of surveys have reported that a high proportion of the people running the *siying qiye* were formerly either cadres in production teams or brigades, or in management, supply and marketing, or technical personnel in state or collective enterprises (*NMRB* 6 December 1983; *RMRB* 16 March 1988; Zheng Xinmiao et al. 1990). These people were able to build up their enterprises by using the skills and contacts developed in their former roles. Some observers have argued that a high proportion of ex-cadres and high-status personnel would suggest significant potential for political influence by successful private entrepreneurs, but others have questioned both the validity of the proportions cited and the degree of political importance attributed to such people in the first place.[6]

I would argue that the real significance of the high proportion of former cadres and skilled personnel among the more successful entrepreneurs is simply that they are the people with the skills, contacts, experience and knowledge necessary to develop larger enterprises. Their political and economic contacts may also be important to their political influence, but, in fact, anyone who runs a large private enterprise in China will have such contacts, either having had them from the start or having built them up along the way. What is more important to the role of private enterprises in society is the relationship between entrepreneurs and the incumbent cadres with whom they have to deal, a relationship shaped by the nature of private sector development under the reforms.[7]

The dynamics of private sector development

The reasons for the exceptional (for a communist-led country) growth in the Chinese private sector lie in the fundamental contradiction between the economic goals of the reforms and the ideologically defined limits on private enterprise. During the 1980s, 'the public economy and the state organs concerned' were themselves subjected to the impact of a range of reforms which began to alter profoundly the economic and administrative structure. The reformist ideology stressed economic performance—in terms of increased output and profitability, increasing employment, and rising standards of living—as the main criterion of administrative or managerial success. The reforms generated strong incentives to promote economic development through market activity, and did so precisely among the people responsible for controlling the private sector: local cadres and managers of state and collective enterprises. These people would often assist the operation and development of private business well beyond the limits of official policy, if doing so offered economic benefits.

This was made possible partly by the somewhat underhand pattern of many reform measures. New practices were tried out first, and confirmed in official policy only after they had shown good results and gained more support. The detailed formulation of new regulations and administrative procedures necessarily came last of all. This was entirely reasonable: the reformists in China's leadership could not be expected to have a detailed blueprint for the transformation of the entire Chinese economic system; if they had, it would almost certainly have been wrong. The experimental 'feeling for stones to cross the river' method meant that official policies and regulations could be made on the basis of some knowledge of real conditions. It also enabled reformers to push changes through without first completing the long process of establishing their ideological credentials. However, this method of reform meant that in many ways the real engine room of the reforms was at local levels. Local authorities were able to use the wide discretionary powers at their disposal to manipulate reform measures in their own interests or those of their communities.

This process has been particularly obvious in the case of the private sector, perhaps because the ideological obstacles in its way have necessitated a particularly large gap between policy statements and reality.[8] The early statements and regulations on private business allowed for only very small, simple businesses run by families or individuals, and there were many restrictions on the trades they could engage in, the number of people they could employ, and their level of technology. But the pressure to provide employment and promote economic growth meant that local authorities allowed the limits to be exceeded very early on. This created an administrative problem of how to deal with the statistical recording, registration, and licensing of businesses, since the Chinese government's need to continue insisting that it would only allow a small, supplementary private sector made it very difficult to formulate procedures to deal with the significant and rapidly growing private sector which in fact emerged. The gap between existing regulations, official policy, and unofficial practice, also meant that private businesses were often able to develop and expand only at the personal discretion of those in authority. This caused them to remain extremely dependent on personal connections and informal agreements, and diminished their inclination or ability to act as independent agents in politics or the economy.

The dual economy of market and plan is, of course, a prime source of many of the discrepancies between regulation and reality in the reform process. Because it is officially only supposed to exist on the periphery of the economy, the private sector has been given scant regard in state plans and has, like its counterparts in other socialist countries, suffered extreme difficulties obtaining supplies of raw materials or goods for resale, as well as business premises, equipment, and energy. But the combination of opportunities for higher-priced market sales, plus the greater degree of self-direction given to public-sector enterprises, has inevitably produced strong incentives for managers and personnel in charge of planned-distribution goods to deal with private entrepreneurs. This has included the diversion of planned quota goods to private sale, a greater willingness to sell above-quota output to private businesses, and a wide range of deals involving the private rental of space or utilities.

However, many of these arrangements are informal or downright illegal, and they often involve the payment not only of quite high prices for the goods or services obtained, but also of assorted bribes, commissions, gifts and return favours. A survey of 600 private businesses in Changde municipality in Hunan reported that their total expenditure on various bribes and favours in 1989 had been around 13 per cent of their gross profits for the same year (RMRB 20 October 1990, p. 5). Of fifty-four rural siying qiye surveyed in Shanxi in 1988, 53 per cent bought their raw materials easily in free markets, but complained at the price, 20 per cent obtained supplies through connections, and still at high prices, and 5.8 per cent said they often had trouble obtaining materials, to the point of having to suspend production due to lack of inputs (NMRB 16 December 1988, p. 2; RMRB 25 December 1988, p. 8). The enterprises, whose average gross annual profit was around 80 000 yuan, spent an average of 10 000 yuan each on cultivating connections; some spent as much as 30 000 yuan. One entrepreneur commented that every road had many 'wealth gods' to whom offerings had to be made if doors were to be opened and business continued.

These entrepreneurs had to make contributions not only to their suppliers but to administrators involved in granting approvals, conducting inspections, and having responsibility for taxation and licensing. In the case of private enterprise, local cadres have particularly strong incentives to maintain the existing informal, poorly regulated situation, as it gives them extensive powers both over private entrepreneurs and in relation to higher levels of government. Because of the secrecy surrounding its growth, the private sector has been particularly under-regulated, making it a sort of frontier territory and the object of a struggle in which various levels of government and different departments all try to stake their claim. The current situation is that many local-level departments and individual cadres are able to extract funds or other benefits from private entrepreneurs, which do not even have to be reported, let alone be handed over, to higher levels. This involves not only personal, illegal pay-offs and favours, but also a wide range of locally set, (more or less) legitimate charges and levies. For example, one survey of a Sichuan county found that township and village levies on private businesses were at least twice as much again as state-set taxes, and that much of this money was never reported to the county level (Odgaard 1990). Throughout the 1980s, and even more since 1989, there have been constant complaints by both entrepreneurs and the central government about administrative departments or individual cadres making unauthorized levies on private business.[9] Thus private businesses in China have become an important source of funds, and therefore of independence, for local authorities. This suggests that local governments in areas with well-developed private sectors will tend to fight to preserve both the private sector itself and their own power over it.

Another area of informal arrangements which enhance local control is the way local officials have handled the problem of registering, licensing and recording private businesses. Given, on the one hand, the official fiction that only small individual businesses existed, and on the other, the advantages to themselves and to their communities of allowing private enterprise to develop beyond the official contraints, local cadres responded with variety and flexibility. Some communities have chosen to restrict the growth of the private sector and leave the field open for collective enterprises instead (Byrd & Lin 1990; Li Jianjin et al. 1989), but many have been keen to develop both or even to concentrate on the private sector. The result has been a number of forms of private enterprise in China, but much of it has gone under the guise of reforms within the collective economy.

The most obvious example is the false registration of larger private enterprises as collectives. The main reason for this was to get around the rule (operating until large private enterprises were legitimized in 1988) limiting to seven the number of people an individual could employ. Private entrepreneurs usually obtained collective registration by arrangement with state or collective enterprises, or with organizations such as street committees or township and village business corporations. For the payment of a regular 'administration fee' (usually 1–2 per cent of output value or 5–10 per cent of turnover) to one of these organizations, a private investor could register the enterprise as its subsidiary. Other private entrepreneurs took steps to give 'collective' features to their enterprise. For example, the owner of one five-factory concern I visited on the outskirts of Chengdu in 1988 had turned over a portion of its assets to the employees as shares. The portion remained no more than 10 per cent and the director retained total control of the enterprise, yet local authorities were able to see his enterprise as a 'collective share company'. The owner of a large clothing retail and manufacturing company in Chengdu, which in 1988 had 440 employees and a turnover of some 4 million yuan, distributed part of the profits to staff as bonuses. Hence this company, too, was 'collective'. Both of these enterprises were quite large by private sector standards, and were able to have a considerable impact in their local economies. In return, the authorities were willing to bend the rules in order to develop industry and commerce in their area.

The false registration of private enterprises as collectives is known to have been quite widespread. The ICB's 1987 estimate that there were at least 50 000 private enterprises registered as collectives nationwide (*RMRB*

24 June 1988, p. 1) was probably too low. Estimates of the proportion of private enterprises registered as collectives in 1987–1988 ranged from 25 to 40 per cent in various provinces and cities.[10] In 1987, in Wenzhou, which was likely to have one of the highest levels of false collective registration, 52.8 per cent of enterprises registered as collectives were reported to be private (*China Daily* 6 July 1988).

There are also other unacknowledged forms of private enterprise in China which provide many loopholes. Many of the specialized rural households, *zhuanyehu*, are run as enterprises and have become so specialized that there is no difference between their activities and those of a recognized *getihu* or *siying qiye*. Some were founded as enterprises from the start, but made use of the *zhuanyehu* classification, just as other private enteprises were falsely registered as collectives. For example, one of my interviewees in 1988 was a man who had left his state job in Chengdu to set up an intensive chicken farm on land leased from a rural township. His business was not by any means a *zhuanyehu*, but it provided jobs for 100 people, bought feed, and paid rent on the land. If it was listed as a *zhuanyehu*, so much the better for local statistics. Joint enterprises run by two or more families have also been listed separately from private enterprises in official statistics, although the larger ones would perfectly fit the definitions given in the 1988 regulations on *siying qiye*. On a visit to the prefecture of Longshui in Sichuan in February 1992, I found again and again that an apparently single-family enterprise, when it had reached a certain size, would find itself a 'partner', usually a helpful relative, and begin to employ non-family labour or buy in machinery. Yet both specialized households and joint enterprises are seen as 'a management level within the collective economy'. This rather artificial delineation of ownership types has arisen from the combination of the Chinese government's insistence on the administration of the economy according to ownership types, the bias in favour of collective ownership forms, and the political need to disguise the degree of privatization engendered by reform measures.

By registering as collectives, joint enterprises or specialized households, private entrepreneurs were able to develop well beyond the scale officially permitted, and also to take advantage of a variety of policies designed to promote these other types of enterprise. For example, they were often taxed as collectives, received tax concessions in the first few years of operation, and found it much easier to obtain supplies and market their products under a collective name. There were also political motives for avoiding registration as a private enterprise. Although it was an open secret that they were private enterprises, it was felt that they would fare better in the event of a sharp policy change. But there were also costs attached to this insurance policy. By entering into an informal understanding with local governments or state and collective enterprises, private entrepreneurs became indebted to them, and could find themselves obliged to provide certain favours—payments to 'directors' or 'consultants', gifts, dinners, jobs and training programs for relatives or for disadvantaged members of the community—to the key parties to the agreement. In some cases, long legal disputes have arisen when local governments have decided to claim ownership of a fake collective enterprise when it has become successful. (*JJCK* 9 December 1990, p. 1, 16 December 1990, p. 4).

This phenomenon creates another division between small *getihu* and larger private enterprises. Small family concerns are often largely ignored by local authorities apart from the collection of fees, and in some areas they are actually exempt from centrally set taxes. But a larger enterprise, which may have a noticeable effect on the community, is a different matter. Local officials will generally be extremely well-informed concerning the enterprise's operations and financial situation, and only very rarely can a private enterprise grow to any significant size without contributing significantly and in non-market ways to the local community. Thus, in many ways, the need for private enterprises to appear to be part of the collective sector actually does result in some blending of private and collective goals.

Support in the state bureaucracy—the ICB

The story of the clothing company mentioned earlier provides a window onto one of the most important relationships in the growth of private business in China: that between entrepreneurs and the State Council's Bureau of Industry and Commerce (ICB). The clothing company entrepreneur had originally left her job because the leaders of her unit were harassing her after she had a child outside the unit's quota. Without, apparently, any special connections to start with, she had built up her multimillion-yuan business from a single clothing stall, was a joint investor with the local ICB in a new warehouse facility, and although everyone knew she was the sole owner of her company, still had it registered as a collective. I was unable to obtain the exact details of how this was done, but it was clear that a major factor was her apparently calculated decision to align herself with the ICB. She took an active role in the Individual Labourers' Association (the organization set up by the ICB to help control private businesspeople) and in the administration and development of the market in which her early stalls operated. She spoke of this involvement as far too time-consuming but 'necessary'; it was the key to building up a good relationship with ICB cadres, keeping well-informed on policy developments, and gaining power and prestige in the market. By 1988, with her involvement in the warehouse project, she and the ICB were openly partners with a common goal.

The ICB, the bureau responsible for the administration and control of the private business sector, has generally campaigned for the sector's greater acceptance and taken active steps to achieve this. Although this is, of course, the ICB's job as an agency implementing the policies of the State

Council, it also corresponds with the ICB's bureaucratic interests. The ICB has been right behind reforms which divert steadily more activity to the market (its own sphere of jurisdiction) away from the plan (controlled by the various ministries). In many of its activities to develop the private sector, such as the organization and building of markets in which private, collective and state enterprises may all rent space, the ICB is indeed implementing policy, but it is also engaging in a little empire-building.

The methods used by local cadres to control this empire are strikingly traditional, in spite of the central push for the more standardized administration required by market reforms. The central regulations which the ICB administers are becoming increasingly more detailed and leaving less room for cadre discretion, and the ICB is closely involved with the market economy. But many cadres appear to be resisting the effort to turn them into Weberian bureaucrats. When central regulations are not fully implemented or market order is not maintained, the ICB typically offers the excuse of insufficient, inadequately trained staff. But ICB officers I have visited did not appear particularly harried and overworked, and all the evidence points to ICB cadres having extensive knowledge of, and power over, businesses in their area. An alternative interpretation of the ICB's failure fully to implement central directives lies in the contradictions between general reform imperatives of local economic development and regulatory efforts to constrain private business, and between the administrators' local authority and the central government's attempt to reduce them to mere functionaries.

A key aspect of the structure of administration has been the importance of local relationships. Inspection by the ICB and other organizations has often been made ineffective by the pressure of personal connections, since inspectors are responsible for a particular area. This enables them to become familiar with the businesses in their district and to have a very clear idea of which are law-abiding and which are not. At this point, however, the complex system of *guanxi*—part personal obligation, part local loyalties—comes into play. Local officials might therefore aim not so much to eradicate illegal business or to force businesses to operate in the way central authorities would like, rather they might seek an equilibrium, an arrangement mutually satisfactory to all sides wherein administrators regularly collect fines or demand that entrepreneurs contribute to their communities.

A major strategy in the ICB's efforts to control private entrepreneurs has been its setting up of the Individual Labourers' Association (*geti laodongzhe xiehui*), which is built along the lines of other 'mass organizations' like the Women's Federation or trade unions and is under the control of the ICB. The Association is funded from the administration charge collected from private businesses by the ICB, and its finances are generally controlled by ICB cadres on branch committees. The ICB uses this organization to publicize government policies and regulations, and to assist in the policing and taxation of private businesses. Thus, to some extent, it is dependent on private operators themselves to assist it in controlling the private sector. This often works quite well, as the ICB and the more professional private entrepreneurs have a common interest in raising standards and reducing illegality and corruption in business. However, it also gives some leverage to those entrepreneurs who co-operate with the ICB in running the association. The ICB is reliant on their assistance, and there is naturally potential for them to use their position to benefit themselves. As was the case with the clothing manufacturer, such involvement can be a way for an entrepreneur to build up a useful relationship with local administrators, not only in the ICB but in street committees and the Tax Bureau as well.[11]

Nor is the Individual Labourers' Association, expanded in 1988 to include associations for 'private entrepreneurs' (operators of *siying qiye*) entirely a one-way mechanism for ICB control. The unusual independence of private entrepreneurs makes them more difficult to manipulate; for example, many are simply not interested in the association, and they are not in a work unit situation where they can easily be organized into taking part. In order to attract them, the association has to offer more than just political education. This, plus the ICB's interest in promoting economic reform, has meant that the association has often acted as a genuine advocate for private entrepreneurs. In spite of the original puposes of the association, there is potential for it to become quite a significant lobby for private sector interests, especially insofar as these coincide with the interests of reformists in China's leadership.

Private entrepreneurs and 1989

The above discussion has described how, in the course of the development of the private sector in China, private entrepreneurs have developed complex relationships with the people at the local level who are in charge of the supplies and administrative approvals they need. These are relationships in which both sides exchange benefits, but in which the private entrepreneurs are disadvantaged by their inferior political–legal status. Because so much of private business activity has not yet been properly acknowledged and legislated for, they must often ask cadres not for rights, but for favours. The result is that the private sector has become a significant economic force, but that the independence and freedom of choice suggested by private ownership have been compromised to some extent. To date, the most striking political effect of the rise of the private sector appears to stem not from entrepreneurs themselves, but from their importance to local-level bureaucracies. This can be seen from the fortunes of private business in the political and economic clampdown of 1989.

The attack on private business after June 1989 has been seen largely as ideologically motivated: a drive against the individualism and capitalist tendencies of private enterprise. Private operators were also made into something of a scapegoat for some of the deep political and economic problems China was experiencing (Chan & Unger 1990). After 4 June there was a marked change in the publicity surrounding private business. Official efforts to popularize private entrepreneurs and justify their high incomes disappeared, and instead private operators were blamed for much of the corruption and profiteering which had become so objectionable to the public. Publicity concerning the annual (but in 1989, exceptionally determined) tax collection drive now implied that most private operators derived their high incomes, not from risk, capital and hard work as claimed before, but from tax evasion (e.g. *JJRB* 14 July 1989, p. 2; *RMRB* 23 July 1989, p. 5; *RMRB* 2 September 1989, p. 6).

In fact, many of the practical measures which were seen as an attack on private business were inaugurated well before June 1989. They were not so much a retraction of reform policies as an effort on the part of the central government to regain some lost control over economic administration. In many ways, the private sector epitomized this loss of control. Private entrepreneurs were outside the regular systems of collective social control, they were difficult to police, they engaged in bribery and corrupted the public economy, they evaded central taxes, and their incomes were outside government control. They were an important part of the growing network of production, marketing and local organization which was not under central direction and which was making the management of a planned economy, even a 'planned commodity economy', progressively more difficult.

Therefore, from late 1988 onwards, there were heightened attempts to improve and standardize administrative control over private business. The ICB conducted a major clean-up campaign, centering on the inspection and relicensing (or not) of all businesses. This was aimed particularly at the false registrations which were so much a part of the informal co-operation between local governments and entrepreneurs. The Tax Bureau, too, conducted its most determined tax campaign since the reforms began, accusing nearly all businesses of tax avoidance and collecting tax at punitive levels. In Chengdu, the proportion of private businesses registered with the Tax Bureau increased from 46.1 per cent in 1988 to 75.5 per cent by the end of September 1989, and even though over 40 000 businesses (16 per cent of the city's 1988 total) closed down, the volume of tax collected increased from 35.2 million yuan in 1988 to over 40 million yuan by the end of September 1989.[12]

Yet this centrally motivated attack was still a traditional drive organized in the usual way, and open to manipulation by local cadres. In some cases local governments, the ICB and tax officials, while fulfilling the demands of the campaign, sought to defend private business from greater central control. The drive to force fake collectives to re-register as *siying qiye*, for example, was sometimes actively obstructed by local cadres. Tax offfficials in Liaoning were reported to have expressed the opinion to higher levels that registering and taxing *siying qiye*-type private enterprises as such would bankrupt them, and therefore should not be done (*JJCK* 15 May 1989; Chen Xiangqing et al. 1989). In Shenyang, a city which had actively developed its private sector, cadres apparently assisted private enterprises to defend themselves against the feared conservative attack by allowing new bogus registrations: a 21 per cent drop in the number of registered *siying qiye* coincided with a 30 per cent increase in the number of new collective enterprises, mostly, it was claimed, the former *siying qiye* (*JJCK* 11 April 1990, p. 1) The drive to inspect and clean up the many trading companies, which served as vehicles for the diversion of planned-distribution goods for private sale, was reportedly blocked by 'leadership at various levels', that is, by the very cadres who were benefiting from them. Many such companies were affiliated with local government departments and had connections to senior cadres (*SWB* FE/0667 B2/7 20 January 1990; *SWB* FE/0669 B2/6 23 January 1990).

By 1990, the attack had died down, having had a varied impact on the private sector. Nationally, the number of registered individual businesses (*getihu*) fell from 14 527 000 to 12 471 000, a decline of just over 14 per cent. (The number of registered *siying qiye* actually rose, but this was because more private enterprises were being forced to register as such at this time.) However, interviews in Sichuan in early 1991, as well as the prompt recovery of the private sector once the main campaign was over, suggest that not all of these businesses really stopped operating. An ICB cadre in the Sichuan county of Mingshan told me that there had been no real decline in private sector numbers there, although some operators had temporarily moved out of the county town. By the time I returned to Sichuan in early 1992 the chill was well and truly over: local officials would barely admit that there ever had been any problem and were anxious to show how keen their locality was to develop private businesses.

Local authorities did use the 1989 attack to increase their control over private business, but they did this in various ways. Some aimed for a real restriction of private enterprise, not only conducting relicensing and tax collection drives to reduce the number of businesses, but also bringing in new regulations restoring some of the old limitations on private business. Fuyang county in Zhejiang, for example, decreed that new private businesses would not be permitted if they competed with state or collective enterprises for materials, and would not be allowed to poach skilled personnel from state or collective enterprises; new commercial businesses would not generally be approved (*ZGGSB* 25 February 1990, p. 3). Other local authorities, judging from the continuation of informal licensing practices and the central government's attack on local charges, used this opportunity to increase private entrepreneurs' obligations to them.

By 1990, there was also clearly a strong local backlash against the attack on the private sector, and a series of new local policies actively promoted the private sector once again. Some offered even better conditions than had existed before 1989. For example, in spite of a central announcement in January 1990 forbidding private wholesaling (a step backwards to 1983), Xingji municipality in Hebei announced in January 1991 that private long-distance wholesalers could even use the words *Xingji shi* (Xingji municipality) in their business name (*ZGGSB* 3 January 1991, p. 1). This was supposed 'to publicise the name of Xingji', but would also imply that the businesses concerned were connected in some way to the municipal government. A number of localities offered to help arrange premises and tax concessions for private enterprises which were engaged in production, especially of new products, or which could provide jobs for young people.[13] The sequence of local implementation of new measures to encourage private enterprise, followed by central ratification, suggests that the same process of local innovation with support from reformists at the centre, is still at work. In these new measures of 1991, it was noticeable that a great deal of discretion—including the percentage and duration of tax concessions to be allowed and exactly how much assistance would be given in finding premises—was left to local authorities. Private entrepreneurs will still have to go begging for these advantages.

Conclusion

Private entrepreneurs now play a significant role in solving China's economic problems: they are a major part of the dynamic rural economy, they are important in providing employment and satisfying consumer demands, and their role in developing new products is now being recognized. But politics has demanded that they reach this stage by informal means, with practice often being many steps ahead of official policy. China's private entrepreneurs are not independent actors in the market section of the economy, for local and middle-level cadres are able to take advantage of the reform process and use their planned-economy powers to manipulate the market and private entrepreneurs with it. The result is that private entrepreneurs, even though they are no longer in a marginal position, continue to behave in a marginal way, and the private sector is marked by a reliance on corruption and a reluctance on the part of many entrepreneurs to commit themselves to long-term goals.

This does not mean that private entrepreneurs are without influence. On the contrary, their importance to local economies, and to the cadres who run them, cannot be ignored. The failure of the conservative swing in 1989 illustrates most clearly that the development of the private sector, like many reform measures, has reached a stage which would be extremely difficult and costly to reverse. As a result of the manner of its development, the private sector has become a major force shaping the direction of reform, and its fortunes during and after 1989 show that this process continues.

Notes

[1]   An exception is Ivan Szelenyi (1988), who sees the rural private entrepreneurs of Hungary in a much more positive light.

2   The more successful private entrepreneurs, of course, had the option of simply leaving China rather than pushing for change. For a case study of one entrepreneur's involvement in the protest movement, see Chan and Unger (1990).

3   The degree of freedom enjoyed by leaseholders varies. Many lease-holders have complained that they do not have sufficient control over key management decisions such as product mix, output targets, and especially staffing and wages. However, I have visited leased enter-prises which are run quite independently: for example, a leased village enterprise in Anyue county in Sichuan, which makes coal carts for the local mines, plus folding chairs and tables. The leaseholder paid rent, but his own equity far surpassed the original brigade assets and he fully expected his son to inherit the lease.

4   Shanghai and Tianjin both publish regular lists of registered *siying qiye* in the ICB's newspaper *Zhongguo gongshang bao* (Chinese Industry and Commerce). For Guangdong see *RMRB* 5 July 1983, p. 2; Pan and Xie (1988); Jia and Wang (1989).

5   In fact there has been considerable publicity given in China to the poor scholastic performance of the children of *getihu*, with teachers quoted as saying, rather snidely, that this was because their parents were uneducated and were too busy making money to look after them properly. But of the urban private businesspeople I have interviewed, nearly all said they would like their children to go to university, even if they did not think this would actually be the case.

6   I am thinking in particular of Ole Odgaard (1991, chapter 9), who has pointed out, firstly, that the definition of 'cadre' used in such surveys is sometimes very broad, including people such as schoolteachers who would not be expected to have much better political and economic contacts than anyone else; secondly, that in some communities nearly everyone has been some sort of 'cadre' at some time or other; and thirdly, that the surveys cited are not representative, and that others can be found, of different localities or at a later date, which do not show a high proportion of former cadres or higher-status employees in private enterprises. I have objected to Ole that some of these latter surveys are of both large and small private enterprises rather than just the large, successful ones, and that he is overemphasising the suggestions of political influence made in the earlier reports: some were simply arguing that the skills and contacts available to both ex-cadres and senior staff were necessary attributes for larger-scale economic success.

7   The potential for former cadres to obtain special advantages through corruption has, of course, been of concern to the Chinese leadership, and there are regulations restricting the business activities both of incumbent cadres and their relatives, and of retired cadres from Party and government organizations at county level and above. The latter

may not engage in businesses with state or foreign investment, in commercial businesses, or in a field immediately relevant to their former work as a cadre (*ZGGSB* 2 May 1991, p. 3).

8   This is discussed in Young (1989).

9   Examples include *RMRB* 27 February 1983, 9 June 1984, 24 January 1985, 27 July 1987. The ICB has conducted a sustained campaign against such exactions in its paper, the *Zhongguo gongshang bao*, throughout 1991.

10 For example: Liaoning, 25 per cent; Shanghai suburban areas, 30 per cent; Tangshan City, Hebei Province, and Jilin Province, 30 per cent; Nanyang city, Henan, 40 per cent. These are all cited in Odgaard (1991, p. 241).

11 Involvement in the Individual Labourers' Association is therefore one way in which entrepreneurs, normally outside the regular paths to official approval, can be 'activists' of the sort described in state industry by Walder (1986).

12 ICB document obtained at an interview, Chengdu, January 1991.

13 Local introduction of these conditions began in 1990 and early 1991; for examples see *ZGGSB* 28 January 1991, p. 3; *ZGGSB* 11 February 1991, p. 3; *ZGGSB* 3 January 1991, p. 1. The tax concessions were decided by the Tax Bureau in January 1991. See *Jingji cankao bao* (Economic Information) 13 March 1991, p. 1; *SWB*, FE/1021 B2/5, 15 March 1991.

References

Aslund, Anders 1985, *Private Enterprise in Eastern Europe: The Non-Agricultural Private Sector in Poland and the GDR, 1945–83*, Macmillan, London.

Beijing Review

Bruun, Ole 1989, 'Business and Bureaucracy in a Chinese Street: The Ethnography of Individual Business Households in Contemporary China', PhD dissertation, University of Copenhagen.

Byrd, William & Lin Qingsong eds 1990, *China's Rural Industry—Structure, Development, and Reform*, Oxford University Press for the World Bank, New York.

Chan, Anita & Jonathan Unger 1990, 'Voices from the Protest Movement, Chongqing, Sichuan', *The Australian Journal of Chinese Affairs*, no. 24, pp. 1–21.

Chen Jianhua 1988, 'Cong wuxu dao youxu—Fujian sheng Changle xian siying qiye fazhan de diaocha' (From disorder to order—an investigation of private enterprises in Changle county, Fujian), *Zhongguo jingji wenti*, no. 5, reprinted in *Fuyin baokan ziliao*, F22, no. 11, 1988, pp. 41–6.

Chen Xiangqing, Li Bojun & Xu Huafei 1989, 'Siying qiye fazhan xianzhuang yu mianlin de wenti' (Current conditions and problems in the development of private enterprises), *Zhongguo nongcun jingji*, no. 2, pp. 24–31.

Grossman, Gregory 1977, 'The Second Economy of the USSR', *Problems of Communism*, vol. 26, no. 5, pp. 25–40.

——1990, 'Sub-rosa Privatization and Marketization in the USSR', *Annals of the American Academy of Political and Social Science*, no. 507, pp. 44–52.

GMRB—Guangming Ribao

He Jianzhang 1981, 'Jiji fuchi, shidang fazhan chengzhen geti jingji' (Actively support and appropriately develop the urban individual economy), *Hongqi*, no. 24, pp. 13–16.

Hegedüs, A. & M. Markus 1979, 'The Small Entrepreneur and Socialism', *Acta Oeconomica*, vol. 22, no. 3, pp. 267–89.

Jia Ting & Wang Ruicheng 1989, 'Siying qiyezhu jieceng zai Zhongguo de jueqi he fazhan' (The rise and development of the stratum of private entrepreneurs in China), in *Zhongguo de siying jingji—xianzhuang, wenti, qianjing* (China's private economy—conditions, problems, and prospects), eds Guojia 'qi-wu' qijian Zhongguo siying jingji yanjiu keti zu, Zhongguo shehui kexue chubanshe, Beijing.

JJCK—Jingji cankao (Economic Information)

JJRB—Jingji ribao (Economic Daily)

JJXZB—Jingjixue zhoubao (Economics Weekly)

Li Jianjin & Zhu Jun 1989, 'Siying qiye lirun liuxiang fenxi' (An analysis of profit uses in private enterprises), *Zhongguo nongcun jingji*, no. 9, pp. 48–52.

NMRB—Nongmin ribao (Peasants' Daily)

Odgaard, Ole 1990, 'Collective Control of Income Distribution: A Case Study of Private Enterprises in Sichuan Province', in *Remaking Peasant China*, eds Jørgen Delman, Stubbe Østergaard, & Flemming Christiansen, Aarhus University Press, Aarhus, Denmark, pp. 106–121.

——1991, 'Private Enterprises in Rural China—Impact on Resource Mobilization and Social Stratification', PhD dissertation, Center for East and Southeast Asian Studies, University of Copenhagen.

O'Hearn, Dennis 1980, 'The Consumer Second Economy: Size and Effects', *Soviet Studies*, vol. 32, no. 2, pp. 218–34.

Pan Zuodi & Xie Jianmin 1988, 'Guanyu siren qiye ruogan wenti de tantao' (An exploration of certain questions regarding private enterprises), *Nongye jingji wenti*, no. 1, pp. 43–5.

Ren Zhonglin 1987, 'Guanyu geti jingji wenti' (On the question of the individual economy), speech at the Central Party School, 7 April 1987, in *Makesizhuyi lilun jiaoyu cankao ziliao* (Reference materials for Marxist theoretical education), eds Guojia jiaowei gaoji chubanshe & Guojia Makesizhuyi lilun jiaowei yanjiu zhongxin, no. 5, pp. 18–23.

RMRB—Renmin ribao (People's Daily)

Sampson, Steven 1987, 'The Second Economy of the Soviet Union and Eastern Europe', *Annals of the American Academy of Political and Social Science*, no. 493, pp. 120–36.

SWB—BBC *Summary of World Broadcasts*—*Part 3: The Far East*.

Szelenyi, Ivan 1988, *Socialist Entrepreneurs*—*Embourgeoisement in Rural Hungary*, University of Wisconsin Press, Madison, Wisconsin.

Walder, Andrew G. 1986, *Communist Neo-Traditionalism: Work and Authority in Chinese Industry*, University of California Press, Berkeley.

Young, Susan 1989, 'Policy, Practice and the Private Sector in China', *The Australian Journal of Chinese Affairs*, no. 21, pp. 57–80.

Yudkin, Marcia 1986, *Making Good*—*Private Business in Socialist China*, Foreign Languages Press, Beijing.

ZGGSB—*Zhongguo gongshang bao* (Chinese Industry and Commerce) (ICB newspaper).

ZGTJNJ—*Zhongguo tongji nianjian* (Statistical Yearbook of China) 1990, Zhongguo tongji chubanshe, Beijing.

ZGXZQYNJ—*Zhongguo xiangzhen qiye nianjian* (Chinese Township Enterprise Yearbook) 1989, Nongye chubanshe, Beijing.

Zhang Hao, Chen Jian & Fang Rong 1982, 'Beijing shi chengqu qingnian congshi geti jingying qingquang de diaocha' (A survey of the conditions of young people doing individual business in the Beijing urban area), *Jingji yanjiu*, no. 5, pp. 55–60.

Zhang Kai 1988, 'The development of private enterprises in China', *Shiyue pinglun*, Hong Kong, June/July, pp. 49–51.

Zheng Xinmiao, Wang Tongxin & Wu Changling 1990, 'Dui nongcun siying jingji fazhan de lilun sikao ji chengce jianyi' (Theoretical reflections and policy suggestions for the development of the rural private economy), *Nongye jingji wenti*, no. 5, pp. 47–50.

7 The social and intellectual elite[1]
Daniel Kane

One of the characteristics of the past decade has been the emergence of the 'third generation', that is, the generation which came to political and intellectual maturity in the years immediately following the Cultural Revolution. This chapter examines three elite groups within this generation. The perspective adopted here is similar to the politico-cultural approach advocated by Pye (1968, 1984, 1985). As summarized in Lieberthal and Oksenberg (1988, p. 6): 'To Pye and Solomon, the communist system was unmistakeably *Chinese*. Certain cultural traits infused and were core to the system, especially the importance of personal relations, the allure of patrimonialism and patron–client ties, and the deep-seated fear of disorder ... ' A similar approach is taken by Moody (1988, p. 8) who 'hypothesizes that the personal relationship is the major political force in Confucian and post-Confucian society, rather than more abstract entities, such as social class or common interest or opinion'.

The princes' clique

The emergence of the 'princes' clique' (*taizi dang*) has recently become quite evident (Sun 1992). These people are mostly related to the present power elite, either by direct family ties or by marriage. The term is used rather loosely. In broad terms it refers to those whose parents or grandparents were at least of ministerial level, who have had privileged lives, and who have now taken up important and influential positions in Chinese society. One of the characteristics of the decade of economic reform era is that a privileged education does not necessarily mean a scientific education, and important and influential positions are not necessarily political ones. Involvement in economic matters has now become the most important road to political power. Before the Cultural Revolution, most of the *gaogan zidi* (children of high level cadres) studied natural sciences; nowadays, they are more likely to be found in various government and semi-government economic and trade organizations (see appendix 1, pp. 234–5).

The scions of the establishment had always enjoyed special privileges, of course, and the term 'princes' clique' emerged in the mid-1980s in connection with various alleged corruption scandals. This generation is now older and more mature, and the formation of the princes' clique, as a political entity with a real interest in acquiring political power in its own right, rather than relying on the prestige and protection of their parents, is a phenomenon of the late 1980s. This, of course, is related to the imminent retirement or demise of the old guard, and the realization on the part of their offspring that they must take steps to protect and consolidate their position as a matter of urgency.

The power of the princes' clique has become particularly clear since the Tiananmen massacre, as the present leadership can count on them as being completely 'reliable'. The collapse of communism in the Soviet Union and Eastern Europe has also convinced the old guard that, after all, 'blood is thicker than water', and *zijiren* (their own people) are still those to be most trusted. Deng Xiaoping's views on 'dynastic inheritance of power' reflect this attitude. Two of his recent injunctions are said to be 'in promoting internally, do not avoid one's relatives', and 'promote cadres' children and one's relatives to important positions in central leadership organizations' (Wu Tiandai 1991). Deng is also reported to have said:

> We might have even greater difficulties in the future. The resistance might be greater ... We must select successors at all levels ... those who are politically unreliable must be dismissed, don't worry that people will criticize the princes' clique, the princely caste and all that ... the reason the Soviet Union is in trouble is because they didn't choose good successors, they let bourgeois individualistic careerists grab political power! (Luo Bing 1991a).

As a result of Deng's remarks, the CCP Organization Department has officially notified all levels of the Party that in the promotion of cadres they should not deliberately exclude cadres' children; they should promote those with a strong commitment to the Party and with a strong sense of political responsibility, and they should also pay attention to the successors' successors over a long period of time (ibid.).

The formation of the princes' clique in its own right (as distinct from the relationships amongst their parents) can be traced back to their school days. The Beijing No. 4 High School, for example, was attended by Chen Yuan, Li Xianglu (Zhao Ziyang's former secretary and Director of the Research Institute of CITIC, now in the USA), Qin Xiao, now Managing

Director of CITIC (Australia) and Qiao Zonghuai, the son of Qiao Guanhua. Another student at this school was Yu Luoke (He Zhenming 1991; Gu Ren 1991). Other important schools linking the new elite are Beijing No. 101 High School, Qinghua School, Beida School, Shida Girls School, Jingshan School and August 1 School. Students of Beijing No. 101 High School included Li Tieying, Ruan Chongwu, Nie Li, Liu Jiyuan (Vice Minister, Aeronautics and Astronautics Ministry), Xu Wenbo (Vice Minister, Ministry of Culture), Lin Ruwei (a film director), Shi Guangnan (composer), Sima Xiaoming (photographer), Li Tuo (literary critic), Ma Dajing [Da Li] (writer), Xie Zichu (geologist), Ke Yunlu (writer) etc. (Yue Xun 1986). Tertiary institutes linking them are the Harbin Military Engineering Institute, Peking University, Qinghua University, the Beijing Aeronautical Institute, the China Science and Technology University and the Beijing Institute of Political Science and Law (Lang Lang 1986).

We can take the career of Chen Yuan, the son of Chen Yun, as being typical of many of the new elite. He was born in 1945, and studied in the Beijing No. 4 High School and later at Qinghua University. He worked in the Ministry of Aeronautics and Astronautics from 1972 to 1988. After the Cultural Revolution he was a research student in the Chinese Academy of Social Sciences, studying technology economics, and earned his MSc degree in 1981. He was then appointed to the State Planning Commission. In 1982 he was appointed Deputy Secretary (later Secretary) of the CCP West Beijing District Municipal Committee, and in 1984 was Director of the Department of Commerce and Trade of the CCP Beijing Municipal Committee and Vice-Chairman of the Beijing Municipal Committee for Economic Reconstruction. He was appointed Vice-President of the People's Bank of China in 1988 (*Who's Who in China* 1989). During his time in Beijing, Chen Yuan concentrated on economic matters, even supporting a group of young economic theorists to establish the Beijing Young Economists Association. He was responsible for drafting the Beijing Development Strategic Research Plan Report, as well as some of the key projects in the Seventh Five Year Plan. In November 1988 he transferred to the People's Bank of China, where his position is of the same rank as a Minister of the State Council. In 1987, he invited a group of economists to a seminar at which he unveiled his own economic policy, designed to strengthen central planning and control.

In October 1990, Chen held another economic seminar, under the nominal chairmanship of the Director of the State Commission for Restructuring the Economy, Chen Jinhua. The Director of the Development Centre of the State Council, Ma Hong, the Deputy Director of the State Commission for Restructuring the Economy, Gao Shangquan, the Minister of Labour, Ruan Chongwu and most of China's most famous economists, including Xue Muqiao, Li Yining, Dong Fureng and Wu Jinglian attended (Lin Wei 1990; He Zhenming 1990). The main purpose of the meeting was to discuss an article Chen Yuan had written. The main thrust of the article was that the 'small-peasant economy' or the 'feudal lord economy' was rapidly leading to economic disintegration, and that it was imperative to bring the economy under control again by strengthening the central government's authority and power (Chen Yuan 1991).

In June 1991, the British government invited Chen Yuan for an official visit of eight days. In April and May 1992, he announced to the International Monetary Fund in Washington and the Asian Development Bank in Hong Kong that the renminbi should be a convertible currency, and that China should 'learn from capitalism' (*Australia Chinese Daily* 9, 10 May 1991). His public speeches on Chinese economic reform are extremely optimistic. Chen Yuan seems to be very confident about his political future (He Pin 1991; Shai Wen 1991).

Individuals such as Chen Yuan can rise or fall as the result of political battles—the important point is that a new caste of political leaders has formed (the so-called princes' clique) and has already been very successful in gaining important and influential positions in the government and Party hierarchy. In 1990, the Central Commission for Discipline Inspection, the General Office of the Central Committee and the Organization Department of the Central Committee conducted a joint investigation into the structure of CCP membership. They found that the children or immediate relatives of 1700 high-level cadres in central or provincial positions occupied 3100 positions of department or bureau director level or above in government organizations, or division commander or above in the army. More than 900 of their relations worked in special economic zones as managers or managing directors in foreign trade companies (Xia Tong 1991).

This group of people are worth noting not only because of their political and administrative appointments and the consequent legitimatization of their power, but also because of the levels of education and experience which their privileged lifestyle has allowed. The leadership, and even run-of-the-mill 'high level cadres', have arranged for their children to study overseas—very often at the most prestigious institutions. After acquiring qualifications in a variety of fields, many of them have returned to China to take up important positions (Mo Ming 1979; Luo Kedao 1988).

Luo Kedao (1988) gives the following examples of such people who were working or studying overseas in that year: Deng Xiaoping's son, Deng Zhifang (Rochester University); Deng Xiaoping's daughter, Deng Rong (US Embassy, Washington), Chen Yun's son, Chen Zhongying (MIT), Chen Yun's daughter, Chen Weili (University of California); Yang Shangkun's daughter, Yang Li (Queens College), Liu Shaoqi's daughter, Liu Tingting (Boston University), Wang Bingnan's son and Liu Shaoqi's son-in-law, Wang Anping (Wall Street), Bo Yibo's son, Bo Xiangjiang (Massachusetts State), Bo Yibo's daughter, Bo Jieying (Landers University, Massachusetts), Ye Jianying's grand-daughter, Ye Xiaoping (Georgetown University), Yu Qiuli's daughter, Yu Xiaoxia (Boston University), Zhang Aiping's daughter, Zhang Xiao'ai (Mary College, California), Chen Yi's son, Chen Xiaolu (University of Texas), Wan Li's son-in-law, Li Andong (New York University). To which one might add Qiao Shi's son, who was formerly at the Australian National University (ANU) and now at

Cambridge. Deng Zhiduan (1991, p. 9) quotes Luo's article with approval, and notes: 'This article did not mention Zhao Ziyang's son, and many other privileged scions of other leaders studying in other countries, including innumerable sons, daughters and relatives of provincial and municipal level cadres'. The dissident journal *Zhongguo zhi chun* (1989) gives an even more amazing list of children of high level cadres in influential official positions, not all of which is accurate (see appendix 2, pp. 235–6).

In the present tension between central power and provincial autonomy, Chen Yuan is very vocal and strong in reclaiming and strengthening the power of the centre. This is partly because he is, after all, Chen Yun's son, and partly because he is the Deputy Director of the People's Bank of China. On the other hand, Ye Xuanping, the son of Ye Jianying, is ensconced in Guangdong, and is equally vocal in supporting local autonomy and resisting central power (Shai Wen 1991; Shi Hua 1991b). It is commonly observed that central power is in the process of disintegration in China, and that absolute authority no longer exists. In this process of constant political struggle, the princes' clique is able to contribute a certain stability. Whatever the differences between their parents, the younger generation share a common recognition that it is in their interests that the present system continue, and that they inherit it. This we might call the 'born to rule' syndrome.

The princes' clique does not necessarily have a political program in the sense of a set of principles. Their program is determined by their own interests—or position—at any particular time. The princes are no-nonsense realists, and in this differ even from the present generation of leaders trained in the Soviet Union, or in the immediate post-liberation period in China. That generation is now in their fifties or sixties. They may (or may not) still have an emotional attachment to 'socialism', but are essentially a transitional generation, necessary until the true inheritors of the CCP dynasty are ready to take over. The younger generation is very different from the old guard: they have a sophisticated understanding of world affairs, and are certainly going to continue with the process of China's 'open door' policy (with all that that entails) if it suits them (Wu Tiandai 1991).

If this analysis is correct, it tends to suggest that the old days of 'line struggle' (on ideological grounds) are over. This hypothesis is supported by the death of Marxism as a political philosophy, the end of the Cold War and, in Fukuyama's phrase, 'the end of history'. This is by no means to suggest that conflict and political strife are likely to cease, but they will certainly be different in nature from the ideological struggles of the past. Chen Yuan and Wang Qishan rose to power through the support of China's most conservative faction (Chen Yun and Yao Yilin), but they have been involved in setting up that most capitalist of enterprises, the stockmarket, in Shanghai and Shenzhen, and possibly soon in Beijing (*Zhongyang ribao* 25 April 1992). Chen and Wang would not be prepared to sacrifice their interests for the sake of the ideological stance of their parents. They have inherited their power, not their ideology; their attitude might be said to be typical of the princes generally.

The advisors

Another road to political power in China is that of the *muliao*, which we might translate 'political advisor'. This group has been insufficiently studied. Such studies as I have seen (Lieberthal & Oksenberg 1988; Halpern 1986, 1989) on the personal staff of the top leadership, and the role of various research centres and research institutes, are very sketchy, and do not mention any names apart from a few well known high-level bureaucrats. 'Political advisors' do not necessarily have an important government position, and often prefer to work behind the scenes. Their position is dependent on the patronage of one or other of the top leadership, though sometimes they are promoted to official positions in the hierarchy.

The role of *muliao* is more part of the traditional Chinese political structure rather than a characteristic of modern states. In periods of reform and political unrest, the *muliao* come into their own, offering advice and strategies to various political leaders. Kang Youwei did not have the official rank to offer advice to the Guangxu Emperor, but he acquired access to the emperor's ear after having submitted a number of memorials, and was then able to push forward his own reform program in the emperor's name. In the early 1980s, the 'Four Gentlemen'—Weng Yongxi, Wang Qishan, Huang Jiangnan and Zhu Jiaming—submitted a series of 'memorials' to Zhao Ziyang (Weng et al. 1981) which led to him relying on their advice to a much greater degree than their official positions would have entitled them. It was Zhao's patronage, in turn, which led to their acquiring official and influential positions. Their names never appeared in official documents, or in the press, but it was they who drafted certain key documents in the early period of economic reform, as those 'in the know' in Beijing were aware. For example, the 'Minutes of the National Conference on Rural Work', a Central document released on 1 January 1982 which is generally supposed to have launched rural reform, was drafted by Zhao Ziyang's 'advisors' (in particular, Chen Yizi and Wang Xiaoqiang), rather than the government departments supposedly responsible for such matters (Chen Yizi 1990b, p. 39). Before the Economic System Reform Institute (ESRI) was officially established, its members could all be considered Zhao's *muliao*. If one were to try to define the difference between the Chinese *muliao* and the Western think-tank, it would be that the personal patronage relationships in the former are stronger, and indeed crucial.

The advisors, as a group, are not necessarily related to the top leadership by direct family ties, though many of them are: Wang Qishan is Yao Yilin's son-in-law, Deng Yingtao is Deng Liqun's son, Tang Xin is Tang

Ke's son—Wang, Deng and Tang were all members of various think-tanks in the 1980s. They have, however, acquired equivalent patronage of one or other of the leadership. The precise nature of their influence on the political process is not easy for those outside their circles to ascertain, but it certainly cannot be underestimated. A number of rather shady personalities were active behind the scenes during the reform period, of whom we might mention He Weiling, who recently died in a car accident in Mexico. He was born in Shanghai, and went to Beijing in 1962 to study physics at Peking University. In 1979 he and Chen Yizi set up the China Rural Development Research Group. In 1985 he went to the USA as a 'visiting scholar', and the following year was appointed the 'representative' of the Research Institute for the Reform of the Economy in the United States (Zhang Ling 1987). According to a note accompanying one of his articles, he was 'the President of the China–U.S. Liaison Committee for International Enterprises and Senior Fellow at the National Economic System Reform Institute in China' (He Weiling 1990, p. 87). Rumours were rife in China and the USA after his death, many people suspecting that he had been murdered by the Chinese Ministry of National Security. Whether or not that is true, the fact that there were such rumours indicates the aura of secrecy and mystery that surrounded him. He spent many years shuttling between China and the USA, and had the nickname 'the unofficial diplomat'. In China, he had the reputation of being somewhat of a mystery-man, well-connected with the top leadership in ways which his official position could not explain (Zhu Jiaming 1991).

Policy makers in China rely on the advice and social contacts of the *muliao* to supplement their own perceptions, or the advice provided by government departments. In 1988, for example, Zhao Ziyang sent Chen Yizi and Zhu Jiaming on a fact-finding mission to South America, to investigate how those countries managed high inflation rates. Their report directly and immediately influenced Zhao's economic policy in response to the record inflation of that period (Luo Bing 1988; Chen Yizi 1990b, p. 136).

The advisors do not form a unified social force, nor do they have a communal cause. They serve (or seek to serve) a particular leader or group of leaders, and their position is dependent on that continued patronage. Zhao Ziyang lent his patronage to advisors such as Chen Yizi and Wang Xiaoqiang; other leaders, such as Hu Qiaomu and Deng Liqun, preferred the advice and views of He Xin. He, a Research Fellow at the Chinese Academy of Social Sciences, took it upon himself to advise the Politburo on how to deal with the mid-1989 popular uprising (He Xin 1990), and continues to offer his opinions on a wide range of national and international interests.

The links between the former think-tanks in China and various dissident groups overseas, in particular the Federation for Democracy in China (FDC), are too well-known to merit detailed discussion here (Barmé 1991). The dissident groups overseas lack any program or sense of direction. This is a fact of life of which many of the previous think-tank members, now in exile of one type or another, are very aware. For example, Wang Xiaoqiang, formerly Deputy Director of ESRI, chose to remain overseas after the 4 June Massacre. He busied himself learning English and studying economics; he is now in England working towards a PhD degree in economics at Cambridge. Many others have maintained a distance from the various Chinese dissident groups. Here one might mention Li Xianglu, one of Zhao Ziyang's private secretaries, who is doing business in the USA, Wang Xiaolu, another member of ESRI (and the editorial board of the *Towards the Future* series), who has been studying economics at the ANU in preparation for a PhD, and Zhou Qiren, formerly in the Research Institute of the Centre for Rural Development (under the State Council), who has made several public speeches critical of the Chinese government, but has not associated with the FDC or other such groups. Zhou Qiren is now studying for a PhD at the UCLA. Their political ambition has by no means disappeared, but they have chosen to use this period of enforced exclusion from Chinese politics to prepare themselves—by studying English and economics, for example—for a possible future role in Chinese politics. It is not inconceivable that a number of these former 'advisors', whether in China or overseas at the moment, may re-emerge into positions of influence over the next decade.

The intellectuals

Chinese intellectuals have traditionally carried responsibility for the moral wellbeing of society, including education and enlightenment of the masses. This tradition produced a number of younger intellectuals who emerged during the early 1980s, who were extremely active publishing journals, series of books of translations and original works, organizing conferences, holding seminars and public lectures, and so on. Their aim was to bring China closer to current international thinking in a wide variety of fields—philosophy, social theory, literary criticism, economics—in other words, to facilitate communication between China and the rest of the world. The intellectuals involved in these activities liked to think of themselves as being involved in a 'new enlightenment' (Wang Runsheng 1991; Lao Siguang 1988).

The two major groups of younger intellectuals involved in the new enlightenment were the *Towards the Future* group and the *Culture: China and the World* group, both based in Beijing. The *Towards the Future* group was the first to form, organized by Jin Guantao. This group advocated the adoption of a 'scientific attitude' in both the natural and social sciences. Their activities engendered great enthusiasm in China in the early 1980s. They published a series of books (The *Towards the Future* series), introducing contemporary Western thought to the younger generation of Chinese. The editorial board of this series included Jin Guantao as chief editor (formerly Bao Zunxin), Chen Yueguang, Jia Xinmin and Tang Ruoxi as deputy editors and Ding Xueliang, Wang Xiaoqiang, Wang Qishan,

Wang Xiaolu, Wang Yan, Zhu Jiaming, Zhu Xihao, Liu Dong, Liu Qingfeng, Yan Jiaqi, He Weiling, Zhang Gang, Weng Yongxi, Huang Jiangnan and Xiao Gongqin as members of the editorial board. Almost all of these distinguished themselves in one way or another during the 1980s, and many of them are mentioned elsewhere in this paper. They published a journal, also called *Towards the Future*, containing articles written by the newly emerging intellectual elite and which circulated mainly amongst them (Kane 1989a).

Another distinct group of young humanists and social scientists came into prominence in the mid-1980s. They were mainly younger research scholars at Peking University and the Chinese Academy of Social Sciences, who shared a common interest in modern Western philosophy and the problems of modernizing China's culture. This group was organized by Gan Yang, who had achieved national fame through his translation of the German neo-Kantian philosopher, Cassirer, and his spirited attack on Tu Wei-ming's advocacy of Confucianism as a living philosophy (Kane 1989b). They also published a journal, *Culture: China and the World*, and a series of books under the same name. The editorial board included Wang Yan, Liu Xiaofeng, Chen Lai, Chen Weigang, Liu Dong, Sun Yiyi, Su Guoxun, Chen Pingyuan and Zhou Guoping. Specialists in Nietzsche, Sartre, Heidegger and the like, they set about translating the works of these and other influential philosophers of 20th century Europe, who were practically unknown in China at the time.

Other young intellectuals in Beijing published their articles in the journal *Du Shu*, and regularly met in the 'cultural salons' of Beijing. One of the deputy editors of *Du Shu* was Wang Yan (also on the editorial board of *Towards the Future* and *Culture: China and the World*) who encouraged other young intellectuals to publish in this journal. Those who did so regularly included He Xin, Huang Ziping, Cheng Pingyuan, Li Tuo, Chen Kuide, Li Ming, Gu Xin, Ding Xueliang, Liu Xiaofeng, Xu Jilin and Xue Yong. Many of these also published elsewhere, and were active in other groups. Chen Kuide and others (including Xu Jilin) founded the Culture Research Institute under the auspices of the East China Institute of Chemical Engineering; this group published a journal, *Sixiangjia*, of which only one issue was published. Chen is now in Princeton. Xue Yong established the New Knowledge Academy (a non-official society) in Beijing; Li Ming was on the editorial board of the *Twentieth Century Series*, another series of translations of contemporary Western thinkers. Other members of that board included Li Shengping, Chen Ziming, Liu Zaifu and Li Zehou. The nominal editor-in-chief was Deng Pufang.

The members of all of these groups belonged to what we are calling the third generation. Needless to say, they all had their *guanxi* networks linking them to other sections of Chinese society. The *Towards the Future* group was more closely linked with the reformist wing of the government; the *Culture: China and the World* group more so with the previous generation of intellectuals in Beijing and elsewhere—their teachers and mentors.

All of them had experienced the Cultural Revolution in one way or another. This gave many of them a certain maturity and sense of purpose; their interrupted education, however, meant that often their own knowledge of various aspects of Western thought was very limited, and they themselves were in no way an integral part of international intellectual discourse (Lao Siguang 1988). Their work resembled that of late Qing intellectuals such as Yan Fu and the translators at the Jiangnan Arsenal. Their task was to introduce rather than contribute; the people they aimed at were mainly university students, even younger than themselves. When China was just emerging from the darkness of the Cultural Revolution, any new information from the outside world was exciting and enthusiastically welcomed. Many of these younger intellectuals were closely involved in the intellectual ferment in the years and months preceding the Tiananmen Massacre of mid-1989, and many are now in exile.

While these intellectuals were working on their enlightenment project in China, large numbers of Chinese students were going abroad to study. It was not long before they were joining mainstream students and postgraduates in the USA and Europe, and studying the latest Western intellectual trends, very often at first hand from the initiators of those trends or participants in the latest intellectual discourse. Their training in specific disciplines raised their expectations of what to expect from a work of scholarship, or an intellectual leader. After the Tiananmen Massacre, many of the most energetic of the younger 'intellectual elite' (in China) found themselves overseas, without a recognized discipline, with an inadequate knowledge of English, and a drop in status from being an 'intellectual leader' to being condescended to, not only by Western scholars, but even by Chinese undergraduates (Shi Hua 1991a). The result of this was a general disillusionment and questioning as to just what had been achieved during the 1980s. They had made no contribution to internationally recognized scholarship; nor had they achieved anything in traditional Chinese scholarship (Wang Runsheng 1991). This realization meant the end of the decade-long enlightenment movement. The intellectual elite of the 1980s must be prepared to acquire internationally recognized qualifications in a recognized discipline. The number of Chinese students studying for doctoral degrees in the West is legion; the former intellectual elite must keep up with and surpass them if they are to maintain their position and reputation, or they will simply fade from the scene.

There are two new organizations overseas which cater for this 'new breed' of Chinese intellectual, and which themselves are very different in character. The first is the Center for Modern China, established in April 1990. According to its brochure, it is a 'non-profit, non-partisan, educational institution' established in the USA in 1990. The Center brings together scholars and experts on China to form a worldwide network for research of basic issues facing contemporary China. Associates of the Center include people who have participated in China's economic and political reforms, Chinese scholars educated in the West, and China experts from the USA, Taiwan, Hong Kong and other parts of the world. Adhering to the principles of academic freedom and objectivity, and serving as a catalyst for change in China, the Center promotes theoretical research that may enrich the literature of China studies as well as practical, strategic, and policy research that may contribute to China's course towards democracy, pluralism and a free market economy. Despite its claim to be a 'non-profit, non-partisan, educational institution', its strong political program is clear. People associated with this Center include Chen Yizi, Yu Dahai, Ding Xueliang, Chen Kuide, Zhu Jiaming and Su Shaozhi. Chen Yizi, their Vice-Chairman, has suggested three aims for this Center (Chen 1990a): the short term aim should be to make the Center a first class internationally recognized research organization on contemporary China (three to five years); the medium term aim is to contribute solutions to China's major political, economic and social problems (five to ten years); the long term aim is to work towards the complete restructuring of China's political, economic, social, legal and cultural system (twenty to thirty years). This group has attracted a number of third generation intellectual leaders of the 1980s, as well as a number of younger students who are currently being trained in precise and rigorous intellectual disciplines.

The second major group is based on the editorial board of a journal, *The Twenty-First Century*. This group has managed to gather together some of the most famous names in the current Chinese intellectual elite, both inside and outside China, including Du Weiming, Gan Yang, Jin Guantao, Jin Yaoji, Lao Siguang, Li Oufan, Li Yining, Li Yiyuan, Li Zehou, Lin Yusheng, Liu Qingfeng, Liu Shuxian, Liu Zaifu, Pang Pu, Tang Yijie, Wei Zhengtong, Yu Yingshi and Zhang Hao. The impetus behind this was again Jin Guantao and his wife Liu Qingfeng, who had been planning such a journal (with the same title, general content and distribution) as early as 1988. Jin and Liu were visiting scholars at the Chinese University of Hong Kong when the Tiananmen Massacre happened, and now the Institute of Chinese Culture, under the directorship of Chen Fangzheng, has become their new base. The general aim and content of this journal is similar to that of the former *Towards the Future*; the major difference is that the former journal was the product of a group of enthusiastic but relatively unsophisticated writers; the main contributors to the present journal are established Chinese scholars. *The Twenty-First Century* is distributed in mainland China, Taiwan and Hong Kong, and among the 'global Chinese' intelligentsia. It is a serious journal dealing with current international intellectual trends; it is comparable to *Dangdai* or *Zhongguo Luntan* in Taiwan (that is in general content, not in political orientation).

Some of the activists during the enlightenment period in China have managed to take up the challenge of acquiring new intellectual skills in the West. Gan Yang, who specialized in Western philosophy in China, is now studying with Edward Shils in Chicago. Liu Xiaofeng, who had written a book in Chinese on Western theology, is now studying theology in the strict German academic tradition. Wang Xiaoqiang is studying economics in Cambridge, and Chen Ping, one of the first of the *muliao*, who became famous in China after the publication of his article 'The crops-only small peasant economic structure is the root of our nation's protracted disorder and poverty' (Chen Ping 1979) completed his PhD under the supervision of Ilya Prigogine at the University of Texas, and is now a research fellow there. Ding Xueliang was a Research Fellow in the Chinese Academy of Social Sciences; he was also on the editorial board of the *Towards the Future* series and regularly contributed articles to *Du Shu*. He is now a doctoral candidate in the Department of Sociology at Harvard, and is an activist in the FDC. Others, however, seem to be anxious to return to China, whenever circumstances permit.

Connections

An important point to make about the the princes' clique, the advisors and the enlightenment intellectuals is that many people are in more than one group, or have close links with more than one group. Wang Xiaoqiang, for example, was a typical *muliao*, but was also on the editorial board of the *Towards the Future* series. Zhu Jiaming was a research fellow in the Chinese Academy of Social Sciences, wrote a book for the *Towards the Future* series, was an entrepreneur, cadre and *muliao*: now he is an activist in the Federation for Democracy in China. Deng Yingtao is one of the princes (his father is Deng Liqun), and also worked in the Economic Systems Research Institute—a think-tank serving Zhao Ziyang. He is now with the Chinese Academy of Social Sciences. He Xin was on the periphery of various intellectual groups, but forged his links with Hu Qiaomu on the one hand, and to Qian Xuesen (and, at least in the past, to Li Zehou) on the other. Wang Juntao was always on the outside, but tried to forge his own base from which he could exert political influence. An important characteristic about the third generation is that the leading people from various fields or disciplines tended to associate with each other across fields, rather than with lesser lights within the same academic discipline, occupation, profession or organization. In this they display the traditional elitism one might expect.

I think it might be possible to detect a new type of Chinese intellectual emerging in the 21st century, which we might call the 'global intellectual'. A new concept has developed amongst some Chinese intellectuals living overseas over the past few years, namely that of 'Cultural China' (Fu Weixun 1988). Chinese culture, particularly elite culture, has always been limited to the political confines of the Chinese state. (Cultures such as those which developed in Japan, Korea and Vietnam might be considered offshoots of Chinese culture—this development was not accompanied by a vast exodus of the Chinese intellectual elite into those countries.) There

may have been some educated Chinese in the overseas Chinese communities of Southeast Asia, but they could hardly be considered an
intellectual elite (Wang Gungwu 1986).

What has happened over the past few years, however, is that (a) a large
number of the intellectual elite of the 1980s is now overseas; (b) large
numbers of Chinese students are receiving training in Western disciplines,
but are concentrating much of their specific research effort on China; (c)
some of the 'second generation' intellectuals (Liu Binyan, Su Shaozhi, Yan
Jiaqi, Ruan Ming, Liu Zaifu) are overseas; (d) established Chinese scholars
in the USA and elsewhere are asserting themselves in the context of
cultural pluralism and efforts to move away from marginalization of
minority cultures; (e) there is a good deal of contact between the 'pro-
fessionally trained intellectuals' and Western intellectuals (teacher to
student) and between the 'established scholars' and Western intellectuals
(as colleagues).

In this context, the role of such organizations as the Chinese Young
Economists Society (CYES) is worth noting. It was established in 1985 in
the USA. The first president was Yu Dahai, the second Qian Yingyi and
the third Chen Ping. Interestingly enough, both Chen Ping and Yu Dahai
originally went to the USA to study physics, but changed their discipline
to economics. In 1985 the CYES had 58 members; in 1988, 325. In 1987,
under Chen Ping's presidency, the CYES established an advisory board,
including Kenneth Arrow, Gregory C. Chow, Robert F. Dernberger, Dong
Fureng, D. Gale Johnson, Liu Guoguang, Ma Hong, Dwight H. Perkins,
Walt W. Rostow and Herbert A. Simon (CYES 1987). The members of the
CYES maintained close connection with former mentors or professors
(Tong Dalin, Ma Hong, Liu Guoguang) while developing new links with
some of the USA's most influential economists. Yu Dahai has since become
the new President of *Minlian*, but the others, although sometimes out-
spoken in their criticism of the present government, do not seem to be
deeply involved in any of the dissident groups. In this context one should
also note that, during the summer vacation period of 1991, ten members
of the Chinese Students History Association and five members of the
Chinese Students Political Science Association were invited to lecture in
universities in China. The Chinese Students Economists Association was
also going to send five members but, for a variety of political and bureaucratic reasons, eventually no-one from that association went. The History
Association received financial support from the Luce Foundation; the
Political Science Association support from the Rockefeller Foundation,
and the Economic Association was promised support from the Ford
Foundation (Wang Hao 1991). These younger scholars are also keeping
their links with their former universities, as well as making new links with
universities in the USA and elsewhere.

All of these groups and individuals are developing strong links with
Chinese intellectuals in Hong Kong and Taiwan, many of whom themselves are Western trained, but whose special area of interest is in China.

In the context of continuing globalization, it seems likely that there will be an international community of scholars scattered around the universities of the world, whose common language is Chinese, who are aware of, and perhaps participants in, international intellectual discourse, and whose particular area of interest or expertise is China. Perhaps the *Twenty-First Century* group is the prototype for this type of global Chinese intellectual. It is hard to tell whether the traditional Chinese intellectual's 'sense of mission' and 'sense of responsibility' will survive in an increasingly commercialized and industrialized world. It would seem likely, however, that the 'new intellectuals'—trained in strict academic disciplines to internationally recognized standards—will continue to offer their services, or advice, to the Chinese government, and will in this way affect the course of Chinese history in the first decades of the 21st century.

Conclusion

China's economic reform has not yet changed China's political structure, though there seems to be some evidence that such a change is under way. At the moment, however, the CCP still monopolizes political power, and this is the power base of the princes' clique. In this transitionary period the interests of the princes are still mainly within the economic sphere, though some well-known names have been appointed to some political or administrative positions. It is this undramatic but inexorable monopolization of influential positions undertaken while the present political power structure persists which will enable them to survive, and indeed to thrive, should the CCP become marginalized in China's economic and social life. The role of the *muliao* cannot be underestimated. Many intellectuals may have become dissidents of one type or another in recent years, and many who remain overseas may become a sort of globalized intellectual. Most Chinese intellectuals, however, will continue to follow the tradition of offering advice to the government of the day. Many of the current exiles are waiting for the chance to be able to co-operate with the government again (Barmé 1991). Inside China, Xiao Gongqin is one notable figure following this tradition. The elite of the third generation, whether as government advisors, academics, exiles or 'global intellectuals', will continue to maintain their links across fields and even political or national boundaries. The same trends which are seeing the inevitable and inextricable economic links between China and the world are also forging inevitable and inextricable intellectual links between China and the world.

Note

[1] This research has been conducted under a grant from the Australian Research Council.

References

Australia Chinese Daily

Barmé, Geremie 1991, 'Baggage of the Chinese Diaspora', *Problems of Communism*, vol. 40. no. 1/2, pp. 94–112.

Chen Ping 1979, 'Danyi xiaonong jingji jiegou shi woguo changqi dongluan pinqiong de binggen' (The crops-only small peasant economic stucture is the root of our nation's protracted disorder and poverty), *Guangming ribao*, 16 November, summarized in *Xinhua yuebao*, no. 1, 1980, pp. 90–2.

Chen Yige 1988, 'Zhengli Kang Hua Gongsi zhenxiang' (Sorting out the true state of affairs of the Kanghua Company), *Jiushi niandai*, no. 11, pp. 26–7.

——1991, 'Gongzimen jinru quanli hexin—Zhonggong yunniang xin zheng-jing luxian' (The princes enter the power centres—a new politico-economic line developing within the CCP), *Jiushi niandai*, no. 11, pp. 32–3.

Chen Yizi 1990a, 'Guanyu dangdai Zhongguo yanjiu zhongxin gongzuo de ruogan yijian' (Some views of the work of the Center for Modern China), *Newsletter of the Center for Modern China*, December, pp. 7–10.

——1990b, *Zhongguo—Shinian gaige yu bajiu minyun*, (China—The reform decade and the democratic movement of 1989), Lianjing pinglun, Taibei.

Chen Yuan 1991, 'Woguo jingji de shenceng wenti he xuanze' (Problems and choices in the deep structure of our national economy), *Jingji yanjiu*, no. 4, pp. 18–26.

CYES (Chinese Young Economists Society) 1987, *Forum of Chinese Young Economists Newsletter*, vol. 3, no. 1, p. 2.

Deng Zhiduan 1991, 'Zhongguo rencai wailiu wenti: Yuanyin, yingxiang ji zhengce xuanze' (China's Braindrain Problem: Causes, Consequences, and Policy Options), *Papers for the Center for Modern China*, no. 11, September.

Fang Li 1991, 'Taizi dang zhi zheng, fu xi huo xi?' (The princes' clique grasps political power—good fortune or a disaster?), *Zhongguo zhi chun*, no. 11, pp. 43–4.

Feng Shengbao 1991, 'Minzhu yundong yu Zhongguo de zhengzhi chulu' (The democratic movement and China's political future), *Zhishifenzi*, Summer, pp. 48–56.

Fu Weixun 1988, *'Wenhua Zhongguo' yu Zhongguo Wenhua* ('Cultural China' and Chinese Culture), Dongda tushu gongsi, Taibei.

Gu Ren 1991, 'Wo suo zhi de Qiao Zonghuai' (The Qiao Zonghuai I know), *Zhengming*, no. 12, p. 95.

Halpern, Nina 1986, 'Making Economic Policy: The Influence of Economists', in *China's Economy Looks Towards the Year 2000*, ed. John P. Hardt, vol. 1, Washington, pp. 132–46.

——1989, 'Scientific Decision Making: The Organization of Expert Advice in Post-Mao China', in *Science and Technology in Post-Mao China*,

Denis F. Simon & Merle Goldman, Harvard University Press, Harvard, pp. 157–74.

He Pin 1991, 'Chen Yuan—Dangqian Zhonggong baoshoupai de redian renwu' (Chen Yuan—a CCP conservative in the hot spot), *Zhongguo dalu*, no. 8, pp. 25–7.

He Weiling 1990, 'The Impact and Influence of the New View of Science on China's Reform', in *Economic Reform in China, Problems and Prospects*, eds James A. Dorn & Wang Xi, University of Chicago Press, Chicago, pp. 87–90.

He Xin 1990, 'A Word of Advice to the Politburo' (translated, annotated and introduced by Geremie Barmé), *The Australian Journal of Chinese Affairs*, no. 23, pp. 49–76.

He Zhenming 1990, 'Jingji zhuanjia chaojia dahui' (Quarrels amongst economic specialists), *Zhengming*, no. 12, pp. 40–1.

——1991, 'Qiao Zonghuai diaoli Xianggang qianhou' (Circumstances surrounding Qiao Zonghuai's transfer from Hongkong), *Zhengming*, no. 9, pp. 47–8.

Jian Jun 1989, 'Zhongguo zhengtan zhinang xinshengdai' (The newly emerging period of think tanks on the Chinese political stage), *Zhongguo zhi chun*, no. 8, pp. 45–7.

Kane, Daniel 1989a, 'Jin Guantao, Liu Qingfeng and Historical Systems Evolution Theory—a New Theory of Chinese History', *Papers on Far Eastern History*, Canberra, no. 39, March, pp. 45–73.

——1989b, 'Gan Yang and the Introduction of Modern Social Theory into China', paper presented to the International Conference on Literature, Politics and Society in Mainland China, Taibei, May.

Lang Lang 1986, 'Cong zhengzhi paibie kan Deng yihou de Zhongguo' (China after Deng, as seen from an analysis of political factions), *Jiushi niandai*, no. 2, pp. 54–9.

Lao Siguang 1988, 'Panguan dalu sichao' (An observation on current thinking in the mainland), *Yuanjian zazhi*, no. 6, pp. 176–7.

Li Oufan 1991, 'Meiguo youpai weijiao 'duoyuan wenhuazhuyi'' (The American Right beseiges 'multiculturalism'), *Dangdai*, no. 8, pp. 20–7.

Li Yan 1991, 'Zai you meng de difang zuo meng huo zuo ren?—Ji Bo'ang Zhong, De tongxue yu Bei Dao duitan wenxue' (In a place of dreams, to be a dreamer or to conduct oneself well?—a dialogue on literature between Chinese and German students and Bei Dao, held in Bonn), *Zhongyang ribao*, 9 June.

Li Yi & Fang Su 1988, 'Sixiang wenhua weiji haishi xianshi weiji' (A crisis of ideology and culture or a real crisis) (Interview with Liu Shuxian), *Jiushi niandai*, no. 4, pp. 82–91.

Li Yi 1990, '"Liu Si" wailiu renshi de kunnao' (Predicaments faced by June 4th exiles), *Jiushi niandai*, no. 10, pp. 32–4

Lieberthal, Kenneth & Michel Oksenberg 1988, *Policy Making in China—Leaders, Structures and Processes*, Princeton University Press, Princeton.

Lin Wei 1990, 'Lao Deng diandian tou, zai cu gaige?—Dangqian Zhonggong jingji luxiang' (Old Deng nods his head—an impetus for reform? Current economic directions in the CCP), *Jiushi niandai*, no. 12, pp. 23–5.

Ling Wei 1986, 'Wenhua da geming he di san dai ren' (The cultural revolution and the third generation), *Zhishifenzi*, Spring, pp. 50–5.

Luo Bing 1988, 'Caizheng jingji weiji chongji xia, Zhonggong jiang da chu san zhang wangpai' (Under the onslaught of a financial and political crisis, the CCP plays three trump cards), *Zhengming*, no. 10, pp. 6–10.

——1991a, 'Beidaihe de zhenli' (Tremors at Beidaihe), *Zhengming*, no. 9, pp. 6–8.

——1991b, 'Dai Qing shijian chufa Yang-Li maodun' (The Dai Qing affair touches off a fight between Yang Shangkun and Li Peng), *Zhengming*, no. 12, pp. 9–10.

Luo Kedao 1988, 'Dalu liu-Mei xuesheng san shi' (Three items about Chinese students in the United States), *Jiushi niandai*, no. 7, pp. 72–3.

Mo Ming 1979, 'Cong jun—shang xue—chu guo' (Join the army, start studying, go overseas), *Qishi niandai*, no. 12, pp. 8–9.

Moody, Peter R. Jr. 1988, *Political Opposition in Post-Confucian Society*, Praeger, New York.

Pye, Lucian 1968, *The Spirit of Chinese Politics: A Psychocultural Study of the Authority Crisis in Political Development*, MIT Press, Cambridge, Mass.

——1984, *The Dynamics of Chinese Politics*, Gunn & Hain, Oelgeschlager, Cambridge, Mass.

——1985, *Asian Power and Politics: The Cultural Dimensions of Authority*, Harvard University Press, Cambridge, Mass.

Shai Wen 1991, 'Dalu "Zhuhou Jingji" jiang fenjie Zhonggong quanli' (Mainland 'Feudal Lord' economics will break down CCP power), *Jiushi niandai*, no. 8, pp. 30–2.

Shi Hua 1991a, 'Bianyuanren de taolun yu jiaoliu—"Wenhua yu shehui: Ershi shiji Zhongguo de lishi fansi" yantaohui ceji' (Discussions and communication between marginalized men—notes on the seminar 'Culture and Society—Reflections on Chinese History in the Twentieth Century'), *Jiushi niandai*, no. 4, pp. 76–80.

——1991b, 'Deng Xiaoping neibu tanhua: Kending Zhao Ziyang' (An internal speech of Deng Xiaoping in support of Zhao Ziyang), *Jiushi niandai*, no. 6, pp. 22–3.

Sun, Lena H. 1992, 'China's Princelings in the Wings', *The Washington Post*, 2 February.

Wang Gungwu 1986, 'Preface' to *Social History of Chinese in Singapore and Malaysia 1800–1911*, ed. Yen Ching-Hwang, Oxford University Press, Singapore, p. xiv.

Wang Hao 1991, 'Liu-Mei zhuanye xuehui huiguo jiangxue jihua' (The scheme for professional associations of students studing in the United States to return to China to give lectures), *Zhongguo zhi chun*, no. 10, pp. 94–6.

Wang Runsheng 1991, 'Cong shehui gongneng kan xin qimeng de deshi' (The achievements and failures of the new enlightenment as a social function), *Zhongguo zhi chun*, no. 8, pp. 59–61.

Weng Yongxi, Wang Qishan, Huang Jiangnan & Zhu Jiaming 1981, 'Dui woguo nongye fazhan zhanlüe wenti de ruogan kanfa' (Certain views on agricultural development strategic issues in China), *Jingji yanjiu*, November, resumé in *Xinhua wenzhai* 1982, no. 2, pp. 58–62.

Who's Who in China 1989, Foreign Languages Press, Beijing.

Wu Tiandai 1991, 'Lun heping yanbian' (On peaceful transition), *Zhengming*, no. 10, pp. 30–2.

Xia Tong 1991, 'Dui gaogan zinü de diaocha baogao' (Report on an investigation into the sons and daughters of high level cadres), *Zhengming*, no. 2, p. 23.

Yue Xun 1986 'Ke Yunlu he tade Ye yu Zhou' (Ke Yunlu and his Night and Morning), *Jiushi niandai*, no. 10, pp. 74–7.

Zhang Ling 1987, 'Chongji zhong de sisuo—fang Tigaisuo zhu-Mei daibiao He Weiling' (Reflections amidst the heat of battle—an interview with the representative of the Research Institute for the Reform of the Economy in the United States, He Weiling), *Mingbao yuekan*, no. 3, pp. 23–6.

Zhong Shutan 1988, 'Taizi dang xi quan yilan' (An overall view of the princes' clique's power-grab), *Zhongguo zhi chun*, no. 8, p. 71.

Zhongyang ribao

Zhou Jixiang 1991, 'Junban qiye xia Zhonggong junren de xintai' (Attitudes of CCP army officers involved in military enterprises), *Zhongguo dalu yanjiu*, 1991, vol. 34, no. 4, pp. 51–61.

Zhou Ming, 1986, 1989, *Lishi zai zheli chensi* (Reflections on History), vols 1–3 (1986) Huaxia chubanshe, vols 4–6 (1989), Beiyue wenyi chubanshe, Beijing.

Zhu Jiaming 1991, 'Daonian wo de pengyou He Weiling' (In memory of my friend He Weiling), *Zhongguo zhi chun*, no. 8, p. 29.

8 Expertocracy and professionalism[1]

Hans Hendrischke

Expertocracy and professionalism originally referred to social and political changes in Western industrializing societies brought about by new occupational groups possessing technical or other formal skills. 'Expertocracy' is used here synonymously with 'technocracy' in the wider sense which includes not only technical expertise, but also, for example, economics and managerially and politically oriented disciplines of the social sciences (Fischer 1990, p. 18). The reason for using the term 'technocracy' below is easier reference to existing research literature. For the Saint-Simonians in the early 19th century, politics would be replaced by technical administration, with industrialists and bankers holding power in society instead of the feudal and aristocratic class, whose only knowledge was how to govern (Carlisle 1974; Savigear 1971). The technocratic movement in the USA took account of the political role of technical expertise during the 'Great Transformation' to industrial capitalism and postulated that government be run by experts. For the former Soviet Union, parallels to these developments were drawn by observers who equated the Communist Party with feudal powers and technically trained bureaucrats with technocrats who could infuse continuity and stability into the political process.

These views have in common the concept that traditional elites faced with the technical complexity of administrative tasks become increasingly dependent on the advice of experts to formulate policy alternatives and eventually have to entrust them with decision-making powers. Professionals able to independently establish their expertise play an essential part in this process. As much as technocracy represents liberal trends in this respect, it incorporates on the other side an authoritarian element in its justification of strong leadership or even dictatorship (Savigear 1971, p. 156). As reforms in China move towards a market economy and technocracy is already used as a cliché in Western press reporting, it seems worthwhile exploring the adequacy of using these terms for China.

Academic research on China, whether on the role of occupational and other interest groups in policy-making (Falkenheim 1987, p. 2ff) or on their broader socio-political contribution to 'civil society' (Kelly & He 1992), is faced with unresolved issues. In line with press reporting, some scholars see China already on the way to a technocratic society imbued with democratic values. Others maintain the view that 'the bourgeois democratic concept of participation, in which individual participants make autonomous political decisions based on their own interest, is rather difficult to assimilate to Chinese political culture' (Dittmer 1987, p. 43).

Have China's reforms produced a technocratic society ruled by experts? Unlike the Soviet Union, where experts found a *modus vivendi* with the ruling party elite (Konrad & Szelenyi 1979), and where the term 'technocracy' has become accepted, intellectuals and experts suffered various degrees of discrimination and persecution during the Mao era. Moreover, their expertise was often purposefully disregarded. With the advent of the reform period they were not only readmitted into the ranks of the working class, but their skills were now also seen as a precondition for the success of the reform program. Furthermore, with the restitution of the status of intellectuals, a number of professional associations were established or revived in the 1980s, and technocracy, in fact, became a topic of public debate.

In the following pages, an attempt will be made to put these developments into a more general perspective in order to determine whether they represent social trends comparable to professionalization and related developments in Western societies. Specifically, are debates about technocracy in the Chinese press an intellectual reaction to Western developments, or is there evidence to suggest that changes in the Chinese leadership warrant reference to technocracy or rule by experts? Have increasingly complex technical, legal, economic and other forms of expertise become recognized as autonomous disciplines and have the holders of these skills been able to gain professional autonomy? If so, this would point to the emergence of a bourgeois democratic concept of political participation which 'would be indicative of a new relationship between state and society in China' (Suttmeier 1987, p. 158).

Technocracy as ideology

The founders of the technocratic movement in the USA in the 1920s understood technocracy originally as 'government by technicians who are guided solely by the imperatives of their technology' (*The New*

Encyclopedia Brittanica 1989, p. 300). The focus here will first be on the political implications of technocracy. Three relevant aspects are generally accepted features of technocracy.[2] First, regarding the role of technical expertise in the process of political decision making, advice by experts is based on their occupational skills rather than on consideration of political opportunity. Second, regarding the actors in the decision-making process, experts are seen as rivals to traditional political parties or the elite with whom they attempt to share power. Third, as experts base their influence on the professional communities of which they are members, they gain increasing autonomy from the traditional elite they formally serve; the elite, in turn, have to accommodate themselves to the experts.

Technocracy can be defined in different ways. Often its use is based only on changes in educational patterns of experts recruited into existing bureaucracies who are referred to as 'the new technocratic elite', 'the technically trained bureaucrats' (Lee 1991a, p. 6) or 'party technocrats' and 'bureaucratic technocrats' (titles of Lee 1991a, 1991b). In order to detect social changes, the definition of technocracy used here stresses the infusion of new professional expertise into administration and the political role of experts rather than changes in the educational background of administrators. Recruitment of technically trained personnel into administration is not automatically seen as a sign of technocracy. In Soviet studies, both Soviet and Western scholars have used the notion of technocracy in the latter sense. Some argue that the technocratic transformation of Soviet bureaucracy was completed as early as the late 1920s (Rowney 1989, p. 4). This use of technocracy will not be adopted here, as it disregards the potential social and political implications outlined above. As a Soviet historian critically put it:

> scientists and specialists are being drawn into the apparat: committees and commissions of experts are being created, but at the same time undemocratic methods of administration remain intact. In other words, the bureaucrats are being replaced by knowledgeable and more efficient technocrats (Medvedev 1975, p. 300).

China's historical situation bears comparison neither with the Soviet Union, where experts were integrated into the bureaucracy, nor with the West where 'the dominant figures of the past hundred years have been the entrepreneur, the businessman, and the industrial executive' and where 'the "new men" are the scientists, the mathematicians, the economists, and the engineers of the new intellectual technology' (Bell 1974, p. 344, cited in Rowney 1989, p. 3). Yet the concept of experts sharing power and status with the political elite and ruling by virtue of their specialized knowledge has fascinated Chinese reformers (Li & White 1990, p. 13ff).

Among Western researchers, Li Cheng and Lynn White (ibid., also 1988) and, more recently, Lee Hong Yung (1991b)[3] have come to the conclusion that technocracy is emerging in China. However, since the reassertion of Party control after 1989, the prospect of China repeating liberal Western developments has become much less probable, and it seems justified to re-evaluate their findings. Li's and White's writings deal with both the ideological and sociological aspects of technocracy. We will first briefly turn to the ideological aspect.

Li and White (1991, p. 362) quote a classical example of technocratic thinking by Qian Xuesen, one of China's leading experts in aerospace engineering, who suggested that the government should be run like a designing department and mainly composed of scientists and engineers. They argue that his views were shared by China's political leaders when they emphasized the role of science and technology for China's modernization. The promotion of technically trained personnel into leadership positions in the People's Republic of China (PRC) is seen as a proof that 'technocratism' has become the dominant ideology for the PRC and, for that matter, under similar circumstances for Taiwan as well.

The question is whether the promotion of technical and scientific training necessarily constitutes technocracy. Li and White (1988) equate technocratic ideology with an emphasis on 'the development of science and technology and the important role of technical intellectuals', combined with a pragmatic outlook and economic determinism. It is arguable, though, whether the propagation of the role of science and technology means that the leadership supports technocracy. The importance of science and technology has undoubtedly been one of the areas on which there was consensus among the leadership. It manifested itself in support for better use of technical expertise and a new policy towards intellectuals, but not in support for an increased political role for experts. We will see that professionals, on the contrary, have a long way to go to assert their status and influence. The leadership and the media stressed the role of experts also because, up to the late 1970s, their social and political status was lower than that of the workers and the peasantry. Without official encouragement they could not be expected to take on a more active occupational role, especially as they still faced hostility and suspicion from the lower levels of party and bureaucracy (Suttmeier 1987, p. 153). The intensive press coverage of experts and their achievements served first of all the purpose of rehabilitating them and raising their status from a very low level. It is not necessarily a reflection of a technocratic reality.

Intellectuals were given ample media support to propagate their own roles and among the ideas they advocated were various technocratic notions. Technocracy, with its emphasis on the role of educated groups, easily lent itself to parallels with traditional Chinese ideas of leadership by an intellectually trained elite. But technocratic elements appeared also in the concepts of democracy, as well as the neo-authoritarianism voiced during the 1980s. The astrophysicist Fang Lizhi, for example, argued that the Party had to grant a dominant position to the scientific elite and that 'the demands of technological modernization would impose political and social reform upon the Party whether it liked it or not' (Buckley 1991, pp. 15–16). Neo-authoritarianism was inspired by Western social scientists as well as by the 'Four Dragons' (Sautman 1992), but its intellectual tradition can be traced back to the authoritarianism of the Saint-Simonians in the early 19th century for whom

> dictatorship offered a double advantage, on the one hand uniting people in contrast to the divisive effects of parliamentary politics, and on the other hand the prospect of increasing the importance of the technocrats in the new direction demanded by the force of industrialization. In both these respects Napoleon Bonaparte had shown the way (Savigear 1971, p. 156).

How the reaction of Chinese intellectuals to Western technocratic thinking has resulted in shifts between democratic and authoritarian positions has been elucidated elsewhere (e.g. Buckley 1991).[4] For our purposes it is relevant that technocracy could be used to justify either position. Attempts to categorize Chinese intellectuals politically as technocrats or democrats, or even as dissidents, simply miss the complexity of discussions among them and 'fail to capture the ambivalences and tensions' in their thinking (ibid., pp. 35–6).

Regarding social values, it is also questionable that the promotion of younger and better educated people implies that technocratic views have become dominant. The move to put experts into influential positions was initiated from the top of the Party hierarchy in order to facilitate technological modernization and economic growth, but not to partake of political power. Recruitment statistics are not sufficiently conclusive once a stricter definition of technocracy is used. If technocracy refers to 'a system of governance in which technically trained experts rule by virtue of their specialized knowledge and position in dominant political institutions' (Fischer 1990, p. 17) and where 'the influence of such experts, moreover, is in important ways increasingly independent of the politicians and administrators they formally serve' (ibid. p. 19), then this latter condition did not exist when the Twelfth Central Committee was elected into office (Lee 1983, p. 686ff) and was clearly not apparent under the circumstances following the Tiananmen incident. Expert advice from influential research institutions was at times used to counterbalance the interests of competing ministries (Halpern 1992, p. 148), but the reinstatement of Party control at all levels, together with ideological objections against a number of factual developments, indicates a move away from the acceptance of technocratic trends that undoubtedly existed prior to 1989.

In intellectual debate, technocratic ideas provided Chinese intellectuals with arguments to assert the social role of experts after years of suppression and to discuss their political role in a reforming society. Technocratic ideas influenced democratic as well as authoritarian alternatives, but the actual technocratic consequences—the replacement of politics by technical administration—never became a real issue. When the Party leadership adopted policies to promote experts from within its own ranks into leading positions and, in addition, to recruit experts and intellectuals, neither policy was easily accepted within the Party. On the contrary, there was considerable resistance which rendered some of these policies ineffective (Ch'i 1991, chapters 4 & 5), as will be discussed below.

Expertocracy as a social trend

In sociological terms, a general shift from revolutionary veterans (mobilizers and ideologues) to a new political elite (managers and technical experts) has occurred during the reform period. Li and White (1988, p. 399) conclude that, with the election of the Thirteenth Central Committee, 'for the first time in the history of the CCP, a managerial–technical elite has come to the fore'.

This argument is based on the educational level of top leaders and on the prevalence of technical graduates among them. However, the rising level of education among Politburo and Central Committee members since the beginning of the 1980s is not in itself an indication of technocracy. It had to be expected as the older generation of revolutionaries with little or no formal education reached retirement age. Moreover, the fact that a large number of people in leadership positions hold engineering degrees results primarily from the Soviet influenced education system in which the vast majority of tertiary students from the 1950s onwards had no choice but to take up engineering as their field of study (ibid., p. 11). An above average education and a degree in engineering can thus be seen as part of the general elite recruitment pattern.[5]

There is furthermore very little evidence that the engineering degrees held by people in the leadership were indeed the qualifications on the basis of which they were chosen. The main recruitment channels for high leadership positions have been the bureaucracy, Party offices, qualification as personal secretaries, or through youth league, military and scientific or scholarly careers (Li & Bachman 1989, pp. 64–94). For the latter category, Li and White cite only one example. The career pattern that these authors have set out does not conclusively prove that it was technical expertise which brought members of the Central Committee or the Politburo into their offices. There is also reason to doubt that a technical education necessarily indicates a technocratic view, as is often cited in the case of Li Peng. Especially since 1989 it can be argued that Li Peng is not primarily a technocrat but owes his loyalty to the preservation of specific Party interests. His education was not the major factor that led to his promotion. People like Li Peng moved into their positions of power because they were members of the political elite. Their political outlook was primarily formed on this basis and only secondarily because of their formal education or their professional expertise.

Li and White also downplay the influence of personal connections by finding no more than twelve members in the 1987 Central Committee with a high cadre family background. From this figure it would appear that recruitment based on merit plays a much more important role than is apparent if one takes into consideration the complex family and group relations which have been well documented by Kane (1992) and others (e.g. Ch'i 1991, pp. 91–7).

The question of technocracy poses itself not only for the central leadership, but also for lower hierarchical levels where experts are closer to their areas of expertise. In 1983 the Party devised a 'third-echelon policy', according to which leadership positions in central and provincial government, as well as in local administration, should be filled by young and better educated cadres (ibid. p. 77ff). As a result, by 1985 close to half a million younger cadres, the majority of them college educated, were reported to have moved into leadership positions above county level. Over ninety per cent of those who had been promoted into the leadership of central or provincial government institutions had college level education, and nearly eighty per cent reportedly possessed technical skills (ibid., p. 79).[6] As part of this policy, twelve thousand college graduates were sent to basic units to be trained as future leaders (Lee 1991, p. 262).

Upon closer examination, these seemingly technocratic changes were fraught with problems, as the promotion of better educated and technically trained personnel faced considerable resistance from the older generation of cadres. The program to send college graduates to basic units for training was discontinued in 1986 (Lee 1991). Its implementation had been distorted by a number of factors (Ch'i 1991, chapter 4). The Party's organization departments resorted to mechanical implementation of policies when they had to find larger numbers of cadres with academic qualifications than were available. In the city of Beijing in 1985, nearly thirty thousand cadres were reported to have been rushed through training sessions that gave them the nominal equivalent of college-level or high-school-level education. Personal loyalties, factionalism and family connections continued to be important factors in the selection of candidates, to the extent that the *People's Daily* printed a popular saying 'age is capital, diploma is indispensable, past work performance provides a reference, but human connections (*guanxi*) are critical' (cited in ibid., p. 90). Ch'i concludes that the Party's efforts to mobilize younger, more professional cadres largely failed because both the selection process and the working environment were biased against bringing professional expertise into play (ibid., p. 114).

The other way to raise the level of technical expertise within the Party was to recruit experts and intellectuals. The background to this consideration was the very low level of education of the Party membership. By 1983–84 only four per cent of Party members had a college-level education in spite of a recruitment drive that had been going on since 1979 (Ch'i 1991, p. 164; Rosen 1990, p. 58). In 1983 and the following years the need to recruit intellectuals and experts into the Party was taken up in the mass media and personally by political leaders such as Deng Xiaoping and Chen Yun (Ch'i 1991, p. 137; Rosen 1990, p. 56). Both emphasized their dissatisfaction with the slow progress of the recruitment drive. Even this support from the most senior political leaders was not automatically converted into support for intellectuals at the work unit level. Those who were recruited found it difficult to reach positions of influence, became targets of criticism or faced other obstacles in their careers (Ch'i 1991, p. 139).

Most recent statistics indicate that the recruitment drive has led to a constant increase in Party members with higher educational qualifications or technical expertise. Approximately eight million Party members are now classified as professionals and technicians (*China Daily* 7 October 1992). This figure looks impressive, but there is no indication as to what percentage of this group has received higher, i.e. college-level, education which would be relevant for identifying them as potential technocrats. Of the more than 7.5 million new Party members enrolled in the years following the Thirteenth Party Congress in 1987, over two-thirds are reported to have an educational background of senior high school or higher, but again no breakdown is given (*China Daily* 7 October 1992).

These figures indicate that the recruitment drive aiming at experts and intellectuals is slowly changing Party membership. This trend is confirmed by other evidence. Surveys of students' attitudes, for example, show that professional proficiency is now seen by many as an important factor in gaining Party membership, whereas political engagement is regarded as a hindrance. Party membership in turn is seen as essential to gaining good job assignments. This points to a trend towards professionalization more than towards technocracy. Technocracy is not a dominant trend so long as the position of experts within the Party can be subject to sudden political changes, as was the case after 1989, and so long as experts are supported more from above than are in demand by work units from below. Professionalization, on the other hand, is an individual quest which, to the dismay of the Chinese authorities, is gaining increasing adherence among Party candidates and young educated Party members, as occupational qualifications provide career advantages inside and outside the Party (Rosen 1990).

There is, therefore, so far no clear basis on which to speak of technocracy in the PRC, either as an alternative ideology or as a social phenomenon. The fact, however, that intellectual debates and educational and occupational changes in the Party as the power structure point in this direction, raises the question of whether preconditions exist for the rise of technocrats or expertocrats. One important element in the emergence of technocracy is the role of groups of professional experts (Fischer 1990, p. 19).

Professionalism

Professionalism has been called an 'Anglo-American disease' in one of the numerous works written on it. It refers to the emergence of occupational groups which have gained special power and social prestige, as well as economic and organizational autonomy and an increasing independence from dominant ideology where their area of expertise is concerned. The specific details that have developed in Western societies, where medicine was one the earliest areas of professionalization, are of little interest for China. Historical research on professionalism has, however, come to some general conclusions which can shed light on the Chinese situation.

Professionalism comprises several elements: the establishment of a body of knowledge, self-government within professional associations, achievement of social status through the marketing of expertise, the ability of professional groups to emancipate themselves from a client relationship with the ruling elite, and increasing independence from the ideology of the dominant social elites (Larson 1977, p. xii). As these elements develop over time, they provide a yardstick for measuring how far Chinese intellectuals have been able to improve their collective status and to constitute themselves as an interest group. It is in this context that professionalism becomes an indicator of political group autonomy and a diversifying political structure.

Autonomy was strictly denied to Chinese intellectuals irrespective of their specific skills, especially during the Cultural Revolution. An exception might be found in the very limited number of persons involved in isolated areas such as defence technologies which have little social impact.[7] At the beginning of the reform period a general reversal of these restrictions manifested itself in the newly announced policies towards intellectuals, especially technical and scientific experts. Not only was the political stigma removed from them; they were also promised better professional and material conditions and allowed to revive professional associations and their activities. Originally set up during the 1950s and early 1960s, professional associations ceased to function during the Cultural Revolution and resumed limited activities in the early 1970s. After 1978 they had a spectacular increase in numbers and activities and embarked on a wide range of activities. A large part of their activity was aimed at constituting a body of professional expertise. To remedy the negative results of the long enforced isolation, internally as well as internationally, numerous conferences and meetings took place. These provided liaison between members of the organizations and allowed their leading exponents to establish links with foreign counterparts and colleagues in China and abroad. Publication statistics show that considerable effort was spent on promoting the interests of the various professions and enlarging their public role. They gained wider public appeal with publications aimed not only at the professional community, but also at a wider, more popular audience. Professional associations received official recognition through public encouragement and ritual meetings with political leaders. However, in the words of an observer, the associations 'have been penetrated by political authorities and thus do not enjoy the authentic autonomy that the concept of professionalism normally conveys' (Suttmeier 1987, p. 128).

Does this indicate a trend towards professionalism? The answer depends on the degree of autonomy achieved by professional associations and the economic independence enjoyed by individual occupations. The following section will consider the role of some occupational groups which in the West have gained professional status.

Apart from Science and Technology (S&T) personnel, lawyers, economists and social scientists are of special interest, as their areas of expertise relate to society as a whole. To accord them the status of professionals in line with the above definition would require them to be able to organize themselves in order to define their own body of knowledge, to practice in their area of expertise on the basis of their own professional criteria, and to operate independently from a client relationship.

Numerous policy declarations regarding the importance of intellectuals in China's modernization program were aimed at scientists and technicians (Simon 1987, p. 122–55). These resulted in marked changes to the institutional working environment of S&T personnel. Demand for scientific advice and science policy analysis arose from newly established research centres and a variety of central and local government institutions which had the means to fund research in order to advise government departments. Institutions such as the National Research Center for S&T Development (NRCSTD) provided advice on policy matters to the State Council and to central ministries, as well as engaging in long-term planning. Nina Halpern (1992, pp. 131–46) has described in precise detail the extent to which research institutions such as the NRCSTD, with its large staff of experts and research associates, could feed its expertise into the governmental process, influence decisions and set research agendas for other institutions. This gave them a significant degree of autonomy which extended to other, more specialized, research institutions, such as the Chinese Academy of Sciences, which co-operated with them.

Scientists gained further autonomy through increasing rights to administer their own affairs. Research planning and project evaluation of the Chinese Academy of Sciences was largely placed in the hands of its Scientific Council, composed of 400 leading scientists and technical personnel (Simon 1987, p. 141). The need for greater autonomy of the S&T community was also recognized by moving the responsibility for staffing decisions from the Ministry of Labour and Personnel to the State Science and Technology Commission. A semi-government institution, the Chinese Association for Science and Technology, was put in charge of disseminating research results and conducting academic exchanges for more than a hundred professional associations. In 1982, the Association of Science and Science Technology Policy was formed which included scientists and technicians. The Association represented the interests of S&T personnel in areas ranging from work to living conditions (Suttmeier 1987, p. 152).

The other path to professional autonomy opened to members of the S&T community was through entrepreneurial activities, primarily on an institutional basis (Suttmeier 1989, p. 1009ff). In 1983 the first consulting organization, operating under the Ministry of Aeronautics Industry, was set up in Beijing. Commercial activities of companies under the Chinese Academy of Sciences and new non-governmental technical enterprises

such as the Stone Corporation signalled a new step towards an autonomous role for scientists and technicians. S&T personnel were given
increased autonomy in providing consulting services in areas of scientific
research, teaching, public health, and agricultural and industrial production. These consulting services allowed scientists to augment their
salaries (Simon 1987, n.56).

None of these developments have led to the changes in the working
environment for S&T personnel that could have been expected from the
policy announcements. Simon (1987, p. 148ff) has compiled a list of
examples where scientists were prevented from making use of their new
rights or where new policies were not implemented. Chinese scientists
have continuously been complaining about their poor living conditions
compared with other groups and changes might have to wait until their
new role becomes socially accepted (Suttmeier 1987, p. 156).

The legal profession has also experienced an impressive growth in the
number of practitioners. James Feinerman (1987, p. 109) has observed a
'penetration of institutions manned by legal professionals into the lowest
levels of local government', where they mainly operate in the areas of
international commercial transactions, representation of criminal defend-
ants, and management of the domestic economy. This, however, has not
given them an independent professional status. China's highest juridical
authority is not a professional legal body, nor are legal proceedings
beyond the influence of the Party or the bureaucracy. Access to legal
practice is defined in loose terms, allowing people with a wide range of
educational backgrounds, including those with no formal legal training at
all, to be engaged in legal work. Furthermore, legal practitioners are
bound by their duties as state legal workers and are not able to operate
independently in their markets. All these restrictions have prevented the
emergence of an independent legal profession.

Economists are another group which in Western countries wields
considerable professional influence. Nina Halpern (1987) has shown that
Chinese economists have been able to influence political decision-making,
but her analysis also reveals that their situation has always been precarious. The economist Sun Yefang was able to voice his dissent and to
participate autonomously in economic debates with the political leadership in the early 1960s, but his limitations became evident when the
politician to whom he had submitted his professional criticisms of
government policies attacked him as 'the biggest revisionist in China' two
years later (ibid. p. 60). Even with a much wider definition of the term
'economist', Barbara Krug (1984, p. 40–67) concluded that there is no
autonomous role for them in the political environment of China's economic sector. All the quoted studies show that the influence of economists
has depended on the support of political patrons. The relatively autonomous and critical economic discussions during the mid-1980s are no
exception as they depended on the patronage of Zhao Ziyang (Hamrin
1992, p. 121). Nonetheless, Halpern (1992, p. 148) observes that pro-

fessional expertise has gained a stabilizing influence amidst political fluctuations, as 'the reliance upon expert advice and the use of such advice to counterbalance the authority of individual ministries appears more stable than the influence of any particular institution'.

Social scientists during the 1980s were able to establish new professional bodies, widen their scope of activities and embark on new areas of research. There are now several hundred research and study associations operating at provincial and central levels. Researchers are able to communicate through numerous conferences and publications (Watson 1987, p. 71ff). Scholarly activities flourished especially during the late 1980s when Party cells in social science academies and research institutes were not under unified coordination and control of research activities was left to the Party cells of the individual units. Central control of Party cells was re-established after 1989 and led to a reduction of research topics.[8]

Social science scholars doing research on foreign countries see themselves as potential innovators through their ability to absorb foreign experience for Chinese purposes. Their case provides an interesting example of how research is structured and how results are handled in a highly bureaucratized and politicized context.[9] In their evaluation, research based on officially approved projects generally has very little impact, with the exception of national key projects which receive large funding and which are meant to provide expertise for the leadership. An example is the 'one country, two systems' project undertaken during the Seventh Five Year Plan by the Fujian Academy of Social Sciences. Another channel for implementing research results is through unofficial contacts. The former director of the Institute for American Studies at the Chinese Academy of Social Sciences in Beijing explained to me that he had been able to present a memorandum to Deng Xiaoping recommending that scientific research institutes should be able to market their results[10]. These recommendations, inspired by his American expertise, were later incorporated into official policies. This success enabled him to extend his influence. A year before his death in summer 1991, he was preparing a campaign to lobby for a ministry-based shareholding system for state-owned enterprises. In anticipation of an enterprise reform he was planning to contact a number of ministries in Beijing and travel to major provinces to explain his ideas, which he would then present as an official recommendation. In this way he would ensure that he had already talked to most of the concerned parties and given them all the necessary information needed for their final consent. Although this is an individual case, it illustrates the informal structure in which professional expertise can be absorbed in the Chinese political system. Chinese and American researchers have discussed a research project to identify the few hundred persons and scholars who are able to operate in the fashion described above.[11]

The point illustrated by the above and other possible examples, such as the journalistic profession,[12] is the transitory state of professionalism in China. Materially, no occupational group with an intellectually based background has been able to secure an independent basis. Politically, all professionals have been subjected to political pressure directed towards intellectuals in general. In terms of professional influence, they have been dependent on a client relationship with individuals or groups within the political leadership. Thus, in a strict sense, none of the conditions for professionalism as it exists in the West have emerged yet. On the other hand, occupational groups have undeniably been able to achieve some autonomy within a diversified institutional framework. Professional organizations have started to publicly redefine and broaden the scope of professional expertise through links and co-operation among scientists and other groups, both nationally and internationally. Through research and policy advising for the administration, professionals have gained public acceptance for the use of their expertise. A diversifying institutional structure has enabled them to reduce their dependence on individual patrons within the administration (Suttmeier 1987, p. 151ff).

Outside this institutional set-up, there are several emerging groups with considerable occupational expertise which should be included here, although they are generally not considered in the context of professionalism. A group with common interests, common upbringing and a relatively coherent educational background is the sons and daughters of higher cadres: the 'princes' party' (or 'princes' clique') (taizi dang). The elder generation has already reached positions of power, with representatives such as Li Peng, Chen Yuan, Zou Jiahua and many others. The next generation has a much different outlook in that they have been able to make use of the connections of their fathers to gain access to work or study experience abroad, in joint ventures or in foreign enterprises in China. The concept of the taizi dang rests on limited scholarly research (e.g. Kane 1992; Rosen 1990) and anecdotal evidence readily obtainable in informal conversations in China. The group is characterized by their close connections to the leadership which provides them with important personal connections and with inside information on the bureaucratic apparatus, including advance information of personnel shifts, etc. Their educational and working background makes them familiar with Western, as well as with Chinese business practices, and thus gives them expertise which could make them indispensable, should they be able to operate in a less restrictive environment in China.

Another little-researched group is the 'compradors'. These are highly qualified Chinese mediators for Western companies operating in China. They have a background in the Chinese bureaucracy or personal connections with influential bureaucrats. They possess an intimate knowledge of the working of Chinese bureaucracies which they can make available to foreign partners who pay them. At the same time, they are conduits for the flow of expertise from foreign sources to the Chinese bureaucracy. They provide information about projects, foreign companies, technological questions etc. which cannot easily be obtained through official channels. These 'compradors', as they are sometimes called by their Western partners, are not an identifiable group in the sense that they have their own structures and organizations. Like lobbyists they operate individually, on the verge of what is officially acceptable and at the risk of falling out of grace with their counterparts in the Chinese bureaucracy. It seems justifiable to mention them in the context of the emerging professions as they fulfil at least part of the definitory conditions for professionals, namely, they possess specific skills and have acquired a market which gives them a degree of independence.

Another group are Chinese students and scholars living abroad and those who have returned from overseas studies and training (Hayhoe 1990, 1989). A large proportion of them are studying scientific and technical subjects, as the limited surveys suggest (Gu 1992, p. 57). The number of qualified people who for the time being have decided not to return to China is, even according to official Chinese statistics, larger than the number of those who have returned. Those who have returned to China have definitely not received the attention and gratification they were hoping for. Chinese universities and research institutes generally complain about working and living conditions, but one of their major problems is that they are unable to bridge the gap between China and what returned scholars have been used to in the West. The most important obstacle, however, seems to be that the returned scholars are generally not allowed to move into positions of responsibility which they consider commensurate with their skills and which would allow them to make use of their expertise. Their formal training, as well as their living experience in the West, makes it highly likely that they harbour strong ambitions to develop a technocratic role for themselves and their cohort.

Conclusion

If one applies a rigid definition, China is not an expertocracy or a techno-cracy. These terms presuppose a strong public role for groups with special professional expertise. The move away from mobilization towards a more predictable, bureaucratic and economically oriented form of governance is in itself not a sign of technocratic government, even though leadership positions have been filled with technically trained persons. Technocracy has been advanced as an ideological argument by intellectuals, but the Party has likewise been promoting a leading role for science and techno-logy. The provision of expert advice has not become institutionalized, and policy options and alternatives continue to be formulated more in the shifting interest of Party rule than by groups with special expertise.

Professionals have so far, only in very limited circumstances and then only with strong institutional backing, been able to emancipate themselves from the client relationship which binds them to their political patrons. They have been able to make increasing use of professional organizations to pursue their interests, but they still rely on political patronage to define the contents of their professional expertise, to be allowed to influence public opinion, and to improve their social and economic standing. In a diversifying economy they have found sources for improving their low private incomes, but market reforms have not reached a stage where the need to improve performance has produced a market for professional advice (Suttmeier 1987, p. 155).

The situation of Chinese professionals shows some similarities to the situation of professionals in the West before they finally established their autonomous status. While they depend on political patrons, the ruling elite, in turn, is increasingly forced to rely on professional expertise to fulfil social demands and to legitimise its own position. Expertocracy and professionalism are only emerging trends in China; they cannot be separated from political reforms. The fact that most developments in this direction have so far been halted on political grounds underlines this point.

Notes

1 The author wishes to acknowledge the support of the Academy of the Social Sciences in Australia, the Australian Research Council and Macquarie University for research visits to China.

2 The following definitions follow Fischer (1990, p. 17).

3 Lee speaks, in fact, of 'bureaucratic technocrats'.

4 For Fang Lizhi's views, see Fang (1989).

5 A similar case was made for the graduates of the French Ecole Poly-technique. See Carlisle (1974, p. 451).

6 For provincial figures see Lee (1991, p. 264, table 44).

7 Military professionalism as a different notion of professionalism falls outside the scope of this study, for this topic see Joffe (1967) and Jencks (1982).

8 According to interviews by the author in China in 1990.

9 Most of the information in this section is based on interviews conducted by the author in China in 1990 and 1991.

10 Interview by the author with Professor Li Guoyu, 1990.

11 This is based on a personal communication from Dr Huan Guocang, Princeton University.

12 For an interesting account of journalists in socialist countries see Curry (1990, chapter 1).

References

Bell, Daniel 1974, *The Coming of Post-Industrial Society*, Heinemann, London.

Buckley, Christopher 1991, 'Science as Politics and Politics as Science: Fang Lizhi and Chinese Intellectuals' Uncertain Road to Dissent', *The Australian Journal of Chinese Affairs*, no. 25, pp. 1–36.

Carlisle, Robert B. 1974, 'The Birth of Technocracy: Science, Society, and Saint-Simonians', *Journal of the History of Ideas*, vol. 35, no. 3, pp. 445–64.

Ch'i Hsi-sheng 1991, *Politics of Disillusionment—The Chinese Communist Party under Deng Xiaoping, 1978–1989*, M.E. Sharpe, New York & London.

Curry, Jane Leftwich 1990, *Poland's Journalists Professionalism and Politics*, Cambridge University Press, Cambridge.

Dittmer, Lowell 1987, 'Public and Private Interests and the Participatory Ethic in China', in *Citizens and Groups in Contemporary China*, ed. Victor C. Falkenheim, Center for Chinese Studies, The University of Michigan, Ann Arbor, pp. 17–44.

Falkenheim, Victor C. 1987, 'Citizens and Group Politics in China: An Introduction' in *Citizens and Groups in Contemporary China*, ed. Victor C. Falkenheim, Center for Chinese Studies, The University of Michigan, Ann Arbor, pp. 1-16.

Fang Lizhi 1989, *China im Umbruch* (China in Transition), ed. Helmut Martin, Siedler Verlag, Berlin.

Feinerman, James V. 1987, 'Law and Legal Professionalism in the People's Republic of China', in *China's Intellectuals and the State—In Search of a New Relationship*, eds Merle Goldman, Timothy Cheek & Carol Lee Harmin, Harvard University Press, Cambridge, Mass, pp. 107–28.

Fischer, Frank 1990, *Technocracy and the Politics of Expertise*, Sage Publications, London.

Goldman, Merle, Timothy Cheek & Carol Lee Hamrin eds 1987, *China's Intellectuals and the State—In Search of a New Relationship*, Harvard University Press, Cambridge, Mass.

Goodman, David S.G. ed. 1984, *Groups and Politics in the People's Republic of China*, M.E. Sharpe, Armonk, New York.

Gu Weiqun 1992, 'Political Attitudes of U.S.-Based Mainland Chinese Students and Scholars', *Issues and Studies*, vol. 28, no. 1, pp. 53–81.

Halpern, Nina 1987, 'Economists and Economic Policy-Making in the Early 1960s', in *China's Intellectuals and the State—In Search of a New Relationship*, eds Merle Goldman, Timothy Cheek & Carol Lee Hamrin, Harvard University Press, Cambridge, Mass, pp. 45–64.

——1992, 'Information Flows and Policy Coordination in the Chinese Bureaucracy', in *Bureaucracy, Politics and Decision Making in Post-Mao China*, eds Kenneth G. Lieberthal & David M. Lampton, University of California Press, Berkeley, pp. 125–48.

Hamrin, Carol Lee 1992, 'The Party Leadership System', in *Bureaucracy, Politics and Decision Making in Post-Mao China*, eds Kenneth G. Lieberthal & David M. Lampton, University of California Press, Berkeley, pp. 95–124.

Hayhoe, Ruth 1989, *China's Universities and the Open Door*, M.E. Sharpe, New York & OISE Press, Toronto.

——1990, 'China's Returned Scholars and the Democracy Movement', *China Quarterly*, no. 122, pp. 293–302.

Jencks, Harlan W. 1982, *From Muskets to Missiles: Politics and Professionalism in the Chinese Army, 1945–1981*, Westview Press, Boulder, Colorado.

Joffe, Ellis 1967, *Party and Army: Professionalism and Political Control in the Chinese Officer Corps, 1949–1964*, East Asian Research Center, Harvard University, Harvard University Press, Cambridge, Mass.

Kane, Daniel 1992, 'The Chinese Political and Intellectual Elite in the Year 2000', paper presented at the conference 'Towards the Year 2000: Socio-Economic Trends and Consequences in China', Asia Research Centre, Murdoch University, Western Australia.

Kelly, David & He Baogang 1992, 'Emergent Civil Society and the Intellectuals in China', in *The Development of Civil Society in Communist Systems*, ed. Robert Miller, Allen & Unwin, Sydney, pp. 24–39.

Konrad, George & Ivan Szelenyi 1979, *The Intellectuals on the Road to Class Power*, Harvester Press, Brighton.

Krug, Barbara 1984, 'The Economists in Chinese Politics', in *Groups and Politics in the People's Republic of China*, ed. David S.G. Goodman, M.E. Sharpe, Armonk, New York. pp. 40–67.

Larson, Magali Sarfatti 1977, *The Rise of Professionalism*, University of California Press, Berkeley.

Lee, Hong Yung 1983, 'China's 12th Central Committee—Rehabilitated Cadres and Technocrats', *Asian Survey*, vol. 23, no. 6, pp. 673–91.

——1991a, *From Revolutionary Cadres to Party Technocrats in Socialist China*, University of California Press, Berkeley.

——1991b, 'From Revolutionary Cadres to Bureaucratic Technocrats', in *Contemporary Chinese Politics in Historical Perspective*, ed. Brantly Womack, Cambridge University Press, Cambridge, pp. 180–206.

Li Cheng & Lynn T. White III 1988, 'The Thirteenth Central Committee of the Chinese Communist Party', *Asian Survey*, vol. 28, no. 4, pp. 371–99.

——1990, 'Elite Transformation and Modern Change in Mainland China and Taiwan: Empirical Data and the Theory of Technocracy', *China Quarterly*, no. 121, pp. 1–35.

——1991,'China's Technocratic Movement and the World Economic Herald', *Modern China*, vol. 17, no. 3, pp. 342–88.

Li Cheng & David Bachmann 1989, 'Localism, Elitism, and Immobilism: Elite Formation and Social Change in Post-Mao China', *World Politics*, vol. 42, no. 1, pp. 64–94.

Lieberthal, Kenneth G. & David M. Lampton eds 1992, *Bureaucracy, Politics and Decision Making in Post-Mao China*, University of California Press, Berkeley.

Medvedev, Roy 1975, *On Socialist Democracy*, Knopf, New York.

The New Encyclopedia Britannica 1989, vol. II, Encyclopedia Britannica, Chicago.

Rosen, Stanley 1990, 'The Communist Party and Chinese Society: Popular Attitudes Toward Party Membership and the Party's Image', *The Australian Journal of Chinese Affairs*, no. 24, pp. 51–92.

Rowney, Don K. 1989, *Transition to Technocracy—The Structural Origins of the Soviet Administrative State*, Cornell University Press, Ithaca & London.

Sautman, Barry 1991, 'Sirens of the Strongman: Neo-Authoritarianism in Recent Chinese Political Theory', *China Quarterly*, no. 192, pp. 72–102.

Savigear, P. 1971, 'Some Political Consequences of Technocracy', *Journal of European Studies*, vol. 1, no. 2, pp. 149–60.

Simon, Denis Fred 1987, 'China's Scientists and Technologists in the Post-Mao era: A Retrospective and Prospective Glimpse', in *China's Intellectuals and the State—In Search of a New Relationship*, eds Merle Goldman, Timothy Cheek & Carol Lee Harmin, Harvard University Press, Cambridge, Mass, pp. 129–55

Suttmeier, Richard P. 1987, 'Riding the Tiger: The Political Life of China's Scientists', in *Citizens and Groups in Contemporary China*, ed. Victor C. Falkenheim, Centre for Chinese Studies, The University of Michigan, Ann Arbor, pp. 123–58.

——1989,'Reform, Modernization, and the Changing Constitution of Science in China', *Asian Survey*, vol. 29, no. 10, pp. 999–1015.

Watson, Andrew 1987, 'Social Science Research and Economic Policy Formulation: The Academic Side of Economic Reform', in *New Directions in the Social Sciences and Humanities in China*, ed. Michael Yahuda, Macmillan, London, pp. 67–88.

Womack, Brantly ed. 1991, *Contemporary Chinese Politics in Historical Perspective*, Cambridge University Press, Cambridge.

Yahuda, Michael ed. 1987, *New Directions in the Social Sciences and Humanities in China*, Macmillan, London.

9 Revolution or corporatism? Workers and trade unions in post-Mao China[1]

Anita Chan

The Chinese workers' message to the authorities in the Beijing mass protest movement of 1989 was loud and clear—they were not satisfied with their lot. It came as a surprise to the intellectuals and students who had occupied centre stage during the upheavals that their 'own' movement could have aroused such a massive response from the workers.[2] But to the national authorities it was a nightmare come true. They had been alert to the frustrations of the Chinese workers and, with their own long-standing interests to defend after four decades of rule, they had grown fearful that the workers might one day turn against their own 'vanguard' (Chan 1991c, esp. pp. 123–9; Chan & Unger 1990b, pp. 78–81).

In 1980–81, not long after Deng Xiaoping and his team took power, a wave of strikes and agitation for the formation of autonomous trade unions swept China (Wilson 1990a). Whether by coincidence, by convergence or by contagion, this unrest had emerged around the same time as the Solidarity movement in Poland, the first successful workers' revolution in a workers' state, and one which aroused great consternation in the socialist world. Thereafter, China's Party leaders had sought to forestall any possible re-enactment of such a movement on Chinese soil.[3] Solidarity, of course, turned out to be a first death knell for the domino-like collapse of communism in Eastern Europe—and, as the Party had feared, in 1989 independent trade unions emerged in China.

There was another reason why the Party elite was alert to the potential threat posed by workers. Whereas most Chinese, and above all the younger generations, generally assumed that 1989 was the first time that Chinese workers had turned upon the Party in protest, the Party elite was painfully aware that this in fact was the fifth time that a portion of the

Chinese working class (at times led by the official trade unions) had asserted itself politically. This lack of knowledge about the earlier protests illustrates how successful the Party has been in controlling the Chinese people's knowledge of recent history,[4] skilfully down-playing and even obliterating any collective memory of the earlier confrontations.

The first conflict occurred immediately after Liberation, when the Communist trade unions, still genuinely representing workers' interests *vis-à-vis* the capitalists and the emerging Communist Party managers, lost out in a struggle for independence from the Party. The trade unions' defeat was signalled by the fall of the union chairman, Li Lisan (Harper 1969; Wilson 1986, p. 221), and the incident went down in popular memory as simply a power struggle among the Party's top leaders. The second conflict erupted in 1956–57 during the Hundred Flowers period. It ended with the imprisonment of workers and union activists[5] and the fall of Lai Ruoyu, the new chairman of the All-China Federation of Trade Unions (ACFTU), who was championing the notion of a more independent ACFTU. The agitation from the workers in this short period of liberalization was completely overshadowed in public memory by the rebelliousness of the intellectuals.[6] The third round of confrontation, this time accompanied by violence on a massive scale, occurred during the Cultural Revolution (1966–69). In terms of the number of people involved, the duration of the struggle, and the number of workers ultimately jailed or killed, it greatly surpassed the 1989 workers' movement. The workers' organizations that arose in 1967 as vehicles for articulating class interests reached a level of sophistication and independence tantamount to 'quasi-political parties' (Xi 1986, p. 14). Yet, in the popular image, the role of the workers is completely overshadowed by the sensationalism associated with the violence of the Red Guards. The fourth period of political confrontation arose when groups of workers took to Tiananmen Square in 1976 to commemorate Zhou Enlai's death. The activities of these workers were subsequently recorded in official histories, but the incident itself was interpreted as a popular rebellion against the tyranny of the Gang of Four, rather than as a movement that had any working-class content. The fifth cycle of confrontation occurred, of course, with the popular protest movement of 1989. Yet once again the role of the workers (and the trade unions) became subordinated in public consciousness to the high profile of the students. The government this time sought to condemn worker participants as unemployed vagrants and hooligans (Chan & Unger 1990a; Chan 1991d).

In this history of sporadic Chinese working-class movements and their recurrent alliance with Communist trade unions, sceptics would surely question whether workers and the official communist trade unions shared similar goals, or whether the trade unions had ever defended workers' rights *vis-à-vis* the Party. Very often, to be sure, the trade unions and their cadres have acted against workers' interests—corrupt, inefficient, ineffectual, functioning merely as an arm of enterprise administration, etc. However, this does not alter the fact that in both China and Eastern

Europe (on the latter, see Sabel & Stark 1982, pp. 444–6) the political structure of a one-party communist state is not totally monistic, and that a bureaucratic organization within it, just as in a pluralistic structure, seeks sometimes to assume its own separate identity. It can act in accordance with the institution's collective interests and/or its members' individual interests. In short, a bureaucratic politics is often at work.

If we recognize this model of a party–state with a multiplicity of bureaucratic interests, then it is easy to understand the logic behind the five conflictual episodes involving Chinese workers and, at times, trade unions. Each of the five upheavals occurred at times when the power of the party–state, for one reason or another, was weak, withdrawn, or internally divided. The first occasion was before the Party had fully consolidated its power; the second (1956–57) when the Party itself, under Mao's prodding, implemented political liberalization from above. Neither of these periods was marked by large-scale street actions (though there was considerable enterprise-level agitation in the second). In both periods, it was the ACFTU which took up the gauntlet. The ACFTU, though weak, played a leading role in trying to wrest some power for itself, and also to protect workers' interests from infringement by the party–state. But once crushed by the Communist Party in 1957–58, it was not able to re-emerge as a bureaucratic interest until more than twenty years later. In those intervening years the ACFTU was consigned to complete oblivion. For the first half of the 1970s it did not even exist as an institution. Thus the workers' upheavals of 1966–69 and 1976 were staged with only marginal involvement by the official trade unions. But like the two upheavals of the 1950s, these were also periods of weakened central control: in the Cultural Revolution, when Mao smashed the power of the Party; and in 1976, when Mao, the source of authority, was dying and the ruling oligarchy was split by internal strife.

During the 1980s, the ACFTU was allowed to reorganize itself. The party–state even granted the ACFTU a certain measure of power to protect workers' rights from being violated by the party–state itself, for reasons discussed below.

Unlike the previous four upheavals, the 1989 workers' movement was composed of two parts: ACFTU institutional agitation from above, and independent spontaneous protest from below.[7] Whether these two elements actually joined together, or whether they merely exhibited tendencies to move in the same direction, will be explored empirically in this chapter. Herein lies a key to the direction Chinese society might take in the 1990s. Before providing empirical evidence, however, I will place the analysis in a theoretical framework.

State corporatism and the ACFTU

For some time after the end of the Second World War, state corporatism was a discredited concept because it had been generally associated with

Fascistic political systems. Philippe C. Schmitter (1974) tried to revive the concept as a theoretical framework for a more general understanding of 20th century state structures, by identifying a variegated form of corporatism:

> Corporatism can be defined as a system of interest representation in which the constituent units are organized into a limited number of singular, compulsory, non-competitive, hierarchically ordered and functionally differentiated categories, recognized or licensed (if not created) by the state and granted a deliberate representational monopoly within their respective categories in exchange for observing certain controls on their selection of leaders and articulation demands and supports (p. 96).

Based on this definition, Schmitter tried to show that even pluralistic societies in the 20th century had evolved corporatist structures.

Daniel Chirot (1980) further developed the concept of corporatism, using Romania as a case study.[8] Chirot argued that communist one-party systems are one variant of corporatist states. The communist state created vertical functional institutions and placed them under central control, with the express purpose of pre-empting any horizontal coalescing of class interests (pp. 367–9). Workers in a communist party–state are not allowed to establish horizontal linkages freely. Their functional interests are to be channelled through the official trade union. In this schema, the differential interests within each corporate group are not recognized; enterprise managers and workers are assumed to have similar interests. This assumption is premised on the overriding socialist mission to which all interests are to adhere, subsumed under the ideological chieftainship of the national Party leadership.

This is to say, the implicit ideology of state corporatism recognizes conflictual societal interests, in that the very purpose of establishing a corporatist structure is to keep these interests under control. The logic of the argument is that whenever central party–state control loosens up, the corporate institutions will dysfunctionally strive to expand their own interests. So too, and worse yet from the vantage point of the Party leadership, class-based interests that had been suppressed would likewise take advantage of a more liberal atmosphere to resurface. In this respect, the brief history outlined above of the Chinese workers and the ACFTU constitutes no more than a classic manifestation of this constant tug-of-war among the three forces—the party–state, the ACFTU, and the workers— within a state corporatist structure.[9] We have, in fact, observed that the Maoist leadership, at once aware and irritated with this potential for jockeying, gradually abandoned the Leninist version of state corporatism after the events of the 1950s, to the point that the ACFTU was dissolved during the last decade of Mao's rule.

Before that, in the 1950s, and again under Deng in the 1980s and 1990s, the ACFTU, just like other official trade unions in the communist party– states, has served as one of the institutions of functional corporatist representation. Based on the generic Leninist 'transmission belt' imagery, in its ideal state of operation the ACFTU provides a two-way conduit between the party centre and the workers. The ACFTU is assigned two functions: by top-down transmission, mobilization of workers for labour production on behalf of the nation's collective good; and by bottom-up transmission, protection of workers' rights and interests. This dual characteristic, which Pravda and Ruble (1986) call 'classic dualism', is inherently contradictory. The party–state's pretence that the arrangement is workable stems from a pseudo-logic that wishes away any inherent conflict between the top and bottom hierarchies of the corporate institution. The reality is that under 'real socialism' an internal hierarchical conflict is always lurking beneath the surface, but because the state is so powerful the top-down transmission of party directives regularly suppresses the bottom-up transmissions relating to workers' interests. The result is a potentially explosive situation that recurrently threatens to burst forth.

The trade union as a transmission belt could play a shifting and occasionally pivotal role in this structure. It could—and this has been seen historically in China—choose to act out one of its ostensible missions, i.e. become an advocate on behalf of the workers, *in addition* to mobilizing labour for production, though any such attempts would inevitably end up being suppressed by the state. This dynamic of communist corporatism, with cyclical episodes of workers' explosions and suppression, abetted occasionally by portions of the trade union, was a pattern that is also familiar to the East European socialist states, particularly Poland.

There is a problem, though, with this model of communist state corporatism in that it is static, with a dynamic that moves cyclically in circles. Empirically, however, the dynamic actually moves in spirals. External factors and internal social developments effect changes in relations among the three main actors: the party–state, the official trade unions and the workers. As Pravda and Ruble (1986, p. 15) note of all communist countries:

> Over the last twenty years, and particularly over the last ten, a number of changes in the environment in which trade unions operate have placed increasing strains on Classic Dualism: changes in the composition of the workforce leading to more demanding memberships, shifts in the economic context shaping labour relations, and a deteriorating economic climate.

An expanded and better educated urban workforce inevitably led to a more powerful working class. The pressure it exerted from below increasingly forced the trade unions to fulfil their dualistic functions. In Eastern Europe the party–states, in order to salvage internal stability, gradually had to compromise by granting the unions and other corporatist representatives increased powers. In so doing, the party–state paradoxically undermined its own dominance over the corporatist edifice, which led again to an expansion in the power of the various corporatist interests, inducing the trade unions and the workers to behave at times in a syndicalist manner (Batt 1991, pp. 3–16). At the enterprise level, trade unions were obliged to become more participatory; at the national level, they played a more genuinely corporatist role (Pravda & Ruble, 1986, p. 20). However, at all levels the room to manoeuvre of both the workers and the official unions remained limited, and the conflictual situations were never fully resolved. The many 'trade union reforms' promulgated in these socialist states never went beyond the model of 'dualistic functions'. When the final implosion in the Soviet bloc came in 1989–90, the trade unions played an insignificant role—despite desperate efforts, for instance, by the official Polish trade union (OPZZ)(Ost 1990, pp. 185, 211) and its Soviet counterpart (AUCCTU)(Roundtable 1991, p. 22) to shed their 'transmission belt' functions and become genuine adversarial unions during the final countdown.

China, of course, shared in a workers' upheaval in 1989, and the liberal wing of the ACFTU tried to play a mediating role between the hard-line party elite and rebellious workers (Wilson 1990b, p. 60). Some ACFTU cadres even instigated and helped organize workers to stage protest actions (*Gongren Qilaile* 1990, pp. 99–109).[10] But most analysts of the movement have failed to note the workers as a powerful social force in 1989; and even the few scholars who have specifically pointed to the workers' role in the movement have not registered the significance of ACFTU's activities (Walder 1991; Wilson 1990b). Jeanne Wilson is practically the only Western scholar who, based on her study of the ACFTU, had become aware several years back that:

> Whatever the inherent tensions of the concept, the dual functioning role, should it actually be instituted in practice as well as articulated in theory, offers the Chinese trade union movement greater autonomy than it experienced in the Maoist era (Wilson 1986, p. 244).

Using a comparative perspective, Wilson was able to see that the ACFTU in the first half of the 1980s was beginning to play a more independent role, much like its counterparts in the Soviet Union and Eastern Europe. But she has not incorporated this concept of the changing dynamism of the ACFTU into her analysis of the 1989 movement.[11] In the second half of this chapter, I will argue that the ACFTU as a corporatist institution played a more significant role than recognized by Wilson. Based on this argument, I will attempt to hypothesize about the future developments of the ACFTU, its relationship with the Chinese working class, and the repercussions of this upon the future of the Chinese socialist system.

Economic reforms, workers and the ACFTU[12]

As noted above, in the Soviet Union and Eastern Europe the official trade unions, by fits and starts since the 1950s, had been more apt to defend workers' rights within the dual functioning model. This became possible with de-Stalinization and the implementation of half-hearted economic reforms, measures which were vehemently denounced by Mao as 'revisionism'. But when Deng came to power, Chinese 'revisionism' quickly surpassed Soviet-style 'revisionism' in the economic sphere, if not in the political. In no other socialist country, not even in Yugoslavia or Hungary, had marketization and devolution of economic decision-making powers to the enterprise managerial level gone as far as in China in the 1980s.

These new policies affected the workers in very specific ways: dramatic improvement in standards of living in the first half of the 1980s, leading to rising expectations, but beginning in the second half of the 1980s an erosion of incomes due to double-digit inflation, along with an erosion of fringe benefits, decreases in job security, etc. The thwarted rising expectations served as one of the causes of popular disaffection, leading to the protests of 1989. This has been dealt with in previous studies (Walder 1992; Wilson 1990b; Chan 1989; Yang 1991)[13] and does not need to be repeated here. What do need to be highlighted are phenomena that were specific to China under economic reform and were not found in the Soviet Union and Eastern European countries. These entailed, first, rapid income polarization among the different social sectors and within enterprises and, second, degenerating labour-management relations in enterprises as a result of rationalization of the production process and the emergence of Tayloristic management practices.

Anger by industrial workers with what was seen as 'unfair' differences in income distribution was causing severe incentive problems in the manufacturing industries by 1989.[14] Factory managers, private entrepreneurs in high-tech industries, self-employed merchants, corrupt officials, and wealthy peasants in suburban agricultural areas—in short, groups that were raking in incomes several times higher than an ordinary blue- or white-collar worker—were the targets of jealousy. But even income differentials that were only marginal, in the order of fifty per cent or at most double, could arouse great resentment so long as the reward structure was perceived as 'unfair'. Thus dyads such as intellectuals/ workers, state enterprise workers/foreign enterprise workers, workers in metropolitan areas/workers in the county towns, tenured workers/ contract workers, workers in money-making/money-losing workshops within the same enterprise—and the list goes on—pointed fingers at each other, complaining that the others were receiving an unfairly large income.[15] It was this kind of divisiveness that gave the authorities, especially the technocratic reform faction, the chance to denounce any expressions of dissatisfaction with income distribution, whether legitimate or unfounded, as caused by a discredited, remnant Maoist-era mentality of 'eating from the same big pot', undue 'egalitarianism', and infection by the 'red eye disease'. Such criticisms, dominating the mass media, relegated defenceless any claims for equity and social justice in a critical time of fundamental redistribution of the nation's wealth. It was not until after the 1989 movement that 'unfair distribution' was recognized officially as a problem that should be 'correctly understood', with Jiang Zemin calling on 'realization of social justice' as a goal of modernization.[16] So, whereas the revolutions in Eastern Europe and the Soviet Union were grassroot uprisings demanding economic and political liberalization, the 1989 upheaval in China was, to a large extent, a result of rapid marketization of the economy and, to a more limited extent, also due to liberalization in the political realm. The way in which these changes led to a new development of sectoral interests and, in this context, to a shift in the stance of the ACFTU will be discussed shortly.

A second important impact of economic liberalization on the workers was, as mentioned, the introduction of more Tayloristic management practices. Taylorism refers to management practices that attempt to rationalize, to 'make scientific', and to intensify the labour process so as to raise labour productivity. It implies a production process that is deskilling: the labourer's motor activities are controlled by the machine. Tayloristic management is seen as undemocratic and extractive, resulting in an antagonistic relationship between labour and management.[17] Thus when Howard and Howard (1989) describe the debate on 'scientific management' that emerged in China's academic and policy-making circles in the 1980s, Taylorism is counterposed against 'democratic management'.[18] The Chinese state has forced state enterprise managers to assume responsibility for the enterprises' gains and losses in exchange for managerial autonomy, achieved by curtailing the Party secretaries' administrative fiats. In turn, managers have shown a great inclination toward use of Tayloristic management techniques. Their measures include tightening labour discipline, imposing heavy penalties, raising production norms, and restructuring the award system. The situation for workers has been aggravated where managers have happened to be tactless, tyrannical, or partial, the changes bureaucratic and unreasonable, and worse yet if the factory director has been blatantly self-serving.[19] The latter half of the 1980s witnessed degenerating management–labour relations, and poor working conditions became one of the main causes of an increasing number of strikes.[20]

Under these rapidly changing conditions both in society and at the enterprise level, workers felt they were receiving short shrift in the new dispensation. In particular, Tayloristic management techniques which were originally meant for unskilled labour-intensive work today find their way most easily into the more labour-intensive industries in China. That is to say, the most exploitative kind of management practices in China are more commonly found in the small and medium-sized factories that are either collectively or privately owned. In some cases these factories are owned by Hong Kong, Taiwanese, or other foreign capitalists (Chan 1991a; Chan, Madsen & Unger 1992, chapters 11 & 12).[21] The sweat-shops that have mushroomed in county towns all over China, employing some

32.5 million people in 1989,[22] about a third of the entire industrial work-force, quite often seem like flashbacks to a 19th century Dickensian industrial revolution.[23] Many of the employees are erstwhile peasants (including children) employed on a temporary or seasonal basis. But despite the poor labour conditions, these mostly first-generation workers are not likely to form a rebellious social sector. Ability to gain access to any type of non-agricultural job is a rise in their station in life.[24]

The case is different with the urban workers in state-run or large collective enterprises. These tend to be second- or third-generation workers. Though their incomes and welfare benefits are better than those of the peasant workers, they are also considerably better educated and better informed, and hold feelings of 'relative deprivation' under the reforms, which continue to threaten their job security and welfare provisions. Working conditions are generally much better in the very large state enterprises, where the bureaucratic structure is well established and management is somewhat more constrained by the rules and regulations set down by the state.[25] But it is also in these enterprises that workers are more likely to harbour feelings of discontent.

It should be noted that while the level of China's economic development is still low and the percentage of industrial workers within the entire populace remains small, in absolute numbers the urban industrial work-force swelled to 70 million by 1986, an eighteenfold increase since 1949.[26] The urban industrial workers comprise a sizeable social force.

The state enterprises and large collectives tend to have more effectively functioning 'staff and workers representative councils' (*zhigong daibiao dahui*), and in these enterprises the grass roots trade unions are better staffed and organized, with greater resources to attend to workers' welfare, and perhaps even to encourage workers' rights.[27] In other words, it is in the state enterprises that the trade unions' dualistic functions could best be developed. At times of tight political control and production–mobilization campaigns they may side with the state and management to push through top-down policies. In politically relaxed and economically liberal times, they are given a chance (if they so choose) to transmit grass roots discontent upwards, or even to play an adversarial role against management—within limits. Given the right climate, trade unions can play a crucial role in the corporatist structure, where their allegiance can swing either way or both ways—and such a climate existed in the 1980s.

Civil society, social discourse and the articulation of sectoral interests

With economic liberalization and limited political liberalization beginning in the late 1970s in China, and with the retreat of central power and a relaxation of vertical control, a new economic structure emerged. Accompanying this, new social groups arose, and there was a proliferation of new group interests. Social groupings (from individuals and work units to bureaucratic organs) which felt they shared the same interests gradually established horizontal, autonomous, self-organizing relations. This is what a number of scholars have described as the emergence of 'civil society' in China (Kelly & He 1992; McCormick et al. 1992; Ostergaard 1989; Fung 1991);[28] though others are somewhat hesitant to acknowledge its existence (Tay 1992), or feel that the nascent civil society in China was nipped in the bud in the 1989 crack-down (Baum 1991). I would not want to enter into a debate on whether civil society exists in China today, but suffice it to say that an 'emergent' civil society can be seen as a sort of game in which neither state nor society is yet the winner.

The relationship between state and society can be framed from yet another angle. Lateral socio-economic associations of interest groups did emerge in China and continue to do so today, but their capacity for self-expression, and their self-identity, organizational cohesion and development are fraught with difficulties. Every time the state tightened the reins by launching a political campaign, such as the crack-down on the Democracy Wall Movement (1980–81), the Anti-Spiritual Pollution Campaign (1983–84), and in the aftermath of the Beijing massacre of 1989, these lateral relationships were weakened or were disbanded voluntarily or by force, only to spring to life again when the pressures receded. In such circumstances, establishment of a full-scale civil society can become an uphill battle that may even involve blood-letting. There is an alternative— by way of 'societal corporatism'.

Like state corporatism, which imposes organizational controls from above through state-created and state-controlled hierarchical institutions, societal corporatism is structured sectorally, but unlike state corporatism, it functions in a manner that represents grass roots interests.[29] In short, societal corporatism entails a form of interest-group politics. Thus voluntary associations, semi-official organizations, or even government organizations could group and regroup horizontally while endeavouring through the corporatist structure to further their own interests and the interests of their assigned constituencies. To a large extent, however, the existing corporatist structure stunts the maturation of horizontally formed class interests, which, as pointed out by Chirot (1980), is precisely what a state corporatist system is designed to pre-empt.

In the 1980s, three broad sectoral interests in Chinese society could be identified, revolving around the issues of industrialization and modernization:[30]

1 **The technocratic-managerial social engineers**. This group generally coincides with the groupings of enthusiastic economic 'reformers', and includes enterprise managers, 'reform'-oriented *nomenklatura* (Hong Yung Lee 1991), economists, well-known academics, 'high-level intellectuals', writers, journalists, etc. They claim that they have an economic formula (or formulae) to modernize China, and privately lambaste the workers for being lazy and being consumed by a dys-

functional 'egalitarianism'. Their social engineering plans for enterprise reforms are to empower the managers at the expense of the Party bureaucrats and, *vis-à-vis* the workers, to employ 'scientific management' techniques (Howard & Howard 1989). They have been able to project a popular image that the economic reforms they advocate are 'liberal' and 'democratic', and that they are the main force challenging the ossified, conservative and self-serving Party bureaucrats who obstruct changes.

An excellent article by Li Cheng and Lynn White forcefully argues, however, that this group of 'reformers' are technocrats, not democrats; that they tend to be more interested in democratic 'noises' than democratic 'values' (Li & White 1991, p. 374). In fact, the solutions they advocate are 'anti-democratic'. Some openly argue for a 'new authoritarianism', for 'elite politics' as opposed to 'democratic politics', or advocate a marriage of the 'knowledge elite' and the 'power elite'.[31] So organized, aggressive and influential has this group been in the 1980s that Li and White refer to it as a 'technocratic movement' (ibid.).

As technocrats both within and outside the bureaucratic structure, these social engineers possess the knowledge and skills to utilize the existing organizational structures and to work the political and bureaucratic systems to their own ends. To the extent allowed by the political climate of the time, they have aired their views vigorously in the print media (the *Shijie Jingji Daobao* (World Economic Herald) being the best known of the publications devoted to their perspective) and in the electronic media (a prime success was their ability to put *He Shang* on the air), or have organized seminars and conferences under private or official sponsorship.[32] To circumvent the stigma attached to 'private' organizations, when they set up private enterprises (be it in manufacturing, like the Stone Corporation, or a private research institute) they seek 'protection' from bureaucratic institutions. For instance, the famous Chinese Social Research Institute was 'hooked up' (*guagou*) with Zhao Ziyang's major think-tank, the Economic System Reform Research Institute (*Tigaisuo*). They are also very adept at making use of their membership in official organizations and of their connections; e.g. they have tried to promote their ideas through 'mass organizations' such as the Chinese Writers' Association or through the so-called democratic parties (*minzhu dangpai*), which have become equivalent to professional trade unions/professional associations/political interest groups all meshed into one,[33] and above all through the People's Congress structure or the prestigious Chinese People's Political Consultative Conference (CPPCC), both of which have a disproportionately high percentage of representation from intellectuals (Chan 1989, pp. 8–13). Joining them in the latter forum is the new *de facto* officially-sanctioned federation of capitalists, the All-China Federation of Industry and Commerce which, having gained a membership of half a million, was granted constituent membership in the CPPCC in 1986 (*Zhongguo Nianjian* 1986, p. 142).[34] Increasingly, as the Bureau of

Industry and Commerce and the private entrepreneurs find that their interests coincide, they band together *vis-à-vis* the state (Young 1991). An implicit alliance is emerging of the 'reform' faction of the elite (those with power), these new-born capitalists (those with money) and the technocratic intellectuals (those with know-how). Through the existing corporatist functional representation structure, these groups were able to exercise considerable influence in the power structure. In this social sector, a form of societal corporatism is helping to articulate sectoral interests.

2 **The conservative social engineers of the party** *nomenklatura*. This group had been much discredited in the 1980s in part because the language of reform that they used was far less radical and less effective than the one used by the reformers: hence, the qualifier, 'conservative'. Many of them had been victims of Mao's attack on 'revisionists', but their 'revisionism' had been comparatively mild. In the 1980s, they could be seen as the 'old' and 'established' power elite. But even this group was undergoing internal stress: infected by corruption, and/or radical 'revisionism', with the latter splitting off to join the 'reformers'. The cohesion of the group is also threatened by their separate bureaucratic interests. The most obvious example is the conflict between central government power and provincial power. They have been faced with three choices: to return to tyranny *à la* Mao; to grant society more freedom by giving the corporatist representatives more power, but stopping short of the point where the fundamental power structure would be threatened; or to forgo efforts to retain power, and divide up the spoils before their time is up.[35] In the 1980s, for those who chose to stay put, the second option seemed the most viable. For survival, this group wanted to maintain state corporatism, but even they realized that to avert upheaval they would need to allow two-way traffic through corporatist channels. (The octogenarian oligarch Peng Zhen has been a major exponent of this line.) The revolution that swept Eastern Europe at the end of 1989 has been an external source of strain to this group.

3 **The labouring classes—the socially engineered—and their allies**. This group includes the industrial workers and most of the white-collar workers. They are of course less educated than the technocrats and *nomenklatura* and their access to inside political knowledge is severely limited. Consequently, their influence by way of the existing political structure is minimal. The ACFTU is practically their only 'legitimate' functional representative. They have pitifully small representation in the People's Congress structure and the CPPCC. Of the 2970 delegates to the Seventh National People's Congress (NPC), 'worker and peasant' representatives together comprised only 23 per cent. This was a decided disadvantage at a time when political institutions such as the NPC were beginning to be granted some influence in the polity.[36] Worse yet, the 'worker-peasant' representatives were often successful factory managers eulogized as 'entrepreneurs', rural cadres, or self-made '10 000

yuan households' (Chan 1989, p. 82; Jacobs 1991, pp. 171–200).[37] In a state corporatist structure they could claim to represent workers and peasants but, very obviously, their interests are diametrically opposed to those of most of the workers and peasants. In this model of tripartite division, the latter groups are subordinated to the above two types of social engineers.

The workers are therefore left with the ACFTU, which, at least as defined by the official ideology, is officially sanctioned to operate partially in the interests of the workers. It shall be seen below how the ACFTU has acted on behalf of its assigned constituency. But throughout the 1980s the ACFTU was at best only a self-imposed ally, for the workers had not been persuaded that the ACFTU could indeed be a genuine corporatist representative of their interests.

During my field research in Beijing in 1991 I came to the realization that the workers also have other supporters and self-imposed allies. These are the intellectuals whose jobs relate to workers and trade unions. They include journalists who work for *Gongren ribao* (The Workers' Daily) or for the magazine *Shidai* (The Times), the ACFTU's journal during the 1980s;[38] academics who undertake research on workers; and teachers and students of the Gongyun Xueyuan (the Workers' Movement College), which trains trade-union cadres.[39] There are others whose jobs are not worker related, but who themselves had been workers for a number of years in the 1970s.[40] No 'intellectual star' has emerged from this group. Their writings reflect an advocacy of workers' interests, with the Workers' Movement College providing the theoretical base for the cause. The College, the ACFTU and groups at various levels of the union hierarchy have carried out repeated surveys to find out the attitudes of workers and to bolster their own arguments. Just as the technocratic social engineers are eager to introduce management techniques from the West, so do these workers' advocates eagerly learn about the organizations and workings of the trade unions of capitalist countries and of the Soviet Union and Eastern Europe. Their professional placement in the corporatist structure has influenced their attitudes and behaviour, much as the enterprise managers, under the economic reforms, have quickly taken on different sets of new attitudes and patterns of behaviour.

A question to confront is: how is it that these workers' advocates have been so unsuccessful in gaining the trust of their constituency? One factor is that there exists a gulf in everyday social contact and a gap in educational level. Ordinary workers are unlikely to read the articles and surveys about themselves that are laced with what seems meaningless jargon, and are unlikely to recognize subtleties in the ways in which the trade unions today are reinterpreting the fall of Li Lisan soon after Liberation. This raises the crucial question of social discourse in China, as an impediment to the ability of the workers' advocates to articulate an independent language and ideology that is morally acceptable and attractive to the workers.

The social discourse of the 1980s was dominated by the language of 'Reform', i.e. the language of the reforming social engineers. That this language could take the offensive and become 'morally correct' was due to the fact that the Marxist–Maoist language of discourse had been discredited. Urban society's vehement rejection of the Maoist economy and political tyranny has relegated the Marxist–Maoist ethos to a defenceless position, repugnant to many urban Chinese. Although the conservative social engineers would have wanted to retain parts of the language of Marxist–Maoist discourse, terms like 'the masses', 'the Party is the vanguard of the proletariat', or 'the working class is the most progressive class' etc. (for it was on the basis of this kind of language that they could lay claims to political legitimacy), they have found that reliance upon such rhetoric only backfires. Still, the conservative social engineers resist discarding the entire lexicon of Marxist–Maoist terminology. Terms like 'socialism', 'Marxism', the 'communist party' etc. have to be preserved, if only to provide a last line of defence against the inroads made by the languages of other ideologies. In their struggle with the reforming social engineers, terms like 'privatization', 'capitalism', or 'human rights' are branded as 'bourgeois liberalism', although in practice these have either been condoned (i.e. private ownership and capitalism), or the discourse of the 'bourgeoisie' has been implicitly accepted (e.g. in Chinese government proclamations on the issue of human rights).

Unfortunately for the workers, the Marxist–Maoist terminology which was so discredited in the 1980s is advantageous to their class positions. A Marxist concept like 'exploitation' that had been rendered unmentionable in the context of 'real socialism' suddenly assumes relevance with the introduction of the economic reforms. Unfortunately for the workers' advocates, who could finally use such language to express real content, this mode of terminology has been undermined and discredited by the reforming social engineers. It is the kind of language the conservative social engineers would have loved to wield, but even they have to use it sparingly and selectively. Faced with this terminology, the ordinary people (and Western scholars as well) must sometimes have found it difficult to distinguish the workers' advocates from the conservative ideologues.

A lexicon that to ordinary people has been reduced to meaningless rhetoric includes words like 'masses', 'socialist democracy', 'democratic centralism'—empty Maoist-era phrases that are sneered at and shunned by the reforming social engineers. Consider, then, the following passage from a book entitled *Socialist Democracy and Trade Union Participation in, and Discussion of, Politics* (Feng & Chang 1987), authored by two staff members from the Workers' Movement College and published by the Workers' Press. The following is extracted from the last two pages of the final chapter:

> The system of assigning grass roots union cadres is currently a vital issue affecting the trade unions' democratic principles. In the early

Fifties, the large majority of our unions' grass roots chairmen were elected by members of the masses. These union cadres had the trust and support of the masses, and even then [i.e., under pressure from the Party] were able to represent and listen to the opinion of the masses. But later the union cadre electoral system was replaced by the 'appointment system'.

[Today], the 'appointment system' is changed, and the 'electoral system' is genuinely being implemented. But in theory there is no breakthrough; in praxis, it cannot be seen as reform. It is no more than reviving the principle of democratic centralism that is set down in the union constitution. The 'appointment system' was a form of appropriation (*buoduo*) of the union members' fundamental rights.

Many trade union organs have come to the full realization that organizing the staff, workers and masses to represent and protect their interests, conforms to the basic demands and mission of the work of the trade unions. To achieve this, it is necessary to put into practice the principle of democracy. Eliminating the union cadre 'assignment system' has become an important part of the content of building up union organizations. Some Party and state organs have issued notices that they no longer recognize Party-assigned union chairmen and union cadres. Some Party and state organs have also sent out documents stating that they will no longer assign union cadres. But we should of course realize that this is only the beginning. The question of building up democracy in the union organs has only recently been brought up. Much as building up socialist democracy is a protracted and difficult task, so is the internal democratization of the trade union a protracted and difficult mission.

While sounding like appropriate language even to a Western ear, to many Chinese the rhetoric in which this quotation is couched resembles the type of sloganeering and ideological nonsense that for decades has filled Chinese books. Yet, on closer reading, several crucial issues can be detected below the surface of the language: the allusion to the fact that even going back to the 1950s is not enough; that real democracy rests with democratizing the trade union, and getting the Party off its back; that there is a possible struggle going on over this, and that some victory has been achieved; and that some people connected with the trade union (at least the two authors and like-minded souls) want the union to become a one-way bottom-to-top 'transmission belt' instead of having the 'traffic' of corporatist representation going both ways. The workers' advocates, too, like the reforming social engineers, understand the value that societal corporatism can bring to their political cause. The problem is the difficulty they have encountered in convincing the workers and ordinary people that they have their interests at heart.

In short, the workers' advocates are confronted with two crippling disabilities: first, the fact that their language of discourse has been placed on the defensive, and that even the constituencies they claim to represent sometimes have difficulty perceiving the real content of their rhetoric; and second, and worse yet, that they have sometimes been mistaken as ideologies working on behalf of the conservative social engineers. It is not unlikely, though, that these two groups will in fact become bed-fellows, albeit strange ones, if the reforming social engineers become politically dominant in the pursuit of marketization and privatization.

Reform from above: the ACFTU articulating corporatist interests

The ACFTU as a state corporatist institution (as opposed to some of its more radical members who advocate societal corporatism) and the conservative engineers realized that unless the ACFTU was allowed to reform itself so as to be able to represent workers' interests, even if only to a limited extent, a Chinese workers' Solidarity movement might emerge. To pre-empt the rise of an independent movement, the ACFTU did undergo a series of organizational reforms, though a detailed discussion of these warrants a separate paper.[41] What can be highlighted here are the aggressively unprecedented attempts by the ACFTU to share power with other bureaucracies in decisions on administrative matters and in drawing up new legislation pertaining to workers' interests.

In 1985, based on an ACFTU proposal, the State Council ordered that henceforth the Council itself and all relevant administrative organs would permit trade unions to take part in their meetings on matters relating to workers' interests (Wei 1990, pp. 2–4). In 1987, the ACFTU tendered to the State Council a whole series of proposals designed to protect workers' rights, including specific legislation to protect the welfare of the disadvantaged (ibid., p. 2). To counteract the erosion of standards of living by inflation, the ACFTU also proposed several times in the 1980s that incomes be indexed to inflation, but these suggestions were turned down by 'some economists', according to a member of the ACFTU executive committee.[42] At the enterprise level, the bureaucratic status of the trade-union chair has been elevated and, at least on paper, the staff-and-workers' councils have acquired an ill-defined 'supervisory' power over management. All these measures, though presently merely on paper, could in future conceivably have repercussions in a new configuration of rights and powers within the corporatist structure and within enterprises.

The ACFTU and workers' advocates channelled a lot of energy into fighting for an input in the drafting of legislation. The 1980s saw the promulgation of a whole series of new laws in response to the new economic situation. It was considered crucial at this juncture to intervene in the legislative process if workers and unions were not to lose out in the redistribution of power and resources.

Four laws were particularly relevant to the workers' future: the Enterprise Law, the Bankruptcy Law, the Trade Union Law, and the Labour Law. During the debates, and drafting and redrafting of these four laws, the ACFTU tried its best to interpose its views. Thus far the Enterprise Law and the Trade Union Law[43] have been passed—in 1988 and 1992 respectively. The Bankruptcy Bill has been tried out at test points, but its broader implementation has been repeatedly delayed.[44] The Trade Union Bill (before it was passed) and the Labour Bill were intensely debated for several years, and the very fact that the ACFTU continued to state how important it was that these laws should be promulgated as soon as possible, and what a pity it was that they had not, is an indication that there has existed a very strong lobby against their passage.[45] The intense struggle over the passage of these bills is clearly revealed in the report of a conference held by the ACFTU on the proposed Trade Union Law (*Gongren ribao* 9 December 1989):

> It is said that the 'Trade Union Law' is being redrafted. But for various reasons it has not been passed. The chairman of the legal advisory committee of the ACFTU said that some time back, due to the pervasive influence of bourgeois liberal trends of thought, the status of the working class had been slighted. Even the redrafting of the Trade Union Law had been affected. Now [after June 1989] that leading members of the Central Committee have reaffirmed their position of complete reliance on the working class and of going all out to exploit the function of the trade union, it is the most opportune time to redraft the Trade Union Law. We should go ahead with it without fail.

The language is coded, making it sound very much like official rhetoric. But, by reading between the lines, it is not difficult to detect the intense conflict that had gone on between the reforming social engineers and the workers' advocates. It is also quite obvious that before 1989 the workers' advocates and the ACFTU had been in a weak position to fight back.

The ACFTU was more successful with the passage of the Enterprise Law, which finally was enacted in 1988 after a decade of debate and intense lobbying from all sides. Never before had the details of intense debates and lobbying efforts during the gestation of a bill been revealed so vividly in the press (see e.g. *Gongren ribao* 16 April 1988, p. 3; *Renmin ribao* 14 April 1988, p. 4). The major issue in contention was which of the three—the enterprise Party secretary, the enterprise manager, or the workers' congress—should hold the ultimate power of authority. The law invested the enterprise manager with the great bulk of the power; but the ACFTU, after much lobbying, was able to make the following substantial amendments to the draft: that the status of the staff and workers as rhetorically the masters of the state is guaranteed; that the legal rights of the staff and workers are protected; that the workers have a right to submit criticisms of management cadres; that women workers enjoy specific labour protection; that the enterprise staff-and-workers' council holds the right to protect the welfare of the staff and workers, and the right to carry out its duties independently (*Gongren ribao*, 16 April 1988, p. 3; also Leung 1988, p. 121).

The views among many of the cadres of the ACFTU have become intense, even radical. According to an internal document released by the CCP's Beijing Municipal Committee Research Office in 1988 (*Diaocha yu Yanjiu* (Investigation and Research), no.5), during thirty forums organized by the city and the city-level union, there were suggestions by union cadres that they should be rid of such mundane duties as overseeing the social welfare of the workers on behalf of the enterprise management in order to free them up to concentrate on protecting workers' rights. Some suggested that union membership be voluntary, which would have meant terminating the unions' dual function, enabling them to become genuine adversarial unions. Some union cadres even wanted to dissociate themselves from the state's administrative structure, and in view of the rapid erosion of Party authority in enterprises, this would have meant a completely new ACFTU, a politically independent union reliant upon voluntary membership. Such voices within the ACFTU structure implied an advocacy of complete societal corporatism at the expense of state corporatism.

Articulation of grass roots interests

Unfortunately, these uphill battles fought by the ACFTU and the radical suggestions made behind closed doors went unregistered by ordinary workers. The ACFTU as a bureaucracy was weighed down by inertia, and grass roots trade-union cadres often have encountered a hostile management if and when they assumed an adversarial role. Workers are basically left with three options: to resort to go-slows and absenteeism etc.; to seek help from existing institutional channels such as the staff-and-workers' councils and the trade unions; or to set up alternative independent trade unions, which would mean violent confrontation with the state and mass arrests. Disillusioned and passive, the first option is definitely a popular choice at some enterprises. The second option seems viable to the workers in about a quarter of the enterprises. These tend to be large state enterprises with reasonably powerful trade unions and with staff and workers' councils; there exists in these enterprises an outlet for frustrations. In other words, a well-functioning state corporatist institution can alleviate the built-up social tensions in some workplaces—mostly the large state enterprises.

As to the third option, the alternative arose with the birth of 'autonomous trade unions' (*gongzilian*) throughout China during the two months of upheaval in 1989. The Beijing Autonomous Workers' Federation, the best organized and best known, did attract a sizeable number of supporters, but did not have enough time to expand and organize itself sufficiently before being crushed (Walder 1992; Chan 1991b). Staff and students of the Workers' Movement College participated in militant activities during this period. It is not clear whether very large numbers of workers and radical trade unionists would have taken this route as the most viable option had the crack-down not occurred; but at least some people risked their safety by going for the third option. Whether the vast bulk of the workforce would have ever joined their ranks is open to question, though; former movement activists have lamented the fact that the workers of Capital Steel and of other large state enterprises were not willing to come out in full support of the Beijing Autonomous Workers' Federation. One reason, I would argue, is that these workers, whatever their complaints about ineffectual unions, were more satisfied with the second option than is generally recognized.

The ACFTU played a role during the upheaval consistent with the stand it had taken over the previous decade. It leaned toward the side of the protest movement, while seeking to serve as a mediator between society and state. Workers who wanted to make use of the state corporatist channel called on the ACFTU to represent them in negotiations with Li Peng and Zhao Ziyang.[46] The ACFTU itself called on the protesters and the government to resolve the conflict through the constitutional process. It organized meetings between 'members of the Central Committee leadership' and 'workers of the capital'; and called on the government to consider the demands of the 'masses' (*Gongren ribao* 19 May 1989, p. 1). In so doing it was able to elevate its status as a representative of a sectoral interest.

In Shanghai, for instance, on 10 May the mayor and deputy mayor, 'braving pouring rain', went to the municipal trade union office to meet with the city trade union chairman (an unusual practice in bureaucratic etiquette; a subordinate goes to the office of a superior, not the reverse). There, the latter introduced to the mayor 'the situation of the workers, and told him that in some enterprises the workers' status has not reached that of the masters of the state, and that the level of workers' participation in management has not been satisfactory'. The union chairman presented a litany of demands. The meeting ended with the mayor 'agreeing that from now on issues raised by the trade union would be given serious consideration. As of now they should talk more about managers' dependence on the workers and masses in managing factories, and talk more about the importance of the working class in the enterprises' development'. The meeting closed with an eight-point pact, which amounted to a wholesale acceptance of the demands presented by the municipal trade union (*Gongren ribao* 13 May 1989, p. 1). The trade union leaders held a trump card, and they knew how to play it. Unlike their radical colleagues, they chose the state corporatist route. They were expanding their corporatist power by laying claims to representation of a restive social force.

The radical elements among the workers and from within the trade unions who rejected this solution of relying on the existing state corporatist institutions sought to set up the autonomous trade unions.[47] Inasmuch as very few of them ever demanded the formation of an independent political party, or a multi-party system, the existing political structure of a corporatist state was in fact their only viable option. But in so far as the new autonomous trade union was to be a voluntary institution representing a sectoral interest, these radicals were aiming for a form of societal corporatism.[48] Yet this was too radical a challenge to the party–state authorities. The movement was crushed in the aftermath of the Beijing massacre, with a ruthless brutality that was spared the students and intellectuals.

The party–state's concession to ACFTU corporatist interests

As the victory of the Shanghai trade union illustrates, the party–state was eager to make concessions to the ACFTU. After severely punishing those who had deviated too far out of line, the conservative social engineers, having defeated the technocratic reformers, set out to pacify the workers. They considered it better to continue to permit the ACFTU to reform and democratize itself rather than to annihilate it, as Mao had done twenty years earlier. The Marxist–Maoist language was revived (and at times ludicrously so, as in a revival of the 'Learn from Lei Feng' Campaign) but minus the orthodoxy that blatantly alienates the non-working classes. So, too, slogans such as 'talents managing the factory' or 'let a few people get rich first', which had been associated with Zhao Ziyang and his think-tanks, were denounced as a denigration of the workers. In their stead, slogans like 'workers are the masters of the nation', 'social justice', 'democratic management' etc., now appeared regularly in the press in an effort by the conservatives to woo back alienated workers. The 'ration-alization and restructuring policy' (youhua zuhe zhengce) which had disconcerted workers so much in the late 1980s was seen as no longer viable.[49] Leasing out of enterprises to individuals is being phased out, moreover.[50]

Although it has not been specified that managers no longer hold supreme command in enterprises, a new push for readjusting power relationships within enterprises has been implemented: the new model of 'the enterprise as a community of mutual interests' (qiye liyi gongtongti). This model is an attempt, at least rhetorically, to replace the Tayloristic scientific-management technique. Thus, instead of the previous 'con-tracting out of factories to an individual' (geren chengbao)—i.e., to the manager—the policy is to 'contract out to the entire workforce' (chuanyuan chengbao). The slogan, the 'enterprise as a community of mutual interests', embodies this form of 'responsibility system'.[51] The enterprise community is to be an autonomous economic entity responsible for its own profits and losses, and within it, manager and workers are to share equal power, rights and duties (*Qiye Liyi* 1989). This model aims to absorb workers' discontent and raise work incentives. Collective contracts are pushed hard by the authorities as a way to give workers more power in the wage bargaining process; a concession to alleviate the situation where the managers had become de facto 'bosses'. Concessions of this sort seem to be standard practices used by Communist governments to pacify workers' discontent. But policy is one thing; implementation is another. With successful devolution of power into the hands of factory managers for a number of years in the 1980s, it is not easy to persuade managers to share any of their power with the employees.[52]

After 1989 the ideas and language used by the conservative social engineers resembled even more than before those of the workers' advocates. Since the adversarial role played by the ACFTU in the 1989 movement has not left any impression on the ordinary workers, and with the strengthened position of the ACFTU since then, it becomes difficult in the popular mind to distinguish between these two sectoral groups. My reading of the situation, though, is that when people realize that the two are in fact only strange bed-fellows, the situation could well develop rapidly in new directions.

Theoretical implications and future scenarios

The conservative social engineers are caught in a catch-22 situation. Not only have they continued with the economic reforms in much the same manner as was advocated by the reformers, they have in addition allowed the ACFTU to continue to expand and consolidate its bureaucratic power and to make appeals to the interests of the workers. But the dynamics of this process of liberalization will reach a critical point when the work of the ACFTU and workers' advocates is recognized by their constituency. This point will crystallize when the existing vertical and emerging horizontal relationships of the ACFTU's structure succeed in reaching down to the grass roots level. So, too, a nascent protective legal structure is there on paper, delineating workers' rights; and more such legislation is in the pipeline. It is now up to the workers to recognize that they can make use of it to further their own interests. In other words, it is now up to workers to effect changes within the existing state corporatist structure, just as the technocratic-managerial reforming social engineers have been exploiting bureaucratic channels.

However, if this did happen in the 1990s, state corporatism as defined in the earlier section of this paper will have been changed in character. In this new development of state corporatism, sectoral interests would provide a linkage between the top and the factory floor, in its ideal form resembling societal corporatism. The difference would be one of origin: the former evolving from a top-down direction, and the latter, through a coalescing of horizontal interests, from the bottom upward.

On the other hand, if a democratized state corporatist system does not materialize in China in the coming decade, another social upheaval might occur. One possibility is a total collapse of central power, with the country plunged into chaos and with myriads of social groups rising up and resorting to violence.[53] Another possibility is that the conservatives will be able to control the situation before it plunges into turmoil, but from a position much weaker than in 1989. In such a circumstance, the con- servatives' need to change course for the sake of self-survival may supersede their will to dominate, and they may prefer to form an alliance with the workers and the workers' advocates against the technocratic reformers. Autonomous trade unions would be recognized and a genuine form of societal corporatism might emerge. But this form of societal corporatism would have evolved in circumstances very different from the societal corporatism (or neocorporatism) Schmitter describes as found in democratic societies. Thus, in terms of the origins of societal corporatism, two variants conceivably could exist: capitalist societal corporatism and socialist societal corporatism. The only precedent for socialist societal corporatism was the short period at the end of the 1980s when the Jaruzelski regime in Poland recognized the legal status of Solidarity as a trade union (Ost 1990, chapters 7 & 8), a new form of socialist governance that collapsed when Solidarity competed in the Parliamentary elections, effectively becoming a political party.[54]

There are other scenarios. The reformers in China may win out in a power struggle with the conservatives. The reform faction is itself a coalition between two types of reformers: the technocratic neo- authoritarians and the liberals. The former, modelling Chinese indus- trialization on the 'Four Little Dragons', would not be supporters of societal corporatism. At the most, they would grant the workers only marginally symbolic representation in a state corporatist structure. Some of the proponents of this group are now in exile, and their silence on the issue of workers' representation in their ideal 'pluralistic' political structure is an indication of their unwillingness to include the workers and the peasants in their 'democratic club'.[55]

If the liberal reformers win out in the struggle, there is the possibility of a more open system. Class interests would be permitted to be articulated. Might China then head the way of capitalist societal corporatism, with workers represented by a labour party, or would it go the road taken by, say, India? With the corruption and nepotism of the upper elite so entrenched, and China still in a Third World stage of development, the latter scenario seems more likely.

The final question is relevant regardless of which of the groups of social engineers wins out: in which of two directions is Chinese political development heading, toward a state corporatist structure or a societal corporatist structure? The recent developments in the former Soviet Union and Eastern Europe provide a possible benchmark. Neither the Chinese elite nor the populace want to see China plunged into the economic and political crises variously plaguing these post-communist countries. For this reason the Chinese conservatives are likely to continue with the renewed policy of gradually liberalizing so as to avert a socio-political explosion. The ACFTU too is learning from the fate of the official trade unions in the Soviet Union and Eastern Europe. The latter came to realize too late that it would have worked to their own advantage had they sided with the workers and dissociated themselves from the communist parties earlier. At the same time, though, the ACFTU should be able to see a glimmer of hope for its future. In the wake of the revolutions in these post-socialist countries, the only once-communist institutions which have been able to survive the confiscation of bureaucratic properties and even obtain some kind of grass roots support are the former official trade unions (Roundtable 1991). If the ACFTU tries hard enough to reach toward its own constituency it may yet succeed. The hope of the ACFTU leadership, and even the hope of conservative leaders, must be that the workers would not opt for militant action if they could help it, and that they would feel that exploiting the existing bureaucratic structure is possibly the most effective means to further their own class interests. It would be a case of evolution of the state corporatist structure, perhaps the least risky and tortuous route visible on the horizon toward worker representation.

Notes

1. I would like to thank the numerous people in Beijing who generously helped to locate informants for this study. My thanks are also due to Jiang Shu for his help in gathering documentary materials, Jonathan Unger for his helpful editing, the two editors of this volume David Goodman and Beverley Hooper, Bill Brugger, Elizabeth Perry and others for their constructive comments. My research trip to Beijing was partially funded by the ANU–Beijing University Scholarly Exchange Program.

2. Liu Binyan is one of the very few Chinese intellectuals who sees this gulf between the intellectuals and the workers. See Tim Nunn's report on Liu's addresses to the Smithsonian Institution and Columbia University (*China Now*, no. 136, 1991, p. 16).

3. Wilson (1990a) has detailed chronologically the effect the Solidarity movement had on Chinese rulers in the decade of the 1980s.

4. There is no space here to go into detail on how the Party was able successfully to distort post-Liberation history, and how the ruled have been susceptible to this manipulation. Readers interested in this line of argument might like to refer to my paper of 1992. For other examples, see Unger (1993).

5. Rebellious workers were imprisoned and sent to labour camps as 'bad elements', as a Party decree had declared that only errant 'intellectuals' could be labelled 'rightists'.

6   I am currently writing a book about the events of this period.

7   For a description of the activities of both the ACFTU and the workers see Wilson (1990b).

8   Other scholars have also argued that by the time of Brezhnev, the Soviet system could more appropriately be described as 'corporatist'. See Brunce and Echols (1980).

9   Readers should note that the concept of 'corporatism' used in this paper is very different from the definition used by Peter Lee (1991). The meaning of 'corporatism' embodied in that paper approximates 'corporatization', a term commonly employed by management studies to denote a process tending towards increasing enterprise-level identity and independence.

10 As yet there is no idea as to what extent the *nomenklatura* in the ACFTU supported the movement. An ACFTU official (someone who fled China after the Beijing massacre) reports that in his office more than half of the staff were supportive of the movement. Among them, the activists 'went out onto the streets and the Square to make speeches, distribute handouts, post up slogans, and send scripts to the Autonomous Workers' Federation's broadcasting station to be read to the public. Our purpose was to arouse the workers and peasants to make suggestions on how to promote democracy' (*Gongren Qilaile* 1990, p. 102).

11 Wilson (1990b) documents some of the independent activities of the ACFTU before and during the 1989 protest movement, but she has not specifically placed them within the framework she had used in her 1986 article.

12 These findings are drawn from a variety of sources, including: newspapers and magazines (1988–1991) directed at Chinese workers, such as *Gongren ribao* (Workers' Daily) and *Shidai* (Times), plus the ACFTU English journal *Chinese Trade Unions*; books on ACFTU history, handbooks for union cadres and textbooks for union cadre trainees; surveys and documents pertaining to Chinese workers' attitudes (1988–1991), printed for limited circulation and presented at academic, ACFTU and Beijing municipal government forums; and interviews with workers and union officials in 1991 in Beijing.

13 A paper by Yang Xiaodong (1991) is particularly interesting in its periodization of the people's declining enthusiasm toward the economic reforms from 1987 to 1989 in keeping with the declining standard of living. This article is of some significance because Yang, who was once a staff member of the 'privately-run' Chinese Social Survey System (which was affiliated with the influential Chinese Economic System Reform Research Institute), has based his analyses on surveys carried out by his office. According to Yang, in 1987 about 20 per cent of the urban population experienced an absolute decline in their standard of living (mostly affecting the lower-income groups), and the figure had jumped to 40 per cent by the middle of 1988.

[14] *Zhongguo xinwen,* (China News), 4 January 1989. The ACFTU reported that according to a survey of 210 000 employees at 400 enterprises in seventeen cities, workers' incentive had reached a nadir due to dissatisfaction with income spreads.

[15] For a more detailed discussion of the perception of the different social groups see Chan (1989).

[16] See *Qiaoshi,* no. 12, 1989 (also reprinted in *Renshi Zhengce Fagui Zhuankan* (Specialized Journal on Policies and Regulations Pertaining to Personnel), no. 10, 1989, pp. 2–7.

[17] It should be noted that this general understanding of Taylorism differs somewhat from 'Taylorism' as introduced by Frederick Taylor in the early twentieth century. When Taylor first campaigned for this new method of 'scientific management' he had argued from his scientific management experiments that the new method was not exploitative and extractive of the labourers' labour because it awarded according to productivity, and its intent was to bring about an identification of interests between workers and management. The result was to be harmonious worker–management relationships, management was not to 'drive the workers like slaves' (Taylor 1911).

[18] The Howards' article is one of the few that focuses on the labour process in Chinese factories. It outlines the debates on Taylorism among Chinese policy-makers and academics and hopefully can stimulate further research in the China field in the 'sociology of work'.

[19] For detailed examples of workers' dissatisfaction caused by enterprise restructuring see Rofel (1989) and Yang (1989).

[20] On the increasing number of strikes see Wilson (1990b, p. 59). In a speech by Ni Zhifu, the chairman of the ACFTU, Ni admitted that poor working conditions had become one of the causes of strikes. (*Chinese Trade Unions,* February 1989, p. 4). In a 1984 survey of workers' and enterprise cadres' attitudes, the two groups gave very different responses to the question as to what workers mainly were seeking in their work. To workers, 'good working conditions' topped the list, while 'high income and a high bonus' came only fourth. The cadres' perception of the workers' needs, on the other hand, placed 'high income and high bonuses' first, followed by good working conditions (see General Survey Team 1986, p. 295). It must be noted, though, that in 1985 inflation was not yet a serious problem, and the economic reforms in enterprises were just beginning, which probably accounts for workers' relative indifference to wage issues.

[21] According to a PRC reporter, the mistreatment of migrant labourers in the Special Economic Zone has become increasingly serious. See *Huangjin Shidai* (The Golden Age), April 1991, pp. 12–14.

[22] This figure comes under the column of 'industrial workers'. In addition there were 15.5 million 'construction workers' in the countryside. See National Statistical Bureau (1991, p. 13).

[23] My thanks to Zhu Xiaoyang for this information. Zhu helped direct an investigative survey (1987–89) of 135 county enterprises. Also see Keith Forster's (1990–1991) description of Wenzhou, the region in China hailed as a model for entrepreneurship.

[24] This rural-based industrial workforce was 31 million strong in 1986, and now much larger. Not surprisingly, almost none of these peasant-workers have a union branch to turn to. As of 1992, only 0.1 per cent of the rural enterprises contained unions (these tend to be the very largest rural factories, representing 3 per cent of the rural-based industrial workers). Moreover, only 8 per cent of the enterprises that are foreign-funded have union branches (*People's Daily* 28 April 1992.)

[25] Leung (1988, pp. 113–18) describes how at the Wuhan Steelworks the workplace union was democratically elected and held regular meetings. Yang's (1989) case study provides a good example of how in a medium-sized collectively owned printing factory, the trade union director fought with great difficulties on behalf of workers' wages.

[26] See *Zhongguo Gongyun Xueyuan Xuebao* (Chinese Workers' Movement Bulletin), no. 3, 1988, p. 51. It is not easy to ascertain the exact number of industrial workers in China because Chinese statistics tend to lump white-collar and blue-collar workers (*zhigong*) into one category. The figure I came across in this journal is not referenced.

[27] There is a general consensus among my informants in Beijing that trade unions are more assertive in state enterprises than in the collective enterprises. In fact, relatively few private rural factories and foreign-owned enterprises have unions on the premises. For example, among the foreign-owned enterprises in Guangdong Province, only 42 per cent contain unions (*Chinese Trade Unions*, no. 9, 1989, p. 23).

[28] For a more critical view of the usefulness of the concept of 'civil society' in understanding social development in China, see Chamberlain (1993).

[29] Like state corporatism, societal corporatism exists in a variety of forms. Schmitter (1983) calls it 'neocorporatism', which he sees as emerging out of pluralistic democratic state structures. Ost's (1989) reference to the Solidarity Movement as an attempt to establish a societal corporatist structure suggests another variant.

[30] By coincidence, this tripartite schema coincides broadly with that of Howards' (1989). Their categories are: the 'bird-cage faction' headed by Chen Yun; the radical reformers, including a sizeable proportion of the economists, social scientists, enterprise managers, industrial engineers etc.; and ordinary people who want a civil society, including an independent labour union.

[31] In this latter respect, their views are similar to those that Konrad and Szelenyi (1970) posited as the hidden agenda of East European intellectuals.

[32] One good example was a seminar held in 1983 to give a theoretical 'Marxist' prop to the issue of privatization (Christiansen 1989). While

in Kunming on a research trip in 1988, I was told that a local millionaire was in the process of sponsoring a conference to which many important intellectuals, among them Fang Lizhi, had been invited.

33 See chapter 7 of Seymour (1987), which describes the changing nature of the 'democratic parties' in the 1980s.

34 For case studies of how former capitalists have become influential today by holding multiple posts in the functional institutions, see *Beijing Review*, vol. 31, no. 39, 26 September 1988, pp. 22–4.

35 The flight of capital from China is a reflection of the vast amount that is being slipped into private pockets. By IMF statistics, in 1990 alone over $8 billion has not been accounted for in China's balance of payments. Another source says that $14 billion of export earnings never made it back to China. (*Associated Press*, 16 December 1991).

36 Readers who are skeptical of the increasingly important role played by NPC representatives should refer to O'Brien (1990).

37 For a detailed discussion of the gross malproportionment of seats in the People's Congress election system, see Jacobs (1991).

38 In August 1991 I was informed that this journal, which was not specifically directed at a workers' readership (though there were articles that appealed to workers' interests), would take on the title *Zhongguo gongren* (The Chinese Worker) as of January 1992. I interpret this name change to have some significance in that the ACFTU was trying to signal that the journal would in future appeal directly to workers' interests. In the 1950s *Zhongguo gongren* played a 'subversive' role and was forced to cease publication during the Anti-Rightist Campaign.

39 I have interviewed ten people in this category. Except for two academics whose work in a social science institute specifically related to management reforms in enterprises, the other eight all showed strong sympathy for the workers. All these interviews were arranged through personal contacts, introduced as a friend of friends. It is by no means a 'scientific' sample, of course, and there is certainly no dearth of people who care not the least for those they are researching and writing about. But a conclusion can definitely be made that among intellectuals whose jobs are worker related, there exists a group of people who are advocates for the workers' cause. A good illustration is provided by an off-hand statement made by a university academic who has been carrying out joint research projects with staff of the Workers' Movement College: he claimed that he had often come into disagreement with researchers from the College because the latter were always concerned to bring up questions pertaining to workers' democratic participation in enterprise management. He thought that as a scholar he himself should remain 'objective'.

40 In China, it is not unusual to find middle-aged intellectuals who were once peasants or workers, given that so many of that generation had been assigned to the countryside or factories during the 1970s.

41 Some of these reforms have been discussed by Wilson (1986, 1990b).

42 This was related to me in an interview I conducted with a member of the ACFTU Executive Committee at the ACFTU headquarters in Beijing in August 1991.

43 The Trade Union Law was passed in April 1992 (*People's Daily* 9 April 1992, p. 3).

44 For interesting details on how a reforming social engineer, Cao Siyuan, lobbied for the promulgation of the Bankruptcy Law, see *Zhongguo zhi Chun* (China Spring) June 1991, pp. 39–42.

45 This can be seen from a discussion paper written by a member of staff of the Chongqing Municipal Trade Union Policy Research Office for the 'Forum on Theoretical Issues Concerning the Working Class' held in 1991. [This document (not dated) was given to me by an academic who attended the conference.]

46 10 000 workers from an electronics factory signed such a petition. (*Gongren ribao* 18 May 1989, p. 1)

47 See a 1989 interview with a rebellious trade union official (*Gongren Qilaile* 1990, pp. 99–110).

48 For an analysis of why the Beijing Autonomous Workers' Federation limited itself to societal corporatism, see Chan (1991b).

49 This information came from an interview with a worker and another interview with two Chinese academic researchers on enterprise reforms. The 'rationalization' campaign disappeared from the press for a while after 1989.

50 This information was provided by an interview with ACFTU officials.

51 The stories of economically successful state enterprises reported in the media are usually enterprises which have attained a harmonious management–labour relationship after granting the staff and workers' council and the trade union participatory rights. For example, see *Shidai*, no. 1, 1991, pp. 2–5, on the success story of the Shanghai Iron Factory. Also see *Chinese Trade Unions*, no. 9, 1989, pp. 9–12, on the management's paternalistic treatment of workers in a plastics factory.

52 According to my interviews with ACFTU officials in August 1991, the ACFTU planned to push forward another model in early 1992. This was the model offered by the example of Teng County in Shandong, which had passed a regulation that all new policies introduced by enterprise management have to be passed by the staff and workers' councils.

53 This scenario is described in Walder (1991).

54 I am indebted to a discussion on corporatism held by the Sociology study group of the Research School of Social Sciences, ANU, for providing this insight.

55 A recent meeting with one of the leading members of this reforming elite confirmed this observation. This individual, in public, stone-walled my inquiries on the position occupied by the workers in his

group's scenario of the future. In private, he commented that my question was 'too controversial' (*jianrui*). I assume he was implying this was not the kind of issue that his grouping wanted to see broached.

References

Batt, Judy 1991, *East Central Europe from Reform to Transformation*, Royal Institute of International Affairs, London.

Baum, Richard 1991, 'The Paralysis of Power: Chinese Politics since Tiananmen', in *China Briefing: 1990–1991*, ed. William Joseph, Westview Press, Boulder.

Brunce, Valerie & John M. Echols III 1980, 'Soviet Politics in the Brezhnev Era: "Pluralism" or "Corporatism"', in *Soviet Politics in the Brezhnev Era*, ed. Donald Kelly, Praeger Press, New York, pp. 1–26.

Chamberlain, Heath B. 1993, 'On the Search for Civil Society in China', *Modern China*, vol. 19, no. 1, pp. 199–215.

Chan, Anita 1989, 'The Challenge to the Social Fabric', in *China at Forty: Mid–Life Crisis?*, ed. David S.G. Goodman & Gerald Segal, Clarendon Press, Oxford, pp. 66–85.

——1991a, 'PRC Workers Under "Capitalism with Chinese Characteristics"', *China Information*, vol. 5, no. 4, pp. 75–82.

——1991b, 'Workers in China and Poland: Comparing the 1989 Beijing Movement and the Solidarity Movement', unpublished paper presented at the Australasian Association for the Study of Socialist Countries, Melbourne.

——1991c, 'The Social Origins and Consequences of the Tiananmen Crisis', in *China in the Nineties: Crisis Management and Beyond*, eds David S.G. Goodman & Gerald Segal, Clarendon Press, Oxford, pp. 105–30.

——1991d, 'Protest in a Hunan County Town: The Profile of a Democracy Movement Activist in China's Backwaters', in *The Pro-Democracy Protests in China: Reports from the Provinces*, ed. Jonathan Unger, M.E. Sharpe, Armonk, New York, pp. 137–49.

——1992, 'Dispelling Misconceptions about the Red Guard Movement— The Necessity to Re-Examine Cultural Revolution Factionalism and Periodization', *Journal of Contemporary China*, vol. 1, no. 1, Princeton, pp. 61–85.

Chan, Anita & Jonathan Unger 1990a, 'Voices from the Protest Movement, Chongqing, Sichuan', *The Australian Journal of Chinese Affairs*, no. 24, pp. 257–79; also in Jonathan Unger ed. 1991, *The Pro-Democracy Protests in China: Reports from the Provinces*, M.E. Sharpe, Armonk, New York, pp. 106–26.

——1990b, 'China After Tiananmen', *The Nation*, vol. 250, no. 2, pp. 78–81.

Chan, Anita, Richard Madsen & Jonathan Unger 1992, *Chen Village Under Mao and Deng*, University of California Press, Berkeley.

CCP's Beijing Municipal Committee Research 1988, *Diaocha yu Yanjiu* (Investigation & Research), no. 5, 3 August.

Chirot, Daniel 1980, 'The Corporatist Model and Socialism', *Theory and Society*, no. 9, pp. 363–81.

Christiansen, Flemming 1989, 'The Justification of Private Enterprises in China, 1983–88', *China Information*, vol. 4, no. 2, pp. 78–91.

Feng Tongqing & Chang Kai 1987, *Shehuizhuyi Minzhu yu Gonghui Canzheng Yizheng* (Socialist Democracy and Trade Union Participation in, and Discussion of, Politics), Gongren Chubanshe (Workers' Press), Beijing.

Forster, Keith 1990–1991, 'The Wenzhou Model for Economic Development', *China Information*, vol. 5, no. 3, pp. 53–64.

Fung, Edmund 1991, 'China In Protest, Spring 1989', *Asia Studies Review*, vol. 15, no. 2, pp. 251–64.

Gongren Qilaile: Gongren Zizhi Lianhehui Yundong 1989 (The Workers Have Risen: The Workers Autonomous Federation Movement 1989), 1990, Hong Kong Trade Union Education Centre Press, Hong Kong.

Gongren ribao (Workers' Daily)

Harper, Paul F. 1969, 'The Party and Unions in Communist China', *China Quarterly*, no. 37, pp. 84–119.

Howard, Pat & Roger Howard 1989, 'China's Enterprise Management Reforms in the Eighties: Technocratic Versus Democratic Tendencies', paper presented at the international conference on 'China 40 Years After the Revolution' held at the Research Institute for Asia and Pacific of the University of Sydney.

Investigation Group of the Chinese Institute of Reform of the Economic System 1986, *Gaige: Women Mianlin de Tiaozhan yu Xuanze* (Reform: The Challenges and Options that Confront Us), Zhongguo Jingji Chubanshe, Beijing.

Jacobs, Bruce 1991, 'Elections in China', *The Australian Journal of Chinese Affairs*, no. 25, pp. 171–200.

Kelly, David & He Baogang 1992, 'Emergent Civil Society and the Intellectuals in China', in *The Development of Civil Society in Communist Systems*, ed. Robert F. Miller, Allen & Unwin, Sydney, pp. 24–39.

Konrad, George & Ivan Szelenyi 1970, *The Intellectuals on the Road to Class Power*, Harcourt Brace Jovanovich, New York.

Lee Hong Yung 1991, *From Revolutionary Cadres to Party Technocrats in Socialist China*, University of California Press, Berkeley.

Lee, Peter Non-shong 1991, 'The Chinese Industrial State in Historical Perspective: from Totalitarianism to Corporatism', in *Contemporary Chinese Politics in Historical Perspective*, ed. Brantly Womack, Cambridge University Press, Cambridge, pp. 153–79.

Leung Wing-yue 1988, *Smashing the Iron Rice Pot: Workers and Unions in China's Market Socialism*, Asia Monitor Resource Center, Hong Kong.

Li Cheng & Lynn T. White III 1991, 'China's Technocratic Movement and the World Economic Herald', *Modern China*, vol. 17, no. 3, pp. 342–88.

Lu Jianhua 1991, '"Chinese Workers" High Expectations of Enterprise Managers', *International Sociology*, vol. 6, no. 1, pp. 37–49.

McCormick, Barrett, Su Shaozhi & Xiao Xiaoming 1992, 'The 1989 Democracy Movement: A Review of the Prospects for Civil Society in China', *Pacific Affairs*, vol. 65, no. 2, pp. 182–202.

National Statistics Bureau (Social Statistics Sector) & Labour Bureau (General Planning Office) 1991, *Zhongguo Laodong Gongzi Tongji Nianjian 1990* (Chinese Labouring Wages Statistical Yearbook), Zhongguo tongji chubanshe, Beijing.

O'Brien, Kevin 1990, *Reform without Liberalization: China's National People's Congress and the Politics of Institutional Change*, Cambridge University Press, Cambridge.

Ost, David 1989, 'Towards a Corporatist Solution in Eastern Europe: The Case of Poland', *Eastern European Politics and Societies*, vol. 3, no. 1, pp. 152–74.

——1990, *Solidarity and the Politics of Anti-politics: Opposition and Reform in Poland since 1968*, Temple University Press, Philadelphia.

Ostergaard, Clemens Stubbe 1989, 'Citizens, Groups, and a Nascent Civil Society in China: Towards an Understanding of the 1989 Student Demonstrations', *China Information*, vol. 4, no. 2, pp. 28–41.

Pravda, Alex & Blair Ruble 1986, 'Communist Trade Unions: Varieties of Dualism', in *Trade Unions in Communist States*, eds Alex Pravda & Blair A. Ruble, Allen & Unwin, Boston, pp. 1–21.

Qiye Liyi Gongtongti Chutan (Preliminary Investigation into the Enterprise as a Community of Mutual Interest) 1989, Zhongguo renmin chubanshe (Chinese Workers' Press), Beijing.

Rofel, Lisa 1989, 'Hegemony and Productivity: Workers in Post-Mao China', in *Marxism and the Chinese Experience*, eds Arif Dirlik & Maurice Meisner, M.E. Sharpe, Armonk, New York, pp. 235–52.

Roundtable, 1991, 'Trade Unions in Post-Communist Society: The USSR Learns from Eastern Europe's Experience', *Report on the USSR*, vol. 3, no. 41, pp. 16–22.

Sabel, Charles F. & David Stark 1982, 'Planning, Politics, and Shop-Floor Power: Hidden Forms of Bargaining in Soviet-Imposed State-Socialist Societies', *Politics & Society*, vol. 11, no. 4, pp. 439–75.

Seymour, James D. 1987, *China's Satellite Parties*, M.E. Sharpe, Armonk, New York.

Schmitter, Philippe C. 1974, 'Still a Century of Corporatism?' in *Social-Political Structures in the Iberian World*, eds Frederick B. Pike & Thomas Stritch, University of Notre Dame Press, Notre Dame, pp. 85–130.

Shapiro, Judith & Liang Heng 1986, *Cold Winds, Warm Winds: Intellectual Life in China Today*, Wesleyan University Press, Middletown, Connecticut.

Tay, Alice 1992, 'The Role of Law in Democratic and Economic Reform in Leninist States', in *From Leninism to Freedom: The Challenges of Democratization*, ed. Margaret Latus Nugent, Westview Press, Boulder.

Taylor, Frederick Winslow 1911, *The Principles of Scientific Management*, Harper & Brothers Publishers, New York.

Unger, Jonathan ed. 1993, '*Using the Past to Serve the Present*': *Historiography and Politics in Contemporary China*, M.E. Sharpe, Armonk, New York.

Walder, Andrew G. 1989, 'Factory Manager in an Era of Reform', *China Quarterly*, no. 118, pp. 242–64.

——1991, 'Popular Protest in the Chinese Democracy Movement of 1989', Paper presented at the Comparative Social Analysis Workshop, UCLA March 1991, and the Regional China Seminar, Center for Chinese Studies, University of California, Berkeley, April 1991.

——1992, 'Workers, Managers, and the State: The Reform Era and the Political Crisis of 1989', *China Quarterly* , no. 127, pp. 467–92.

Wei Feng 1990, 'Chinese Trade Unions Make Press Progress in Participation', *Chinese Trade Unions*, November, pp. 2–4.

Wilson, Jeanne L. 1986, 'The People's Republic of China' in *Trade Union in Communist States*, eds Alex Pravda & Blair A. Ruble, Allen & Unwin, Boston, pp. 219–51.

——1990a, '"The Polish Lesson": China and Poland 1980-1990', *Studies in Comparative Communism*, vol. 23, no. 3/4, pp. 259–80.

——1990b, 'Labor Policy in China: Reform and Retrogression', *Problems of Communism*, vol. 39, no. 5, pp. 44–65.

Xi Guang 1986, 'Zhongguo Wenhua Dageming dui Shehuizhuyi Zhidu de tupuo' (The Chinese Cultural Revolution Raises the Socialist Structure to a Higher Plane), *Zhishifenzi* (The Intellectuals), no. 4, pp. 10–16.

Yang, Mayfair Mei-hui 1989, 'Between State and Society: The Construction of Corporateness in a Chinese Socialist Factory', *The Australian Journal of Chinese Affairs*, no. 22, pp. 31–62.

Yang Xiaodong 1991, 'Dashed Expectations: The Ten Years of Profound Social and Economic Changes in Communist China and Changes in Popular Opinion', *Mingbao Yuekan* (Mingbao Monthly), October, pp. 24–8.

Young, Susan, 1991, 'Private Business and the State in China's Reforming Economy', Working Paper Series of the Chinese Economy Research Unit, University of Adelaide.

Zhongguo Nianjian 1986 (Chinese Yearbook 1986), Xinhua Publishing Co., Beijing.

10 Prospects for civil society: a case study of Xiaoshan City[1]

Gordon White

'Civil society', 'the market' and 'democracy' are the conceptual 'good guys' that dominate current Western thinking about China's present and future in the social, economic and political realms respectively. Though these ideas are often used in imprecise and tendentious ways, they have considerable analytical and practical power; they reflect real processes and point toward real solutions. This chapter sets out to examine how useful the notion of 'civil society' is in describing and explaining social change in contemporary Chinese society. I shall proceed, first, by clarifying the specific way in which I intend to use the term 'civil society' and, second, by investigating the empirical utility of the idea through a case-study of one Chinese city.

'Civil society': a protean idea

It is worth considering why the term 'civil society' has come to prominence in general discourse about social and political change over the past decade. It is clearly part of a broader re-evaluation of the role of the state in society and the economy, a sociological adjunct to the conventional state–market paradigm familiar to economists and political scientists. At its vaguest level, 'civil society' reflects the desire to curb the power of overweening states through a sphere of social organizations enjoying more or less autonomy from the state. It is not surprising, therefore, that the term gained prominence following the rise of social movements against communist states in Eastern Europe in the late 1970s and early 1980s, particularly with the emergence of Solidarity in Poland. In

Hungary, it was given intellectual substance by Elemer Hankiss' notion of the 'second society'[2] and by an upsurge of theorizing about its role in socio-political change in Eastern Europe.[3] To the extent that the same problematic of changing state-society relations was important elsewhere in the real world, 'civil society' appeared as a convenient analytical 'hat-stand' in contexts as wide apart as sub-Saharan Africa and Taiwan.[4]

Given that the issue of overweening state power and the need to change the balance of power between state and society/economy through fundamental reforms have dominated thought about China for at least the last fifteen years, it is to be expected that the idea of 'civil society' has gained currency both within China and abroad.[5] The events of early to mid-1989 in China gave particularly strong impetus to scholarly use of the term, because of the widespread attempts then, in Beijing and in other cities, to construct a sphere of autonomous organizational space outside of and in opposition to the party–state.[6]

In analysis of China, as in the broader comparative literature, the term 'civil society' has been used to mean a variety of things. Underlying the often bewildering diversity, there are certain common elements. First, the use of 'civil society' reflects an attempt to define a type of relationship between state and society, regarding them as separable, distinct spheres roughly to be equated with the 'public' and 'private' spheres; second, it implies a certain power relationship between state and society such that there are limitations on the state's capacity to pervade and control society, and a certain power on the part of members of a society to insulate themselves from, and exert influence upon, the state; third, in this realm of autonomous social power and space, 'civil society' denotes an associational realm in which autonomous organizations are formed through voluntary association to represent the interests and aspirations of members of society.

In spite of these common elements, however, the term 'civil society' is commonly used, in the analysis of China and elsewhere, to denote two broad categories of meaning:

1 **'civil society' = 'political society'**. In this concept, following the tradition of liberal political theory embodied in theorists such as Locke and the historical evolution of liberal democracy in Western Europe and the USA, 'civil society' describes a particular type of political relationship between state and society based on the principles of citizenship, rights, representation and the rule of law.[7] In Chinese terms, 'civil society' in this sense would be translated as *gongmin shehui*; it would be a concern *par excellence* of political analysts; and it would focus squarely on the nature and feasibility of political democratization along liberal lines.

2 **'civil society' = intermediate social associations**. This draws loosely on the Hegelian notion of 'civil society' as in some sense intermediate between the state and the family[8] and refers to organizations and associations enjoying some autonomy *vis-à-vis* the state and formed

voluntarily by members of society for their own protection or self-interest. This broad 'intermediate' notion itself translates into three specific usages. 'Civil society' can connote

a **all social organizations**, whatever their nature, including 'uncivil' entities like the Mafia, 'primordial' nationalist or religious fundamentalist organizations, or kinship units from the nuclear family on up, as well as 'modern' organizations such as trade unions, chambers of commerce or professional associations. This usage essentially conflates 'civil society' with society and makes the term 'civil' redundant. In Chinese, this might translate roughly as *minjian shehui* (a usage common in Taiwan).

b **bourgeois society**, the sense in which it was used by Hegel and Marx (*bürgerliche Gesellschaft*) to denote the particular form of society which emerged with the growth of capitalism, rooted in an autonomous sphere of economic activity based on private property and regulated by markets.[9] As such, the institutions of 'civil society' are to be distinguished from 'affective institutions' based on kinship and from pre-capitalist forms of organization of the primordial *Gemeinschaft* kind. As such, 'civil society' is inextricably bound up with the notion not merely of capitalism but also of modernity, these two concepts being embodied in the term *bürgerliche Gesellschaft*.[10] The notion of 'bourgeois' or *bürgerliche* is also linked to the world of cities or towns since capitalism developed out of the particular environment created by late medieval towns. This finds expression in the Chinese translation of 'civil society' as *shimin shehui*. This concept of 'civil society' is more precise than the foregoing in that it directs attention to a specific type of social organization that arises symbiotically with the emergence of a market economy and a capitalist mode of production.

c **mass organizations** which arise in opposition to the state, the product of a contradiction between a dominating state and a dominated society. These are to be found in a particularly pure form in state–socialist contexts. Solidarity in Poland is a clear example, a social organization constituted through its opposition to state domination.[11] It is primarily to this kind of organization that writers are referring when they allude to the rise of 'civil society' in China in the context of the mass mobilizations of 1989. The nomenclature of these organizations is complex—they were variously called 'corps' (*dui*), 'societies' (*hui*), 'brigades' (*tuan*), 'alliances' (*lianhehui*), etc.—but they can be referred to collectively as 'citizens' groups' (*gongmin tuanti*), 'mass organizations' (*qunzhong tuanti*) or 'social organizations' (*shehui tuanti*).[12]

In retrospect, the Hundred Flowers Movement and the Cultural Revolution also contained strong elements of 'civil society' in this sense, and a comparison between the successive patterns of mass organization in these three movements would prove instructive.

As one can see by now, the use of the term 'civil society' involves both unanimity and confusion. However, if one is hoping to find the notion useful in understanding social change in contemporary China, something within the ambit of the second category, particularly sub-category (b), would appear to recommend itself. Unlike (1), it directs attention to an intermediate realm of organizational growth outside the realm of 'politics' proper. This may be 'non-political' in the short term, but it may play a cardinal role in the longer term evolution of the Chinese political system, in the sense that it provides the social underpinning for eventual democratization along the lines of (1).

Moreover, unlike mass organizations of an explicitly political kind— sub-category (c)—civil society organizations of type (b) have received inadequate attention in both Western and Chinese scholarship. It is my hypothesis that there is a close relationship between the spread of market relations and the differentiation of ownership brought about by the Chinese economic reforms on the one hand, and the rise of new forms of social organization and the adaptation of existing social organizations on the other. While this process is not isomorphic with the relationship between the rise of bourgeois civil society and the emergence of capitalism out of feudalism in Western societies, it does bear strong similarities in the sense that market-oriented economic reforms, be they 'socialist' or not, would bring about a radical transformation of the economy and its relationship with the state, with equally radical social and ultimately political repercussions. One can expect 'civil society' in the sense of a change in the balance of power between state and society in the latter's favour, a clearer separation between the spheres of 'public' and 'private', far greater scope for the expression of individual and group interests, and the ability of social interests and organizations to acquire greater autonomy from and influence over the state. In short, the central emphasis here is on 'civil society' as an organic accompaniment of the spread of market relations and the consequent emergence of a new realm of social organizations based on voluntary participation and enjoying some autonomy from the state.

Preliminary research at the national level has revealed that a new layer of just such organizations has in fact emerged in China, spontaneously or through state action or a mixture of both. I hypothesize that this process can be identified in two spheres. First, the socio-economic changes wrought by the reforms will bring pressures to change the behaviour of existing participatory organizations, such as the official 'mass organizations' that involve specific sectors of the population: e.g., the trade unions, the Women's Federation and the Communist Youth League. Here we would be looking for signs within the organization of a recognition of a changing environment, a redefinition of organizational goals, changes in organizational structures and modes of recruitment, and attempts to redefine the organization's relationship with its members, the Party and state authorities and society at large.

Second, I hypothesize that the new relationship between state and society emerging from the economic reforms and the resultant changes in social structure will provide space and impetus for the formation of new organizations of an associational character. The specific functions of these organizations will be: (a) to act as a new form of intermediary linkage between state and society that the state may attempt to control to varying degrees; (b) to represent and protect an increasingly atomized population in its relations with a still relatively monolithic state; (c) to provide means of co-ordination and co-operation to transcend the atomizing effect of markets; and (d) to defend sectors of the population against the instabilities, insecurities and inequalities of the market or to achieve sectional advantages therein.

It is with these issues in mind that this chapter will investigate the rise of the new 'intermediate organizations'. A number of questions suggest themselves: how did these organizations come into being (were they state-sponsored, spontaneous, or a mixture)?; how were they organized internally?; how do they relate to their own constituency and to other such organizations?; how much autonomy do they enjoy?; and how much influence do they exert in relation to the party–state? Also, to what extent are these organizations taking on an intermediate role between state and economy: between the plethora of state institutions charged with specific regulatory responsibilities on the one side, and the various constituents of a semi-reformed command economy on the other, be they individuals, households or enterprises? This latter concern reflects an interest on the part of the state, sparked by a proposal made by Xue Muqiao in 1988, that such intermediate organizations could become part of a new system of 'indirect' economic regulation: what could be called 'socialist corporatism'. In Xue's view, such organizations are valuable because they help to prevent the potential anarchy of the market and 'serve as a bridge between the state and the enterprises' (Xue 1988). If this were to transpire, the Chinese politico-economic nexus would more closely resemble certain of its capitalist East Asian neighbours—Japan, South Korea and Taiwan— whose pattern of development has been characterized by strong corporatist elements.[13]

The research site

The site chosen to examine such questions was Xiaoshan City in Zhejiang Province, a relatively rich area in the suburbs of Hangzhou municipality that developed rapidly during the 1980s through small-scale industry, commercial agriculture and production for export. Xiaoshan was converted from a county to a city in 1988 in recognition of these achievements and is known as one of China's 'ten great Gods of Wealth' (*shi da caishen*) counties, with a 'GLP' (Gross Local Product) per capita in 1990 of 2702 yuan. Out of the total population of 1.153 million in 1990, about 51 per cent was still classified as 'rural', though if one includes the agricultural population living in the urban areas (*chengzhen*), the total 'rural' population is much higher (87 per cent). In 1990, 654 000 people were listed as 'rural workers'. Of these, 37.1 per cent were working in industry and construction and a further 14.3 per cent in the tertiary sector. The agricultural sector produces grain, cotton, hemp and oil-seed, with a particular specialization in 'red hemp' (*hongma*) and silk-cocoons. Xiaoshan also has a historical reputation as a producer of poultry, dried radishes, silk and Chinese medicine, while new specialities have been developed recently, such as a variety of aquatic products, melons, milk, mushrooms, etc. The city's industry is also highly diversified, dominated by light industries producing watches, toys, textiles, hardware, clothing, artwork, paper and food products, with a rapidly expanding export sector. The city seems a suitable place for investigation, since it has developed rapidly over the past decade of economic reforms through a dual process of economic diversification and commercialization in both urban and rural sectors.

The research covered the period September 1990 to September 1991, with two field visits in March 1991 and May 1991. This entailed structured interviews according to a protocol agreed upon in advance, accompanied by the collection of background statistical materials on Xiaoshan in general and its social and mass organizations in particular.

The development of social organizations in Xiaoshan

There appears to have been a flowering of associational life in Xiaoshan County during the Republican period, but this could only be explored through a detailed historical study. The *Xiaoshan County Gazetteer* is brief and selective on the issue, mainly stressing organizations connected with the CCP, which was active in the area (*Xiaoshan xianzhi* 1987).[14] China's first peasant association was established there as early as 1921, and a peasant association continued to exist in the county until as late as 1965, when it was converted into a 'Poor and Lower-Middle Peasants' Association'. Trade unions were established by the CCP in 1927 and there were also numerous trade and religious organizations. After 1949, however, these organizations were either abolished or replaced. For example, the Federation of Industry and Commerce, established in 1919, was abolished and replaced by a new Association of Industry and Commerce in 1950. The Women's Federation was set up in 1951 as a successor to women's organizations that had existed since 1927, and the previous unions were replaced by a county branch of the General Trade Union Federation in 1950. A number of new associations were established in the 1950s, including the Handicraft Workers' Association in 1955, which ceased operation in 1966 with the onset of the Cultural Revolution; the Workers' and Labourers' Association in 1966 for workers in the private and collective sector, which also lapsed during the Cultural Revolution;

and the Science and Technology Association in 1957, which disappeared during the Cultural Revolution and was revived in 1980. To a greater or lesser degree these organizations shared a common characteristic: they were set up under the Party's initiative and largely functioned as Leninist 'transmission belts' between the Party and sectors of the population. With the possible exception of the immediate post-Liberation period, they did not enjoy any significant autonomy; the flow of power and influence was overwhelmingly top-down.

As can be seen from Table 10.1, the picture changed dramatically during the post-Mao era. New social organizations emerged, slowly in the early years but gathering pace after 1984, reaching a high point in 1988–89 and then declining drastically in 1990. The latter phenomenon can be attributed to the general tightening of political controls after Tiananmen, the consequent scrutiny and restructuring of some organizations, and the introduction of more detailed requirements for registration and supervision.

At the time of the survey in 1990, ninety-three social organizations that had come into being during the reform era were registered with the Social Organizations Registration Office of the city's Civil Affairs Bureau. Another six mass organizations had either existed before the reforms (the trade unions, the Women's Federation, the Communist Youth League and the Science and Technology Association) or, though established after the reforms began, were, like the preceding four organizations, under the direct leadership of the municipal Party committee (i.e., the Cultural and Arts Federation and the Overseas Chinese Federation).

The emergence of these organizations can be linked to the economic reforms in three broad senses. First, a process of accelerated social

Table 10.1: New social organizations established in Xiaoshan each year, 1979–1990

Type of Organiz- ation	1978	1979	1980	1981	1982	1983	1984	1985	1986	1987	1988	1989	Total 1990
Political	4					1	1		1		1		8
Economic							6	1	3	2	5	3	20
Science and Technology	3	3	3	1	7	5	4	2	4	3	4		342
Culture and Education								1	6	1		1	9
Sports							4	1			2	2	9
Health											2		2
Social Welfare											1		1
Religious						1					1		2
Friendly											2	1	3
Public Affairs											1	2	3
Total	4	3	3	3	1	8	17	7	12	7	18	13	399

differentiation has occurred in both city and countryside. This has been based on an increasing sectoral differentiation in the economy through growing specialization and through diversification of the ownership system, with the rapid spread of non-state economic institutions, notably township and village enterprises. Second, a process of decentralization or dispersion of power over economic resources has occurred as a consequence. Third, with the spread of market relations there has been an increasing atomization of economic agents and, in reaction, a growth in horizontal ties between them which cross the traditional vertical state-structured boundaries between sectors and areas.

More and more economic actors are now outside the old protective shells of the work unit, be it a state enterprise or an agricultural collective. But separation brings isolation, and decreased dependence brings increasing vulnerability. This generates both a greater consciousness of individual interests and greater awareness of the need to protect them in the context of pressures from both the state and the market. Since the individual economic agent is powerless against both the market and a still powerful state, there is a trend toward a recognition of a group interest (*quntide rentong*) and, in turn, pressure for a social organization (*shetuan*) to act on behalf of this group interest.

From the perspective of the party–state, too, there has been a recognition among reformers that in the new context of an increasingly marketized economy the old forms of control and regulation are increasingly ineffective and new organizational forms have become necessary, to bridge the gap between the state and economy and to act as a crucial agent on behalf of the state. It is not surprising, therefore, to find that the state has been the dominant force behind the establishment of new organizations. This is not merely a question of vertical control; in an economic context in which market relations rupture the old boundaries between 'systems', such organizations can play an important role, not merely in linking the state with the independent economic actors, but also in co-ordinating between different economic 'components' (e.g., forms of ownership) and different state departments. Individual state agencies not only find these organizations useful as an instrument of regulation and control over 'their' sectors of the economy, but also in facilitating communication and co-operation with other agencies (more on this below) in the context of a politico-economic system which is as yet semi-reformed—half-planned and half-market.

The nature and types of social organizations

What exactly are 'social organizations' (*shehui tuanti*)? Are they in some way different from the old-style mass organizations, and, if so, how? The official regulations issued by the Ministry of Civil Affairs in 1989 (Law concerning the Registration of Social Organizations) define them as 'mass organizations' (*qunzhong zuzhi*) and they were specifically prohibited from engaging in profit-making activities. The latter criterion distinguishes them from the plethora of new types of profit-making enterprises and companies which have emerged over the past dozen years, but it is hardly informative since it does not distinguish them from official 'mass organizations' (*Shehui Tuanti Guanli Shouce* 1990). They are generally seen as occupying an organizational space between a state organ proper and an enterprise, an intermediate position that gives them, in theory at least, some degree of formally recognized autonomy and status as a 'popular' (*minjian*) or 'people-run' (*minban*) organization as opposed to an 'official' (*guanban*) organization.

It is possible to classify social organizations, both old and new, according to their functions, under ten different headings:

Political: This category of organizations—which includes the General Trade Union Federation, the Communist Youth League, the Women's Federation, the Science and Technology Association, the Cultural and Arts Federation, the Overseas Chinese Federation, the Individual Labourers' Association and the Private Enterprises Association—primarily functions as an instrument of political–administrative regulation, mobilization, communication and control, and as 'transmission belts' linking the party–state with specific social groups, both old and new.

These institutions characteristically are organized hierarchically from the national level downwards; they are established on the initiative of the authorities; and their organizational structure is defined, their key personnel selected and their expenses provided by the government. As such, they function in ways similar to the 'old' mass organizations, bearing in mind that the role of the latter has changed during the reform era. Rather than functioning merely as instruments of political communication and control, they have had an opportunity to expand their 'mass' role in the sense of representing the interests of their members more effectively in relation to the party–state, broadening their activities, increasing their membership, and (in the case of the Women's Federation) encouraging the establishment of new social organizations to further the interests of their constituency.

The most effective among the 'old' mass organizations have been the trade unions, which began pushing for more autonomy in the mid-1980s under the impetus of higher levels of the organization. Locally, this has meant greater freedom in internal election procedures; a membership drive among township and village industries; publication of two periodicals (the *Xiaoshan Workers' Review* and the *Xiaoshan Workers' News*, though the latter was cancelled after 4 June 1989); and an opportunity to raise extra income through various revenue-generating activities, including a travel agency. It has also meant more influence within the local party–state structure (see below). The trade unions' expansion drive has brought them into conflict with two other 'old' mass organizations. The Women's Federation, under prompting from its national organization, has also sought to expand its membership by setting up its own basic-level organizations in government departments and enterprises. It was successful in setting up a branch in the city government organs, but its efforts to expand into enterprises brought it up against the trade unions which, unlike the Women's Federation, had substantial financial resources at their disposal (they receive 2 per cent of the total wage bill of an enterprise). The unions responded by establishing women-workers committees within their own enterprise organizations and argued that this was enough to safeguard the women's interests (the Women's Federation has a representative on this committee) but the issue is still a live one and is currently being negotiated by the city branches of the trade unions and the Women's Federation.

On another front, the Women's Federation has been more immediately successful. It has sought to reach out to the growing numbers of women (particularly rural women) who are working outside the home in small-scale enterprises or who are engaged in some specialized form of commercial agriculture or sideline. To lay an organizational base for this effort, the Federation has sought to establish branches at the city district (*qu*), township (*xiang*) and town (*zhen*) levels. Moreover, it has encouraged the establishment of two new organizations for working women: one, a women's individual business association (*nüde geti gongshang xiehui*) which plays a particular role at the village level; and two, an association of women factory directors (*nüchangzhang lianyihui*) for women managers in all types of enterprise, from state to household.

These examples suggest how the traditional mass organizations are attempting to seek greater independence and to find new roles for themselves, operating within the more permissive political environment of the 1980s up to 1989 and in response to the impact of rapid socio-economic changes on their own specific constituencies. To this extent, my first hypothesis about the breathing of new life into the traditional mass organizations does receive some support, notwithstanding the efforts by the post-Tiananmen leadership to bring them to heel.

This case is even stronger for the new social organizations within this category, most notably the Individual Labourers' Association and the Private Enterprises Association. There has been a systematic effort by the state (through State Council regulations) to incorporate and control these organizations: e.g., by controlling their leadership and finances or by making membership obligatory. But the organizational base rests on individuals and enterprises that control their own economic resources and that play a growing role in the local economy. As such, though the state may attempt to use the association to organize and control them, this can only have limited success. There is an ineluctable amount of compromise and give-and-take involved in the relationship—as such, they are in fact only 'semi-official' organizations, as will be shown below.

Economic: There were twenty of these organizations in Xiaoshan as of 1990, including sixteen engaged in agriculture, stock-breeding, industry and commerce, and four for quality management, enterprise management, economic information and consumer affairs. The membership of organizations that are based directly on production tend to be enterprises, and as a whole their activities are relatively specialized, being oriented toward exchanges of information, technology and management expertise and co-operation in the management of markets. Unlike the political organizations listed above, they do not play a role in representing the interests of a particular group (*qunti daibiao*) *vis-à-vis* the authorities (even the Consumers' Association only handles individual complaints and deals mostly with enterprises rather than government departments).

Science and technology: There are forty-two such associations in Xiaoshan, of which twenty-four are based on particular disciplines (such as the Construction and Accounting Associations), seven on specific skills (such as Standards-And-Measurement and the Abacus Association), and ten on specific topics of research (such as the Public Transport Study Association). Twenty-two of these associations deal with the natural sciences and twenty with the social sciences. The main functions of the organizations involve raising professional standards through regular exchanges of information, training, conferences, etc. Though they are professional associations in the sense that they are based on particular professions or specialized skills, they apparently do not (as yet) act as fully-fledged professional organizations (*zhiye zuzhi*) in the sense of representing a professional group interest (*zhiye liyi*) on behalf of their members.

As for the rest, there are nine **arts and culture** associations and nine **sports** associations; two **health** associations (the Qigong Research Association and the Old People's Exercise Association); two **social welfare** associations, including the Red Cross; two **religious** associations (the Catholic Patriotic Association and the Christian Association); **friendly** associations (*lianyi xiehui*), such as the Female Factory Managers' Friendly Association and the Retired Teachers' Association, which at present function mainly as social clubs; and **'public affairs'** associations, i.e., namely three family planning associations that are attached to the city bureaux of industry and commerce and to the family planning committee (see Table 10.1).

We can press our pursuit of 'civil society' by asking how much autonomy these organizations enjoy in relation to the party–state. A classification of social organizations in terms of their 'popular nature' (*minjianxing*) produces three categories—'official', 'semi-official' and 'purely popular'. The main leaders and work personnel of an 'official' (*guanban*) organization are appointed by a specific state agency as part of its official establishment (*bianzhi*) of posts, and its finances are either paid directly by the state or are subject to strict legal regulation. The six 'official' organizations in Xiaoshan—the General Trade Union Federation, the Communist Youth League, the Women's Federation, the Science and Technology Association, the Culture and Arts Federation and the Overseas Chinese Federation are distinctive in that they have a 'special' relationship with the Party. Their cadres are selected and appointed by the organization department of the city Party committee, with some important examples of 'double posting' (*jianzhi*) occurring between the Party and

Table 10.2: Types of social organization

	Official	Semi-official	Popular	Total
Political	6	2		8
Economic		20		20
Science and Technology		42		42
Culture and Education			9	9
Sports			9	9
Health			2	2
Social Welfare		1		1
Religious			2	2
Friendly		1	2	3
Public Affairs		3		3
Total	6	69	24	99

three of the key mass organizations: the chairman of the city Trade Union Federation is a member of the standing committee of the city Party committee; the director of the Women's Federation is a member of the city Party committee; and the head of the Science and Technology Association is a vice-secretary of the city Party committee.

In the case of a 'semi-official' (*banguan*) organization, the link with a state organization (administrative or other) is looser. Its main leaders hold concurrent posts in their sponsoring organization (which could, in turn, be an 'official' social organization) and its finances can come from either the state or its own revenue. Last, the 'purely popular' (*chun minjian*) social organization has no overlapping of personnel with its sponsoring state organization and depends on its own finances.

As Table 10.2 shows, the predominant type is 'semi-official', a category which includes all of the more important economic and professional associations which have emerged during the reform era. Since my primary interest here is these types of organizations, attention will be focused on the nature of the 'semi-official' social organizations in an attempt to assess their degree of autonomy from the state, their influence over the state, and the extent to which they play an intermediary role between the state and their membership in a new system of politico-economic regulation.

Relationships between social organizations and the state

This section looks at relations between the state and social organizations primarily from the state's perspective; in the next section this perspective will be inverted.

Although the impetus toward the formation of social organizations may come either from 'below' and 'above', to take on a regular organizational existence the social organization must receive official recognition from the state and must be subordinated to a network of state supervision. In Xiaoshan, the Poultry Raising Association, the Dried Turnip Association, the Poets Society and at least seven other organizations were formed by pressure from below. With the Private Enterprises Association, for example, pressure came from the private owners, who sent a representative to the Industrial and Commercial Management Bureau to raise the issue. Something similar seems to have occurred with the Individual Labourers' Association, which built itself upwards from basic branches. In both cases, however, the groups concerned were responding to national initiatives from the State Council, which had published documents calling upon them to organize themselves. By contrast, the Cement Industry Association was formed on the initiative of local officials who were concerned about the unco-ordinated growth of cement firms and saw an association as a useful way to bring order into the industry. The county Party secretary and a deputy secretary met with an official from the county's Economic Commission and then called a meeting with cement companies to get the association under way.

To receive official recognition, the social organization must receive approval from the state agency that regulates its sphere of operation (*zhuguan bumen*). It must then find a state organization to which it can be formally affiliated (*guikou* or *guakao danwei*) and then initiate an official registration procedure with the Civil Affairs Bureau. This set of formal procedures was not set fully in place in Xiaoshan until 1990. The framework of regulation had built up gradually from the early 1980s onwards as the utility of social organizations obtruded into the government's consciousness. It was given further impetus by the upheavals of early 1989 (Whiting 1989). The details of the procedures vary from region to region within China. Even in Xiaoshan the regulations are not clear: e.g., the distinction between 'departments in charge' (*zhuguan bumen*) and 'affiliated departments' (*guikou bumen*) is messy in practice and may include a variety of 'official' sponsoring institutions, not merely state administrative organs; such as corporations (*gongsi*) like the Foodstuffs Company or the Animal Products Company, and mass organizations like the Women's Federation or the Science and Technology Association, which is itself the 'department in charge' of fifty-six organizations in the social and natural sciences.

This process should not be seen merely as a means of control, since the nature of the department in charge and the affiliated unit are important to the well-being of the social organization. If the agency is well endowed and well situated, it can provide strong support to its affiliated social organization in terms of finance, materials, office space, connections and politico-administrative access. This is referred to as a 'support-drawing' relationship (*jiezhu guanxi*) (discussed later in the chapter). From the opposite perspective, moreover, an effective social organization may have many potential benefits for state agencies in helping carry out its regulatory responsibilities, by organizing the intermediate space between state and economic agents which the state organization cannot directly occupy itself. This distinct role means that it is counter-productive for a state organ to attempt to subordinate a social organization totally to its own control since the performance of the intermediary's mission requires a degree of autonomy. There is thus a role of complementarity between the state and social organizations, engendering a relationship which is to some degree co-operative rather than merely subordinate.

This relationship is cemented with the 'semi-official' social organizations through 'double posting'(*jianzhi*), whereby all or a portion of the leading positions in a social organization are filled by people who also hold formal positions in the department in charge or in an affiliated department. In the case of certain associations, all major posts are occupied in this intrusive fashion: e.g., the Individual Labourers' Association, the Private Enterprises Association and the Consumers' Association *vis-à-vis* the municipal Industrial and Commercial Management Bureau; the Enterprise Management Association and the Quality Management Association *vis-à-vis* the city's Economic Commission; the Agricultural Study Society *vis-à-vis* the Bureau of Agriculture; the Poultry Raising Association *vis-à-vis* the Foodstuffs Company; the Dried Turnip Association *vis-à-vis* the Local Products and Fruit Corporation; and the Rabbit Raising Association *vis-à-vis* the Animal Products Company. In the case of other, less important associations, this intersection of leadership is more limited, such as the Cement Industry Association and the Accountants' Association. In the case of certain sports and cultural associations, there is no intersection at all.

In general, as one might expect, the amount of direct organizational intersection between the state and a social organization (and in the case of 'official' organizations, between the Party and a social organization) varies in keeping with the perceived political and economic importance of the organization.

A social organization is supposed to provide a crucial communications channel between a state organ and the organization's members, thereby helping the state to get across ideological points or specific policies. Second, by bringing together otherwise unco-ordinated economic actors, a social organization can facilitate the state's management of, and policy implementation within, a given sector. For example, the local government has enlisted the aid of the Cement Industry Association in a drive to improve product quality across the local cement industry so as to increase its competitiveness with other districts. Third, associations take over or share certain specific functions formerly monopolized by state agencies. For instance, the Enterprise Management Association and the Quality Management Association share, with the enterprise management section of the city's Economic Commission, the task of upgrading and technically transforming enterprises. Or, as another example, the Individual Labourers' Association and the Private Enterprises Association help state agencies to evaluate the tax liabilities of member enterprises, to maintain health and safety standards, to implement the regulations concerning standards and measurements, etc.

Fourth, an association may bring together otherwise unrelated government agencies in ways which may benefit its members. This is achieved organizationally by the presence within an association's leadership of many of the relevant institutional parties, both governmental and non-governmental. One good example is the Private Enterprises Association. Fifteen of the twenty-five members of its administrative committee are private entrepreneurs while the other ten are representatives from the Industrial and Commercial Management Bureau, the Tax Bureau, the Public Security Bureau, the Land Administration Bureau, the Electricity Bureau and the Township and Village Industry Management Bureau. This enables a range of questions central to the development of the private sector to be addressed across administrative boundaries.

Thus in Xiaoshan the two sets of organizations—state and social—are acting as complementary parts of an evolving new network of management. Though there are conflicts between and within levels, this organizational arrangement rests on certain common interests shared by the state's economic organs on the one side and the members of the associations on the other. At the deepest level, there is a common interest in the development of the local economy in competition with localities elsewhere in China. There is also a common interest in handling multiple conflicts of interest between the state and its economic agents, among state agencies with overlapping responsibilities, among economic actors in a specific sphere and between them and actors in other sectors or regions. There is a common interest also in managing emerging markets so as to minimize damaging fluctuations, bottle-necks and informational shortages. As such, the state–social organizational nexus embodies both complementarities and conflicts and represents the emergence of a dualistic mechanism of institutional integration, parallel with and in response to the emergence of an increasingly dualistic economy.

This integration is both vertical and horizontal: vertical in that the state and an increasingly disparate economic structure are brought together through the intermediation of a social organization, and horizontal in that a social organization can act to bring together both the scattered elements within a complex economic field and the unco-ordinated state agencies which may be involved in that field. Given the realities of China's semi-reformed economy, if such an organizational nexus (and the role of the social organization within it) did not exist, it would have to be speedily invented.

The role of social organizations in representing social interests and influencing government

The relationship between a social organization and its membership varies a great deal according to the type of organization and its specific functions. In some organizations, membership is voluntary, such as various hobby or special interest associations. In others, it is legally compulsory, such as in the Individual Labourers' Association, in which self-employed workers automatically become members when they are issued business permits. The Private Enterprises Association operates along the same lines. In other organizations, notably trade associations (*hangye xiehui* or just *hanghui*), membership is formally not compulsory but pressures may be brought to bear on potential members to make them join. Alternatively, in some trade associations, such as the Poultry Raising Association, membership is used as a control device to exclude new entrants to the market in the manner of a guild.

Where constituents, be they individuals or enterprises, have an element of choice, they can calculate the costs and benefits of membership. With regard to the trade associations, for example, there are certain costs in not participating. In the case of the Cement Industry Association, all sixteen of the cement factories in Xiaoshan joined not only the Xiaoshan association but also higher-level associations for Hangzhou City and Zhejiang Province. Some of them did this with reluctance, but as far as Xiaoshan was concerned, the local government was intent on rationalizing and upgrading the industry, and enterprises were subject to a three-line whip. The reason they joined the higher-level associations, however, reflected the fact that the latter were involved in the process of upgrading cement enterprises, a process which brought substantial benefits to the enterprise concerned. Indeed, membership in not just one but in a number of conveniently situated associations may bring a wider range of benefits to the participating enterprise.

'Famous' enterprises may be courted by associations seeking prestigious members, particularly higher-level associations. One such enterprise in Xiaoshan, a rural township firm which produces spare-parts for vehicles, is a member of the local Science and Technology Association, but also the Chinese Public Bus Association, the Chinese Factory Directors' and Managers' Research Association, and the China Joint Automobile Association. Moreover, some individuals in the firm were themselves members of other associations: e.g., its director was a member of the standing committee of the council of the Chinese Enterprise Management Association and vice-secretary of the Chinese Peasant Entrepreneurs' Association. Clearly an enterprise of this calibre can afford to pick and choose its associations; in fact, this plant had already left several associations which it did not find useful. But membership, particularly in the national associations, did bring its benefits. As one of the firm's officials remarked, 'One advantage of belonging to associations is that it means you must be quite a good enterprise and known to be operating well. For example, to be in the Chinese Enterprise Management Association means you must be good'.

In the context of a semi-reformed economy in which economic relationships are highly politicized and the power of the state is still massive, clearly the greatest potential advantage in joining an economic association is as a channel of access to the government (and the Party) and to the favours that only government can dispense. For example, leaders of official mass organizations cite improvements in their direct access to the local Party leadership as one of the achievements of the reform era. Such access, for example, means that an organization can 'issue orders through a different bugle' (*jiehao faling*), as the chairman of the Science and Technology Association put it. The director of the Women's Federation argued that 'to get as close as possible to the city Party committee is exactly what we want for the sake of women's interests and to improve their status'.

Members of economic associations hold hopes that their association can act as a broker between them and the state in dealing with business problems. One businessperson referred to this triadic relationship in familial terms, from the perspective of a woman married into another household: the association is the 'mother's home' (*niangjia*) while the state is the 'home of the husband's mother' (*popojia*), a distinction which carries with it differences in intimacy/distance, friendliness/hostility, support/control and weakness/strength. The vice-director of an urban private enterprise went even further:

> This factory wanted the Xiaoshan City government to form an association. An association can help out an enterprise like mine through its 'connections' (*guanxi*). If you have problems, the association can help you contact government departments. Private enterprises don't have their own government department, so they see the association as playing this role. They feel as if they have no 'parents'. We're not like a village enterprise which can lean on the village leadership. So we would like the Private Enterprises Association to become a government department or for the government to create a department which takes care of the interests of private enterprises.

The power of an association in this 'support-drawing relationship' (*jiezhu guanxi*) is partly, as noted, institutionalized through overlapping leaderships between the association and its in-charge department and the relevant affiliated (and therefore potentially useful) government agencies. These formal relationships not only bring new opportunities for formal access to the state via the association, but also open up opportunities for informal 'connections' (*guanxi*) with individual state personnel. Extra efforts are made to mobilize connections by inviting retired government cadres from relevant state agencies to work in the association in order to make use of their personal relations. For members of an association, it may open up a new arena within which to form a 'relational network' (*guanxiwang*) involving other members of the association, leaders of the association and influential officials.[15] This can complement the pre-existing networks they had been using to facilitate their business and can be parleyed to good effect in contexts outside the ambit of the association.

An especially obvious advantage of a trade association is where the state is a total or partial monopsonist of the goods produced by its members. A case in point is the Poultry Raising Association, which is able to negotiate on behalf of its members with the state Foodstuffs Company, which buys a large percentage of their produce (e.g., 95 per cent of duck eggs were sold this way in 1991). Fluctuations in the free market price of duck eggs have caused problems for both the Foodstuffs Company and the producers (mostly specialized households) who lock themselves into contracts before the point of sale. In 1984, for example, the contract price turned out to be lower than the free market price at the time of delivery. Some producers ignored the contracts and began to sell eggs on the open market. The state called in the Poultry Raising Association to help persuade recalcitrant members to meet their contractual obligations. In the following year, the situation was reversed as the market price fell below the contractual price and the Poultry Raising Association intervened to persuade the Foodstuffs Company and other state purchasers to respect the original contract price. Though the result was a compromise, duck egg producers still received a guaranteed price which more than covered their costs (0.988 yuan as opposed to 0.96 yuan per kilo) whereas the market price (0.95 yuan) would have led to losses. In this case, the Foodstuffs Company tried to recoup some of its own losses by selling to other areas where prices were higher. Another case is that of the Cement Industry Association which intervened in 1989 in a situation where the price of cement sold to priority local enterprises was being set below average production costs (150 yuan and 190 yuan per ton respectively) by the local Commodity Price Bureau. Member enterprises complained to the Cement Industry Association, which contacted relevant government agencies and sent a formal report to the Commodity Price Bureau suggesting that the stipulated price should cover production costs. Again the result was a compromise—the price was raised (to 177 yuan per ton), still below production costs.

Leaders of both associations and enterprises cited many other examples of this kind of assistance, along with a long list of other economic and technical services which trade associations had provided for their members. Underneath all this, however, one senses that a trade association is like a double-edged sword, with the state edge being considerably sharper than the members' edge. In interviews with both leaders and members of trade associations, however, the leaders seemed more inclined to be up-beat about their association by emphasizing its achievements in its relations with the state and its overall usefulness to members, while the members seemed inclined to be more dismissive, believing that their association had only been able to help them with relatively minor problems. The major problems facing enterprises in the non-state sector—those of procuring raw materials, securing bank credits and finding markets—are matters for which they must largely rely upon their own devices, particularly their personal connections with officials in the relevant departments.

While the organizations nonetheless are able to be of benefit to their members by drawing resources from the state, are they at all able to exert positive influence on state agencies and sway policy in favour of their members? Clearly the leaders of some of the official mass organizations— notably the trade unions and to a lesser extent the Women's Federation— feel that their power increased during the 1980s. This was by no means true across the board: e.g., the Communist Youth League had virtually been abandoned by the Party and had sought a new role as a politically insignificant, mainly sports and entertainment organization. League cadres confessed that they felt neglected by the Party, like children abandoned by adults. The League did not know which way to turn, since few young people wanted to join the organization any longer. By contrast, officials of the Xiaoshan General Trade Union pointed proudly to the fact that there was now a trade union representative on the city Party committee's standing committee, which had not been the case until very recently. Moreover, for the first time ever in May 1991, the union was holding a joint meeting with the city government to discuss issues of common concern, and it was hoped that this would become an annual event. This too was evidence, argued a union official, that 'now the unions have influence in Xiaoshan and people listen to us'.

Given the fact that the union has a stable financial base, it can afford to maintain a sizeable full-time staff and pay for services such as policy research. This may provide it with some leverage in local policy-making. For example, the union did some research on medical fees, which have risen rapidly in recent years, while the limit on payments to state workers has remained fixed. In practice, workers were now spending between 200 yuan and 300 yuan a year on medical expenses, while they were only covered for a maximum of 120 yuan. Based on their research, the union sent a document to the city government proposing that the maximum be relaxed for ill workers and that the government increase its investment in health via its enterprises. As of our last field visit in May 1991, the city government had not yet taken action on this proposal.

The potential impact on local policy-making of the research conducted by associations is not confined to the Xiaoshan General Trade Union. It is increasingly common for government agencies to commission specialized associations to conduct such policy-relevant research. For example, since Xiaoshan is short of land, the government is eager to ease the problem through land reclamation. The staff of the Science and Technology Association were consulted on this issue, and produced a report which was converted into an official government document; a similar process of consultation and advice took place on the issue of land drainage. It seems that other associations in Xiaoshan were involved in similar work in their own particular spheres.

Having an informational input into policy is one thing, but actually contributing to a change in established policy is another. The potential does exist because of the difference in interests between the locality and higher levels of government and the need to convert national policies into 'local policies' that may differ significantly but work better. There is some limited evidence that local economic associations do play a role in the shaping of local policies, given the contiguity of interests in local development between the local state and business. For example, private enterprises have not been able formally to occupy land for long periods (a limit of three years has been set) or to erect permanent structures, whereas enterprises owned by rural townships and villages can. The Private Enterprises Association took up this issue on behalf of some of its members and liaised with the major parties concerned: township governments, village governments, the county-level Rural Enterprise Management Bureau, and the Land Administration Bureau. The result was a proposal that villagers' committees would occupy land on behalf of private enterprises and the latter could then 'borrow' it and erect permanent structures on it. There was a happy coincidence of interests here: the rural township governments agreed because they obtained revenue from private enterprises, which relieved the tax burden on their own collective enterprises; village leaders agreed because 'their' economic assets increased and they could parley this into getting grants for infrastructure; and the Private Enterprises Association was able to bring together the government agencies concerned (including the Industrial and Commercial Management Bureau), all of whom were represented in its leadership, so as to get a new policy implemented to its liking.

This is an interesting example of the ability of an association to influence policy on behalf of its members, but one swallow does not make a spring. Cases of this kind appear to be rare as yet, although they may be a harbinger of things to come if economic reforms continue to progress. At the present stage, the independence and the influence of the associations are too weak to allow us to call them 'pressure groups' (*yali qunti*) or even 'interest groups' (*liyi qunti*). As organizations they are far too deeply penetrated by the state, and the leadership in consequence has too dominant a position over the membership. And yet there is movement.

Conclusion

What light has this case-study shed upon the initial questions and hypotheses posed at the start of this chapter? First, the Xiaoshan case would support the argument that, with the socio-economic changes wrought by the economic reforms, a social space has begun to open up between the state and economic agents, and a parallel shift has occurred in the balance of power between the state and the new non-state sectors. However, in the context of a semi-reformed economy, the state continues to retain a great deal of its power and has moved to occupy this space and organize the newly emergent, dispersed sources of economic power by encouraging the establishment of social organizations to act as intermediaries. Though there has been some impetus for their formation from below, the dominant impulse has come from above.

In consequence, a new type of social organization has emerged which embodies contradictory elements (one of which is still dominant); social organizations are a dualistic institutional form that mirrors the increasing dualism of China's economy and society. The particular mix of these contradictory elements varies between organizations of different types and functions. Let us concentrate here on the newly formed organizations rather than the 'old' mass organizations and return to our indices of the presence or absence of 'civil society'. First, these social organizations do not reflect a clear distinction between 'public' and 'private' spheres; rather they represent a mixture of public and private in which the public continues to dominate. Yet this very mixture creates a distinct organizational form different from the old-style mass organizations before 1978, which were essentially links in a chain of hierarchical statist controls.

Second, these cannot be described as 'independent' organizations, but they do exercise (to varying degrees) a limited sphere of autonomy which reflects their intermediary status. From the point of view of the state, any attempt to extend controls over social organizations to the point of virtual étatisation would be counter-productive because, in the context of economic dualism, there is a trade-off between control and compliance. The gap between state and enterprise would not be bridged; it would merely be displaced downward by one institutional rung.

Third, these organizations cannot be described as 'pressure groups' or 'interest groups' in any credible sense, since the pressure is still mainly one-way. Yet social organizations are not entirely dependent on, and subordinate to, their bureaucratic 'minders'. As observed, they do have limited scope to influence state organizations and state policy in the interests of their members. However, from the point of view of the social organizations, there is a trade-off between autonomy and influence; their leaders often feel that the best way to increase their influence is to get closer to and become more intermeshed with state and Party organs, compromising their autonomy in the process.

Fourth, in general, membership in these organizations cannot be described as 'voluntary' although, again, there are voluntary elements. Even where members cannot exercise the option of exit, they can exercise their voices, and the leaders of an association, to remain credible to both of their constituencies, cannot afford to ignore this.

To summarize, one can detect only embryonic elements of anything that could be described as 'civil society' in the precise sense discussed earlier in this chapter. Nonetheless, though its presence varies greatly from organization to organization, elements of 'civil society' can be found in both major categories of intermediate organization—the 'old' mass organizations and the new associations. That these elements are embryonic is hardly surprising inasmuch as the phenomenon of intermediate social organizations is so very recent, essentially beginning in the mid-1980s.

This relative weakness of 'civil society' must be situated in the context of a semi-reformed command economy in which the state retains its dominant position in the economy. Its weakness must also be perceived within the context of the dynamics of reform, in which this dominance is gradually being undermined as the number of participants in the non-state sectors increases. One can hypothesize, therefore, that to the extent that the economic reforms continue and economic development proceeds apace, these socio-economic forces will grow in strength and a more powerful 'civil society' will emerge in their train.

In the short and medium term, this could involve a growing role for social organizations as intermediaries between the state and the society/economy, in a socialist form of corporatism comparable to those of other East Asian countries and as envisaged by Xue Muqiao. Yet the dynamics of economic reform and development would lead one to expect that the nature of any such corporatist arrangement would undergo constant change, in the general direction of a more developed form of civil society: they would become more distinctly 'private', more autonomous from the state and more influential over it, and more accountable to their members, who would enjoy greater powers of voice and exit. Ultimately, the very notion of corporatism may disappear as these organizations cease to be intermediaries between the state and China's society/economy and become genuine representatives of society in its dealings with the state. In light of the recent sudden breakdowns elsewhere in state socialism, such a scenario may seem bland and quietistic. But it may be preferable to an alternative scenario of radical rupture followed by an institutional vacuum, of the kind currently visible in Eastern Europe and the former Soviet Union.

Notes

1   The research project upon which this chapter is based was sponsored and supported financially by the United Nations Research Institute for Social Development in Geneva, to which thanks are also due (with particular thanks to Ann Zammit). The project was designed by the author as one part of a wider comparative research program covering socialist and post-socialist societies. It was adapted to the Chinese situation and carried out by a research team that also included Dr Jude Howell of the University of East Anglia and a group of researchers from the Institute of Sociology, Chinese Academy of Social Sciences, Beijing, which was headed by Zhe Xiaoye and included Li Peilin, Sun Bingyao, Tang Jun, Wang Ying and Xia Guang. While the material on which this chapter is based reflects the work of all these participants, the author takes sole responsibility for the views expressed.

2   For discussions of the notion of 'second society' and the relationship between the 'second economy' and civil society in the Hungarian context, see Dent (1986), Szelenyi (1989) and Hann (1990).

3   For example, see collections in Gathy (1989) and Keane (1988). For post-1989 views, see Miller (1992).

⁴   For Africa, see Bayart (1986) and Booth (1987). For Taiwan, see Hsiao (1990) and Chou (1988).

⁵   For a review of the Chinese debate, see Wang (1991).

⁶   Western scholars have used the idea of 'civil society' to analyse the Beijing Spring of 1989. For examples, see Ostergaard (1989), Gold (1990) and Sullivan (1990). Solinger (1991, p. 46) has applied the concept to her analysis of the urban 'floating population'. Bonnin and Chevrier (1991) have also used the concept in their discussion of the relationship between Chinese intelligentsia and the state. The applicability of the concept to the analysis of contemporary China has recently been discussed in greater depth by Kelly and He Baogang (1992).

⁷   Hugh Roberts (1987, p. 4) makes a strong case for viewing 'civil society' in these terms.

⁸   For the *locus classicus*, see Hegel (1991).

⁹   For a critical evaluation of Marx's view of 'civil society', see Gouldner (1980).

¹⁰   This raises certain thorny issues, which centre not only on whether one should equate 'civil society' with 'bourgeois society', but also whether one should equate 'modern society' with 'bourgeois society'. As Roberts (1987, p. 4) argues, while it is true that the rise of 'civil society' has gone together with the development of capitalism, the dominance of capitalism as a mode of production does not guarantee the existence of 'civil society'. Moreover, while there have been forms of 'modern society' which are not capitalist, it is true that, in the real world, most 'modern' societies are in fact based on advanced capitalism, and the alternative form of modernity (until very recently), the communist or state-socialist, did not have a 'civil society' worth the name.

¹¹   Bayart (1986, p. 111) defines 'civil society' in the African context in similar terms, as 'society in its relations with the state insofar as it is in confrontation with the state'.

¹²   For a detailed analysis of one of these organizations, see Walder and Gong (1993).

¹³   For analyses of the East Asian states which stress their corporatist aspects, see Deyo (1987) and Choi (1989).

¹⁴   There is also a gazetteer for the main urban area in the former county, Chengxiang Town, i.e., *Xiaoshan Chengxiangzhenzhi* (Xiaoshan Chengxiang Town Gazetteer), Zhejiang daxue chubanshe, Xiaoshan, 1989.

¹⁵   For an exploration of networks in China, see Ruan (1993); also Ruan et al. (1990).

References

Bayart, Jean-François 1986, 'Civil Society in Africa', in *Political Domination in Africa*, ed. Patrick Chabal, Cambridge University Press, Cambridge, pp. 109–25.

Bonnin, Michel & Yves Chevrier 1991, 'The Intellectual and the State: Social Dynamics of Intellectual Autonomy during the Post-Mao Era', *China Quarterly*, no. 127, pp. 569–93.

Booth, David 1987, 'Alternatives in the Restructuring of State–Society Relations: Research Issues for Tropical Africa', *IDS Bulletin*, vol. 18, no. 4, pp. 23–30.

Choi, Jang Jip 1989, *Labor and the Authoritarian State: Labor Unions in South Korean Manufacturing Industries, 1961–1980*, Korea University Press, Seoul.

Chou Yangsun 1988, 'Social Movements and the Party–State in Taiwan: Emerging Civil Society and the Evolving State Corporatist Structures', PhD thesis, Columbia University, New York.

Dent, Bob 1986, 'Knowledge on the Black Market', *Times Higher Educational Supplement*, 7 March.

Deyo, Frederic ed. 1987, *The Political Economy of the New Asian Industrialism*, Cornell University Press, London.

Gathy, Vera ed. 1989, *State and Civil Society: Relationships in Flux*, Ventura, Budapest.

Gold, Thomas B. 1990, 'The Resurgence of Civil Society in China', *Journal of Democracy*, vol. 1, no. 1, pp. 18–31.

Gouldner, Alvin 1980, *The Two Marxisms*, Macmillan, London.

Hann, C.M. 1990, 'Second Economy and Civil Society', in *Market Economy and Civil Society in Hungary*, ed. C.M. Hann, Frank Cass, London, pp. 21–44.

Hegel, Georg W.F. 1991, *Elements of the Philosophy of Right* (first published 1821), ed. Allen P. Wood, Cambridge University Press, Cambridge.

Hsiao, Hsin-Huang Michael 1990, 'Social Movements and the Rise of a Demanding Civil Society in Taiwan', *The Australian Journal of Chinese Affairs*, no. 27, pp. 163–80.

Keane, John ed. 1988, *Civil Society and the State*, Verso, London.

Kelly, David & He Baogang 1992, 'Emergent Civil Society and the Intellectuals in China', in *The Development of Civil Society in Communist Systems*, ed. Robert F. Miller, Allen & Unwin, Sydney, pp. 24–39.

Miller, Robert F. ed. 1992, *The Development of Civil Society in Communist Systems*, Allen & Unwin, Sydney.

Ostergaard, Clemens 1989, 'Citizens, Groups and a Nascent Civil Society in China: Towards an Understanding of the 1989 Student Demonstrations', *China Information*, vol. 4, no. 2, pp. 28–41.

Roberts, Hugh 1987, 'Editorial' in *IDS Bulletin*, vol. 18, no. 4, p. 4.

Ruan Danqing 1993, *The Australian Journal of Chinese Affairs*, no. 29, pp. 89–106.

Ruan Danqing, Lu Zhou, Peter M. Blau & Andrew G. Walder 1990, 'A Preliminary Analysis of the Social Network of Residents in Tianjin and a Comparison with Social Networks in America', *Social Sciences in China*, vol. 11, no. 3, pp. 68–89.

Shehui Tuanti Guanli Shouce (Social Organizations Management Handbook) 1990, Renmin chubanshe, Beijing.

Solinger, Dorothy 1991, *China's Transients and the State: A Form of Civil Society?*, Hong Kong Institute of Asia-Pacific Studies (USC Series no. 1), Chinese University of Hong Kong, Hong Kong.

Sullivan, Lawrence R. 1990, 'The Emergence of Civil Society in China, Spring 1989', in *The Chinese People's Movement: Perspectives on Spring 1989*, ed. Tony Saich, M.E. Sharpe, London, pp. 126–44.

Szelenyi, Ivan 1989, 'Eastern Europe in an Epoch of Transition: Toward a Socialist Mixed Economy?', in *Remaking the Economic Institution of Socialism in China and Eastern Europe*, eds Victor Nee & David Stark, Stanford University Press, Stanford, pp. 208–32.

Walder, Andrew G. & Xiaoxia Gong 1993, 'Workers in the Democracy Movement: The Politics of the Beijing Workers' Autonomous Union', *The Australian Journal of Chinese Affairs*, no. 29, pp. 1–29.

Wang Shaoguang 1991,'Some Reflections on Civil Society, *Ershiyi Shiji* (Twenty-First Century), Hong Kong, no. 8, pp. 102–17.

Whiting, Susan 1989, *The Non-Governmental Sector in China: A Preliminary Report*, Ford Foundation, Beijing.

Xiaoshan xianzhi (Xiaoshan County Gazetteer) 1987, Zhejiang renmin chubanshe, Hangzhou.

Xue Muqiao 1988, 'Establish and Develop Non-Governmental Self-Management Organisations in Various Trades', *Renmin ribao* (People's Daily), 10 October, translated in Foreign Broadcast Information Service, *China Report* 88/201.

11 New conservatism: intermediate ideology of a 'new elite'[1]

Gu Xin and David Kelly

In June 1992 the ambitions of Chen Yuan, a son of Chen Yun, and several other 'princelings'—offspring of high officials in party, government and military—were apparently set back: they failed to be elected deputies to the 14th National Party Congress (NPC) held on October 12–18 of that year[2]. Often speaking through an intellectual client group, they had been warning against accelerated economic reform in the interests of central balance and control. They appeared, then, to have been wrong-footed by Deng's strategic switch from the post-Tiananmen emphasis on orthodoxy to a renewal of acceleration in early 1992.

In what sense conservative princelings like Chen Yuan are themselves orthodox is, though, open to question. That they should appear to be so is in part for tactical reasons, calculated to retain the patronage of elders of the paternal generation like Chen Yun. On the other hand, much of their non-official ideological stance would never have emanated from Chinese Marxists of the old school. Of course, their admonitions against seeking rapid economic growth at too high a cost in central administrative control are not without a rational basis. The conservative princelings' present reversal of fortune could well be recouped handsomely if, as seems possible, the problems that beset China's economy in the late 1980s return in the future (Reuters 1992a, 1992b, 1992c). They could point to their previous warnings as evidence of foresight, prudence and leadership. For this reason alone the princeling's broad ideological stance should not yet be consigned to the historical wastebasket.

This stance emerged most clearly in an internal document entitled 'Realistic responses and strategic options for China after the Soviet coup', circulated by the Ideological and Theoretical Board of *China Youth Daily* in September 1991 (Lilun Bu 1991; Kelly 1994). Among the responses called for was the adoption of a philosophy somewhat confusingly known in Chinese as 'new conservatism', together with 'Western rationalistic philosophy'. Along with a tough attitude to controlling masses and some very realpolitik specifications in foreign policy, these prescriptions tried to supplement a perceived deficit in the Party's legitimacy, and to ward off the temptations of radical reformism, particularly in the political sphere.

According to a former senior cadre in the propaganda department of the Central Party School (now expatriate liberal democratic activist) Ruan Ming, the 'realistic responses' program stood a real chance of official acceptance (Ruan Ming 1992). Ruan quotes a 'publicist for the Princelings' as follows:

Chen Yun and other CCP elders basically adopted an approving attitude toward 'Realistic responses and strategic options', and requested the Politburo to give advice on revising it as soon as possible. It was then to be given to the original drafting group to discuss it and make theoretical elaboration; it would then become the blueprint for the political report of the 14th National Peoples Congress. They also requested that the Central Administrative Office instruct Chen Yuan to coopt the main writers of 'Realistic responses and strategic options' as members of the 14th National Party Congress political report writing group.

Since Deng Xiaoping was unable to put anything new forward, it was quite likely that he would finally identify himself with the majority of the views of 'Realistic responses and strategic options', and thus Chen Yuan and other Princelings would become successors with real work experience and their independent theoretical thought.

We shall return to an analysis of 'Realistic responses and strategic options' later. For the moment, its status, even if notional, as runner up policy document for the 14th NPC, lends it some importance. It will be viewed here as an intermediate ideology, containing highly equivocal formulae for political legitimacy. Both strength and weakness, we believe, lie in this equivocality. The princelings' blueprint breaks dramatically with Marxism–Leninism–Mao Zedong Thought (MLM), but seeks to preserve by other means those aspects of MLM that supported the Party's claims to legitimacy. While doing so, they beckon to new friends with appeals to both cultural nationalism and a marketized economy. Thus, while new conservatism attacks liberal intellectuals and their program of democratic reform, it makes crucial concessions to liberal values and practices. Whatever the motive, this potentially results in a shift of the locus of debate, creating more opportunities for others to make liberal arguments (Kelly & McCormick 1994, forthcoming). Like the proverbial glass of water that may be called half full or half empty, the result is open to rival perspectives, and can thus provide a *modus vivendi* for a number of interests. In this chapter we shall survey the intellectual background and contents of new conservatism and its acceptance in the 'Realistic responses and strategic options' program, in order to examine these constituencies and their prospects.

From new authoritarianism to new conservatism

Xiao Gongqin, an associate professor of history at Shanghai Normal University, first used the term 'new conservatism' at an informal conference on 'China's traditional culture and socialist modernization' in early December 1990. This conference was held by the ideological and theoretical section of *China Youth Daily*; others present included the then rapidly rising intellectual apologist for the regime, He Xin, and, significantly, several 'princelings', younger cadres with family connections to the leadership (He Xin 1989; Kelly 1991).

While informal, this conference had a degree of support from the Chinese Communist Party (CCP) ideology and propaganda departments. Xu Weicheng and Yuan Mu, two leading officials in ideological affairs, took part in the conference. The other attendees were for the most part members of a group of middle-aged and younger scholars enjoying the government's approval, called the 'new elite' (*xin jingying*). This new elite differed from the older generation of orthodox Marxist–Leninists raised by the CCP in the 1950s. Influenced by Western social science to varying degrees, they were able to express their ideas in new language. The older generation on the other hand, could only recite by rote a few 'original expressions of Marx and Lenin' from textbooks. They tend to reject or find incomprehensible the ideas of Western social science. They habitually conduct criticism in the manner which became common in the Cultural Revolution; argument becomes a matter of determining class attributes (if something belongs to a revolutionary or progressive class, it must be 'correct'). Most Chinese audiences are familiar with this practice to the point of disgust. Orthodox Marxist–Leninist criticism campaigns are no longer well received, as even the CCP's ideology departments have become aware. Hence the high expectations they place on the new elite.[3]

After this meeting the new elite remained visible, finding semi-official outlets in the newspapers *Zhongguo qingnian bao* (China Youth Daily) and *Beijing qingnian bao* (Beijing Youth Weekly). Their ideas were also promoted by Yang Ping, a publicist who is himself an enthusiast for new conservatism.[4] While not always using the 'new conservatism' rubric in a consistent fashion, this new elite evidently find something in common with Xiao Gongqin. Most fundamentally, centralization of state power is regarded as necessary in the face of reform-driven fragmentation.

New conservatism is obviously a reworking of new authoritarianism. Xiao's study of the Hongxian Emperor, Yuan Shikai, inspired his formulation both of authoritarianism and of new conservatism. Understandably, given the suppression of new authoritarianism after 4 June, Xiao makes scarce mention of it. In fact, the term 'authoritarianism' was first proposed by Xiao in an academic conference on problems facing intellectuals. This conference was held by the *World Economic Herald*, *China Youth News*, the theoretical section of *Guangming Daily* and the Xingzhi Institute in Beidaihe from 30 July until 3 August, 1988. In this conference, Xiao described the period of Yuan Shikai's rule as one of new authoritarianism, and the period after the 1911 revolution and before Yuan's rule as one of political romanticism. In Xiao's view, the essential point of new authoritarianism was that no break with the 'traditional' political system should be made; instead, the organized forces of tradition ought to be respected and their potential function in the integration of a modernizing society utilized (Gu Xin 1989; Xue 1990). The change (or perhaps development) from new authoritarianism to new conservatism, shows that not only the existing political order (or expression of the 'political system' in Xiao's vocabulary) but also traditional values have been accommodated within his theoretical framework.

While new conservatism has an uncertain identity and many an intellectual inconsistency, it is by no means a figment of the imagination. Nor is Xiao Gongqin entirely alone. Many intellectuals hold views similar to Xiao's, but for various reasons (in most cases moral indignation arising from the 4 June massacre) prefer to bury themselves in their studies rather than publish in outlets of a markedly official character. Several of these refused to take part in the conference mentioned above (for example, a friend of gaoled democratic activists Wang Juntao and Chen Ziming was invited but refused to participate in this conference).

The emergence of this undercurrent is inseparably linked to the intellectual context during the late 1980s. In the 'culture fever' (*wenhua re*) of the period 1985 to 1988, major polemics took place on the relationship between tradition and modernization in China. In late 1988, new authoritarianism emerged with the apparent backing of official circles, leading to another intense controversy. While those taking part were few in number, they were among the more influential (Gu Xin 1989; Waterman 1990; Ting Gong & Feng Chen 1991; Ma Shu-yun 1990; Kelly & He 1990; Rosen & Zou 1991, 1992; Sullivan 1992). It is worth noting that Xiao Gongqin himself was one of the main initial exponents of new authoritarianism (Xiao 1989).

The new conservative outlook

To date, there have been no systematic expositions of new conservatism in open circulation. Indications of its general thrust must be gathered from a few speeches and essays, the most important of which is Xiao Gongqin's essay published in *China Youth Daily* titled 'Yan Fu's reflection on China's modernization and its inspiration', which is the enlarged version of his speech at the informal discussion reported above (Xiao 1990). In this publication, Xiao does not use the term 'new conservatism', preferring instead 'new gradualism' (*xin jianjinzhuyi*). While it is couched as an essay in modern intellectual history, it is in fact a customary mode of expression for Xiao, as for many contemporary Chinese intellectuals, to deliver opinions through the mouths of historical personages. It is not misleading for us to read 'the views of Yan Fu', mentioned in Xiao's address as well as his essay, provisionally as the views of Xiao's himself.

Xiao is concerned with three perennial sources of controversy among Chinese intellectuals (not only during the past decade, but throughout the modern history of China): which strategy, radicalism or gradualism, is appropriate to China's modernization? What role, if any, is to be played by traditional Chinese values in this process? And does the modernizing social force privilege the state, or forces outside it?

In general, new conservatism is made up of a series of oversimplified—and as we shall see, generally radical—responses, consisting of statements supporting controlled or selected introduction of Western institutional civilization, supporting traditional values and the status quo as the lever and medium of modernization, and which depend upon the new-style authority already found, or possibly appearing, within a given system to implement modernizing strategies.

Xiao sums this position up thus:

> Make use of a transitional authority with a modernizing orientation; make use of mediating traditional values to bring about the internal social change; when the success of this internal social change is assured, gradually introduce Western democratic institutions, and thus bring about a steady impetus towards modernization in Chinese society (Xue Yong 1990).

Opposite new conservatism Xiao Gongqin poses 'radicalism', also termed 'political romanticism', the main features of which are: (a) treatment of China's traditional values and the existing order as an obstacle to modernization; hence the claim that their elimination is the starting point for modernization; and (b) advocating rapid, widespread and total introduction of Western institutional culture (Gu Xin 1989). For conservatives such as Xiao, then, radicalism comprises at least two theses, 'Overall Westernization' and 'Totalistic Anti-traditionalism'. As to whether it is basically elitist or populist, Xiao does not make clear.

Put differently, in the new conservative mind the difference between new conservatism and radicalism is that the former places faith in nurturing and shaping a modernizing elite corps within the status quo (i.e. within the CCP). Radicalism, on the other hand, regards certain elite corps (intellectuals, intelligentsia) or popular mass external to the system as the motive force for modernization. Needless to say, Xiao adopts a completely negative attitude toward radicalism.

In early 1989, Xiao Gongqin had already criticized the radical reform strategy as 'institutional determinism'. He argued in an influential journal that rapid marketization, even if totally supported by the administrative authorities, could not play the role of integrating the economic order as efficiently as it does in the West; it would risk inducing social *anomie* because in Chinese society there is not an independent middle class. For Xiao the latter is a prerequisite for introducing an economic system chiefly dependent on market forces (Xiao Gongqin 1989, 1992a, 1992b).

'Realistic responses and strategic options:' the new legitimacy[5]

After the failed coup against Gorbachev in August 1991, an internal document appeared, reportedly commissioned by Chen Yuan and Deng Yingtao. The document, 'Realistic responses and strategic options for China after the Soviet coup' covers a lot of ground in its dozen or so brief pages, including systemic differences between China and the then Soviet Union, causes of the debacle of Soviet communism, and the conclusions to be drawn for China (Lilun Bu 1991). More than an analysis of international relations, 'Responses' is an account of the basis for the CPC's legitimacy and means for revitalising it. As the astute analyst Chen Kuide points out, 'the Princelings are relatively unencumbered by the past compared with their elders. The space of possibilities open to them to make choices in is therefore larger' (Chen Kuide 1992a). As he notes further, however,

> when boiled down their economic program differs little fundamentally from Chen Yun's 'birdcage economy', their foreign policy is extremely similar to Deng's, and domestically they copy the comparatively tolerant policy towards intellectuals of Deng in the early 1980s when he had just returned from the wilderness. Rather than 'supporting neither Chen nor Deng', it would thus be truer to say they 'half support Chen and half support Deng'.

Chen Kuide usefully summarizes 'Responses' as follows:

1 Statism to replace communism;
2 Right-wing dictatorship to replace left-wing totalitarianism;
3 Geopolitics to replace ideological principles;
4 A ruling party defending its power monopoly with realpolitik to replace the romantic egalitarian revolutionary party;
5 Party ownership to replace public ownership by the state.
6 Strengthened power of the Centre to replace regionalist tendencies.

The paper tells us that after forty years it is time for the party to rationalize its approach to government (Lilun Bu 1991, p. 37):

The socialist political party differs essentially from the bourgeoisie, but when in the ruling phase it faces many tasks in common with the latter; for example social stability, gradual reform, etc. If certain techniques of governing are not grasped, if it does not become both in theory and in practice a ruling party, it will be hard to ward off the destructiveness of radicalism and 'populism' among the masses.

The legitimacy of socialism, the document asserts, had two broad sources. The first was the success of the Bolshevik Revolution in 1917; the second was Mao's peasant-based, sinicized Marxism–Leninism. The first of these sources was now, in the hour of Yeltsin's triumph, a liability; if dogmatically clung to it would hand a weapon to the rightists and cause loss of broad mass support. This meant that the second source of legitimacy had to be strengthened through a process of 'creative reinterpretation'. The key to this is the notion of Chinese exceptionalism, of China's unique 'national condition' (guoqing). Emphasizing China's size, poverty, over-population, relative lack of resources, its history of division and foreign humiliation in the last century is 'the most effective means of persuading the people at present' (Lilun Bu 1991, p. 37).

The prime lesson to be drawn from study of the national condition is the need for gradualism: for staying with socialism as opposed to its radical abandonment. China, we learn, is under pressure from an endemic radicalism (no doubt the democracy movement of 1989 was a case in point). Two additional prescriptions are offered to stem the radical thought-tide: new conservatism and Western rationalist philosophy. Western rationalism is described in the document as a main philosophical current, distinct from both romanticism and irrationalism. 'It advocates proof, instrumental reason, order and gradualism, it is opposed to romanticism and violence, irrationalism, disorder, anti-social and anti-cultural behaviour' (Lilun Bu 1991, p. 37). The reference to new conservatism is, as we have argued at the outset, the clearest signal of quasi-official support for the ideas of Xiao Gongqin. This does not imply, of course, that he personally supports the extraordinary Machiavellianism of the writers of 'Responses'. To become a genuine ruling party requires, in addition to appeals to tradition and instrumental rationality, the mastery of 'certain political expedients', what is elsewhere in the document referred to as 'draconian rule' (yanzheng) which will replace the policy of 'aggrandizing the masses'. Regardless of Xiao's own views, the existence of a quasi-fascist stream of thought among the princelings who echo him cannot be dismissed.

'Party control of the asset economy'

We are in agreement with Chen Kuide that the document abounds with contradictions. Some of the above points are incompatible with the others.

In the case of point 5, it is worth citing the 'Responses' document more fully (Lilun Bu 1991, p. 38)[6]:

The CPC must control not only the gun, but the asset economy as well

Some scholars hold that a major reason our Party was able to grow large and strong was its grasp of the gun barrel, 'the Party controls the gun'. But this is only one aspect. Another still more important one is that the Party has to control the asset economy (*caichan jingji*). This is especially important under the present circumstances.

The Party's thinking about controlling the asset economy has the following grounds: (1) a major problem in reforming and opening up is that no one is responsible for state assets. Short term behaviour is rampant, and various interests erode it. Who is to guarantee that asset owners play the most appropriate role? The answer is whoever is most closely united with the process of economic circulation, and can guarantee that state assets multiply in circulation should be in charge.

Who carried out the 156 projects of the First Five Year Plan? Who grasped and managed rural enterprises? Who took responsibility for China's agricultural assets? Who took responsibility for regional projects? All of these were in essence run by and the responsibility of the CPC. (2) Government actions in reforming often induce conflict between the functions of manager–supervisors with those of asset owners. In the exercise of management and supervision, when the functional departments are suppressed by the regional government for reasons of regional or sectoral interest, the evils of protectionism and backwardness, duplication in construction, and over-investment are produced. If the Party is in charge of the asset economy, becoming an owner, it can adjust the arrangement and orientation of productive forces rationally on the basis of the circumstances of the subordinate enterprises, and can form an owner/manager relationship with government. When the government carries out planning and supervisory functions, enterprises attached to the Party will operate within the bounds of the law. But when regional governments engage in short-term behaviour, transactions through mandatory planning (*yiping erdiao*), they will be subordinated to the Party's interests. (3) Party control of the asset economy is advantageous in stabilizing and advancing reform of the political system. If the Party owned the assets, political stability would have a carrier. Social progress can be guided by a powerful corporate interest and not evidence loss of control. At present Party and government form a single entity such that an attack on the government implies an attack on the Party, leaving the latter no room for manoeuvre. If the Party were to become a huge corporate interest, it could exert all kinds of influence on the National Peoples Congresses, and gain a larger political space in which to operate. (4) A reform philosophy of the Party controlling the asset economy is easy to operate and carry out. In the ten years of reform, a major failing was that we did not pay attention to nurturing our own personalized representatives of the property associated with advanced forces of production, but expected to follow the old path of capital accumulation, with the result that the drainage out of wealth far exceeded its accumulation. The new corporate interests thus nurtured had nothing in common with the Party. But under Party control of the asset economy, these evils will not be able to repeat themselves. Still more important, Party control of the asset economy is simply and inexpensively done. Authority over personnel matters of enterprise cadres rests with the Party committee. If certain responsibilities concerning management of state-owned property are returned to the Party committee, and corresponding Party economic committees are set up, the institutional structure will be rational, the demarcation of interests will be clarified. A market will gradually emerge from this.

(For instance, if the economic committee of some city is placed under the jurisdiction of the municipal committee, this will mean it will have operating authority, without any change to the government jurisdiction in terms of supervision and control. It will simply mean that enterprise management must be carried out subject to the indirect control of the CPC committee. Superficially the difference is slight, but the difference in long range terms would be very great.

The principle of Party control of the asset economy should be 'strict separation of government and enterprise, but only moderate separation of Party and government'.)

Chen Kuide notes that this policy, if put into effect

would in a twinkling transfer the assets nominally belonging to 1.1 billion people to a communist party making up just 4 percent of this number, and make the CPC the owner of these vast assets. Such an uncompensated transfer (or seizure) of property rights would not only have no legitimacy (who would confer the rights? would the present owners consent?), but at the same time it would still be no solution to the cancer afflicting the Chinese economy: the problem of the lack of clear ownership (who are 'the whole people'? and who is 'the Party'?). Even in nominal terms it contradicts their basic orientation (of statism replacing communism).

Against Chen Kuide's interpretation, and once again noting the equivocal nature of the formula, we would point to the acceptance explicitly of enterprise autonomy, implicitly of an economic arena dominated by the market, and by further implication of 'nomenclatura capitalism'. Party control of assets would make the CPC a legitimate player in a widened environment, and would remove the stigma of corruption from many present practices.

'New Elite' intellectual background

The constituency to whom new conservatism appeals include a number of intellectual strata. Potential support may also include elements of the rural population, and others with traditional stakes in the politics of culture and national identity (Wang Zhaojun 1992b). Beyond the political machinations of the princelings there is a broad undercurrent among Chinese intellectuals, the broader intelligentsia, and other 'thinking elites', to use the nomenclature of Yoshino (1992, p. 6), in business and politics. Some of these form what is widely perceived to be a 'new elite' with a stake in China's immediate and long term future. Chen Kuide describes these strata as follows (Chen Kuide 1992b, p. 3):

> What characteristics will be manifested by this (post Tiananmen) China, red on the surface but white at heart? One unavoidable social result is the rise of a middle class. Going by the trends of economic development on the Chinese mainland, this nascent interest group is emerging much faster than in any other nation in history. Its basic elements come from the bosses and senior and middle management of non CPC organs such as private enterprises and companies, rural enterprises, joint ventures, direct foreign ventures and banks. In the process of expanding the economy, they must develop conflicts of interest with the incompatible political power system and non-marketized legal framework, so that they will inevitably produce their own political spokesmen. Further, there is evidence that following June 4, these organizations unobtrusively absorbed a number of 'liberalizing elements' (*ziyouhua fenzi*), people of talent whom the regime was unable to tolerate.

Wang Zhaojun, a former editor with a Beijing publishing house, now based in Canada, regards the 'pledge' of eventual democracy as sincere in the case of some the intelligentsia attracted to new conservatism. (Wang Zhaojun 1992a, 1992b). Wang finds that attitudes towards the rural hinterland are a major determinant of the three major political outlooks which dominate active thought among today's intellectuals. These three are liberalism, radicalism, and new conservatism.

Radicalism in Wang's usage refers to advocates of direct democrat-ization, for whom the countryside is the gravest concern. The small peasant mode of production is for them the hotbed of new authorit-arianism. Peasants prefer enlightened bureaucratic management to the direct application of their democratic rights.

The new conservatives overestimate the efficacy of the apparatus of dictatorship in controlling society, while underestimating the learning capacity of political movements under a democratic system. Meanwhile their pleas for caution in economy policy represent no real advance over the liberal position. The majority of China's rural masses, according to Wang, will succumb to the lure of new conservative approaches, while their younger generation members will be attracted to radicalism.

'Eventually, the road they actually take will be liberalism' (Wang Zhaojun 1992a, p 41).

Conclusion

In modern Chinese history, the regimes of Yuan Shikai and Chiang Kai-shek have some salient points of similarity. They both attained national supremacy on the back of revolutionary movements which they subsequently turned against in bloody repression. They shared grandiose reformist ambitions. Both tried to blend ideas and symbols of the Confucian/legalist traditional polity with contemporary political and developmental notions. Both aspired to exert a finer degree of control over the population than their predecessors had achieved (Duara 1988). Both felt either contempt or fear of autonomous popular movements, for what is now termed civil society, i.e. for any sphere of organization not within the government's purview. National strength was, in both cases, the goal, but in neither case was it the result. Their reformist accomplishments were, to say the least, disappointing (Young 1977, p 249).

It is not difficult to see that contemporary new conservatives share many common points with their ancestors in modern China. Indeed, Xiao Gongqin himself acknowledges the lack of success of conservative modernizing movements. Among the major reasons, he borrows from the American scholar Lin Yusheng the formulation that the conservatives' 'contributions to the creative transformation of traditional values were very few' (Lin Yusheng 1990).

The contemporary new conservatives operate, to be sure, in a different milieu. Their attitude to Chinese traditional culture supports a version of nationalism which is evidently acceptable to the Communist Party. Of course, this attitude differs somewhat from nationalism as an official ideology. It is safe to assert that the emergence of new conservatism is a direct consequence of a reaction to the democratic movement during the spring of 1989 in China. Indirectly, however, it rises in intellectual reaction to certain major trends of thought prevalent during the period before 4 June, the main and most influential branch of which can be called 'New Enlightenment' liberalism. The main features of 'liberalism' prevalent in past decade of China can be described as stress on freedom, acceptance of democracy, reason and science as the keys to modernity, and enthusiasm for Western institutions both in the arena of economy and in that of politics. However, the new conservatism critique of Chinese liberalism as taking a nihilistic attitude with regard to the problem of cultural inheritance cannot be sustained. Since Lu Xun it has been understood that received culture was distorted, even perverted, but that foreign institutions would inevitably have to seek universal meaning in terms of a 'creatively reinterpreted' framework of traditional values. The question has been, which values, those of authoritarianism or those of democracy? A full development of this point lies beyond this present chapter.

In opposition to 'liberalism', the new conservative ideologues view their task not simply as the perpetuation of the established order, nor even as the restoration for their own sake of traditional values. Rather, they seek to create a new and modern order aiming at achievement of modernization in China. In this sense, the proponents of new conservatism might simply be labelled 'conservative' in its limited sense. The Maoist criticism of bourgeoisie liberalization was an earlier conservative response to modernity in many ways comparable to religious fundamentalism. New conservatism represents a second, arguably higher phase of this pattern of response. It appeals to those elements of the past that are really alive and still have a real social basis, but have to transform and adapt themselves to the new stage of social and mental development. It is not beyond the bounds of the imagination that the new conservatism may develop as a conscious political ideology opposed to liberalism in China, and play a dynamic role within the future struggle of factions within the CCP. But what a dramatic step away from orthodox Marxist anti-liberalism it is. New conservatism preserves new authoritarianism's deep structural concession to liberal values. Democracy is alluded to as the admittedly ideal form of political rationality, sadly impracticable in China as a result of the 'national condition'. Private property and the middle class are not promoted as openly as in new authoritarianism, but there is a clear sense in which failure to condemn their political value amounts to their approval by default.

All this makes it very difficult to accept the view cited by Ruan Ming in our introduction, that the Party elders around Chen Yun looked with approval upon 'Realistic responses and strategic options' as a potential blueprint for the political report of the 14th National Party Congress. It would surely have required extensive dilution and emasculation to serve as a Party document of any kind. Even the notion of redefining the Party's basis of legitimacy would have been highly explosive in factional political terms, no matter how realistic an assessment it actually is.

We propose an alternative interpretation here, namely that new conservatism is a broad principle of class collaboration in a post-Deng world. The doctrine is likely to re-emerge, no doubt updated and altered, in China after the departures of Deng, Chen Yun and the other original Communist veterans from the scene. Rather than definitively excluding liberalism, as its surface claims would have us believe, it may in fact offer a *modus vivendi* between an array of new elite groups. One would clearly be the widening circle of 'nomenklatura capitalists' identified elsewhere in this book, linking provincial interests, private capital and politically legitimized actors. Another would be the ruling circle in Beijing, a grouping of princelings ruling in the name of an essentially developmentalist ideological charter. Other more liberal groupings of intellectuals would have a claim to be heard in view of their technocratic functions in a modernizing state. The *modus vivendi* between these groups would be explicitly non-Marxist and developmentalist. New conservatism would be invoked to restrict the principle of democratic accountability and voice to the elite strata, and prevent its extension to wider popular constituencies. If history is any guide, however, this process of extension will be driven by forces beyond the ability of any such ideological formula to stop.

This is all clearly speculative. A fundamental obstacle to its success is the weakness of the central pillar of new conservatism, namely the Communist Party itself. The Beijing massacre showed how deep-seated was opposition to the party, even among its own staff. Legitimacy is parlously predicated on personal loyalties among Party and military, loyalties which have not so far yielded a stable institutional order.

Notes

1 This paper draws broadly on research forming part of the project on 'China's Modernization: Comparative Patterns of Cultural and Economic Change', headed by Professor Helmut Martin of the University of the Ruhr, Bochum.

2 They included Deng Yingtao (son of notorious conservative leftist ideologue Deng Liqun), Liu Yuan and Bo Xicheng, sons respectively of late president Liu Shaoqi and CAC vice-chairman Bo Yibo. Chen Yun is a nonagenarian conservative and Chairman of the Central Advisory Commission (CAC): see discussion below. Willy Wo-Lap Lam cites a variety of explanations for their failures (Lam 1992).

3 The term 'elite' is frequently used in CCP propaganda to attack intellectuals who participated in or would not oppose the democratic movement of the Beijing Spring. 'New elite' ironically extends this label to pro-government middle-aged and younger intellectuals.

4 Yang Ping, originally the director of the theoretical section of a local newspaper *Beijing Youth Weekly* has become a leading manager of the ideological and theoretical section of *China Youth Daily*. At a conference in early April 1989, he told one of the authors, Gu Xin, that he prefers conservatism.

5 The following section draws freely on David Kelly 1992. See also *Ouzhou ribao* 1991; *Jing bao* 1991.

6 Reprinted by permission of M.E. Sharpe, Inc., Armonk, New York, 10504.

References

Chen Kuide 1992a, 'Wangchao moride xinzheng' (New Deal of a Doomed Dynasty), *Zhongguo zhi chun* (China Spring), no 1, pp. 24–5, January 1992; translated in David Kelly 1994.

——1992b, 'Wuse shenhua' (The myth of colourlessness), *Minzhu Zhongguo*, no. 12, pp. 2–3, October.

Duara, Prasenjit 1988, *Culture, Power and the State: Rural North China*, 1900–1942, Stanford University Press, Stanford.

Furth, Charlotte ed. 1976, *The Limits of Change: Essays on Conservative Alternatives in Republican China*, Harvard University Press, Cambridge, Mass.

Gu Xin 1989, 'Xin quanweizhuyi de lilun kunjing' (The theoretical dilemma of new authoritarianism), *Mingbao yuekan*, 6 June, pp. 46–50

He Xin 1989, 'A word of advice to the Politburo', translated, annotated and introduced by Geremie Barmé, *Australian Journal of Chinese Affairs*, no. 23, January 1990, pp. 49–76.

Jing bao 1991, 'Beijing chuxian "disan shili" zhiguo lilun' ('Political theory of "the third force" appears in Beijing'), *Jing bao* (HK), no. 12, December, pp. 48–9.

Kelly, David 1991, 'Chinese Marxism since Tiananmen: between evaporation and dismemberment', in David Goodman and Gerald Segal, eds, *China in the Nineties: Crisis Management and Beyond*, Clarendon Press, Oxford, pp. 19–34.

——1992, 'Philosophers revisited', *China News Analysis*, no. 1453 pp. 1–9.

——1994, 'Realistic Responses and Strategic Options: An Alternative Communist Ideology and its Critics', *Chinese Law and Government* vol. 27, no. 1, Spring.

—— & He Baogang 1990, 'Emergent civil society and the intellectuals in China', in *Civil Society in Communist Systems*, ed. Robert F. Miller, Allen & Unwin, Sydney, pp. 24–39.

—— & Barrett McCormick 1994, 'The Limits of Antiliberalism', *Journal of Asian Studies*, forthcoming August.

Lam, Willy Wo-Lap 1992, 'China's "Gang of Princelings" Miss out on Top Posts', *South China Morning Post* (HK), 3 July.

Lilun Bu 1991, *Zhongguo Qingnian Bao* Sixiang Lilun Bu, 'Sulian jubian zhi hou Zhongguode xianshi yingdui yu zhanlue xuan ze' (Realistic responses and strategic options for China after the Soviet coup), text as reprinted in *Zhongguo zhi chun*, January 1992, pp. 35–9. Full translation in David Kelly 1994.

Lin Yusheng 1990, *Zhongguo chuantong wenhua de chuangzaoxing zhuanhua* (The creative transformation of traditional Chinese culture), Sanlian Shuju, Beijing.

Liu Jun & Li Lin, eds 1989, *Xin quanweizhuyi* (New Authoritarianism), Jingjixueyuan chubanshe, Beijing.

Ma Shu-yun 1990, 'The rise and fall of new authoritarianism in China', *China Information*, vol. 5, no. 3, Winter, pp. 1–18.

Ouzhou ribao 1991, 'Zhonggong taizidang guiyin weixian de sandian xuanze' (Three risky choices adduced by the CPC Princelings), *Oushou ribao* (Paris), 26 November, p. 20.

Reuters 1992a, 'China Finance Minister Warns on Deficit Danger', 24 July.

——1992b, 'China Party Paper Warns Economic Problems Ahead', 15 November.

——1992c, 'China Study Sees Inflation Rising in 1993', 17 November.

Rosen, Stanley & Gary Zou 1991, 'The Chinese debate on new authoritarianism', *Chinese Sociology and Anthropology*, vol. 23, nos 2,3,4 and 5

(Winter 1990–91, Spring 1991, Summer 1991 and Winter 1991–92) (parts I, II, III and IV).

——1992, 'The road to modernization and democratization in China debated: the neoauthoritarian and direct democracy schools', unpublished paper, Department of Political Science, University of Southern California.

Ruan Ming 1992, '"Taizidang" de Disandiguo meimeng' (The 'Third Reich' Fantasies of the Princelings), *Zhongguo zhi chun*, no. 10, October, pp. 39–41; translated in David Kelly 1994.

Sullivan, Michael J. 1992, 'The authoritarian route to the reform of Leninist states: the 1988–1989 Chinese neo-authoritarianism debate in comparative perspective', unpublished paper, Department of Political Science, University of Wisconsin, Madison.

Ting Gong & Feng Chen 1991, 'New authoritarianism theory in mainland China', *Issues and Studies*, pp. 84–98, January, Taibei.

Wang Zhaojun 1992a, 'Xiangcun beijing yu Zhongguo dangdai sichao' (The rural background and contemporary Chinese intellectual trends), *Zhongguo luntan* (Taibei), vol. 32, no. 8, May, pp. 34–43.

——1992b, 'Xinbaoshouzhuyi yu dalu zhishifenzi' (New conservatism and the intellectuals in mainland China), *Zhongguo luntan* (Taibei), vol. 32, no. 10, July, pp. 106–14.

Waterman, Harold 1990, 'Which way to go? Four strategies for democratization in Chinese intellectual circles', *China Information*, vol. 5, no. 1, Summer, pp. 14–33.

Xiao Gongqin 1989, 'On the romantic approach to reform in contemporary China: a critique of institutional determinism', in *Zhishifenzi* (The Chinese Intellectual), *Liaoning renmin chubanshe*, Shenyang, January.

——1991, 'Yan Fu dui Zhongguo xiandaihua de sikao jiqi qishi' (Yan Fu's reflections on China's modernization and its lessons), *Zhongguo gingnian bao* (China Youth Daily), 6 February, p. 3.

——1992a, 'Lishi jujue langman: Xiao Gongqin Fujiaoshou tan jijinzhuyi siwei fangshi' (History rejects romance: Associate Professor Xiao Gongqin on the radical mode of thinking), *Beijing qingnian bao*, 19 January, p. 6.

——1992b, 'Dalu xinbaoshouzhuyide jueqi—zhuanfang dalu 'dier sichao' lilunjia Xiao Gongqin' (Emergence of new conservatism on the mainland—interview with theorist of the mainland's 'second intellectual wave' Xiao Gongqin), *Shibao zhoukan* (China Times Weekly) 26 January, pp. 66–9 and 2 February, pp. 98–100.

Xue Yong 1990, Transcript of conference speeches (manuscript).

Yoshino, Kosaku 1992, *Cultural Nationalism in Contemporary Japan*, Routledge, London.

Young, Ernest P. 1977, *The Presidency of Yuan Shih-k'ai: Liberalism and Dictatorship in Early Republican China*, University of Michigan Press, Ann Arbor.

Appendices

Appendix 1

The *gaogan zidi:* shift from natural sciences to government and semi-government economic and trade organizations.

Before the Cultural Revolution, Deng Xiaoping's son, Deng Pufang, was studying physics in Peking University; during the 1980s he was the general manager of the Kang Hua Company (Chen Yige 1988). Another son of Deng Xiaoping, Deng Zhifang, returned from eight years in the USA with a PhD in laser physics; he is now the Deputy Managing Director of a subsidiary of CITIC (*Zhongyang ribao*, 9 May 1992). Chen Yun's son, Chen Yuan, studied science at Qinghua University and worked for some time in the Ministry of Aeronautics and Astronautics; he is now the Deputy Director of the People's Bank of China. Other important positions in economic organizations are also occupied by princes. Wang Qishan, Yao Yilin's son-in-law, is the Deputy Director of the China Construction Bank (Chen Yige 1991). Zhou Xiaochuan, the son of the previous Minister of Mechanical Industry, Zhou Jiannan, was formerly in the Economic Systems Research Institute, a Zhao Ziyang think-tank; he is a Deputy Director of the Bank of China. The Baoli Investment Company, under the Headquarters of the General Staff of the PLA, one of three companies which specialize in the export of military equipment, is controlled by Deng Xiaoping's son-in-law, He Ping (President), Wang Zhen's son, Wang Jun, (Managing Director), and He Long's son, He Pengfei (General Manager). He Pengfei studied natural sciences in Qinghua University before the Cultural Revolution; now he has an essentially administrative position in a commercial company. The other specialists in this field, the Changcheng Company, under the Ministry of Aeronautics and Astronautics, and the Xinxing Company, under the General Logistics Department of the PLA, are also managed by cadres' children (Zhou Jixiang 1991). Deng Xiaoping's daughter, Deng Nan, is now the Deputy Director of the State Science and Technology Commission. Nie Rongzhen's daughter, Nie Li, is the Deputy Director of the Science and Technology Commission (and a Major-General in the PLA); she is married to Ding Henggao, the Minister in charge of the Committee of Science, Technology and Industry for National Defense (and a Lieutenant-General). Zhang Xiaobin, the son of the former Minister of Public Health, Cui Yueli, is the Secretary General of the Stock Exchange Council of China and the Chairman and President of China Venturetech, a government-run investment company similar to CITIC. The Deputy Managing Director and Deputy General Manager of Venturetech is Chen Weili, Chen Yun's daughter. Both Zhang Xiaobin and Chen Weili had studied in the USA for some time before returning to China to take up their present positions (Luo Kedao 1988). It is also reported that a considerable number of third generation establishment figures have been appointed as heads of various departments and bureaus in government ministries (Zhong Shutan 1988).

Appendix 2
List of children of high level cadres in influential official positions.

1 Yang Baibing (younger brother of Yang Shangkun, Director, Political Department, PLA)
2 Chi Haotian (Yang Shangkun's son-in-law, Chief of General Staff, PLA)
3 Jiang Zemin (Li Xiannian's son-in-law [?])
4 Zhao Dajun (Zhao Ziyang's son, Managing Director, Huahai Company, Hainan)
5 Ye Xuanping (Ye Jianying's son)
6 Wu Xiaolan (Ye Jianying's daughter-in-law and Wu Yuzhang's daughter, Vice-Mayor, Shenzhen)
7 Liao Jun (Liao Chengzhi's son, Director, Overseas Chinese Office, State Council)
8 Liu Yuan (Liu Shaoqi's son, Vice-Governor, Henan)
9 Ding Henggao (son-in-law of Nie Rongzhen, Director, Science and Technology Office, Ministry of Defense)
10 Nie Li (Nie Rongzhen's daughter, Deputy Director, Technical Engineering Section, Ministry of Defense)
11 Deng Pufang (Deng Xiaoping's son)
12 Li Ruihuan (Wan Li's son-in-law [?])
13 Wang Jun (Wang Zhen's son, Deputy Political Commissar, Chengdu Military Region)
14 Bu He (Ulanfu's son, Chairman, Party Committee, Inner Mongolia)
15 Wu Jie (Ulanfu's son, Mayor of Baotou)
16 Bo Xicheng (Bo Yibo's son, Director, Beijing Tourism Bureau)
17 Bo Xilai (Bo Yibo's son, Mayor of Dalian)
18 Zou Jiahua (son-in-law of Ye Jiangying)
19 Ye Chumei (daughter of Ye Jianying, Deputy Director, Technology and Engineering Committee, Ministry of Defense)
20 Chen Hansu (Chen Yi's son, previously Vice-Mayor of Beijing)
21 Chen Yuan (Chen Yun's son)
22 Yu Zhengsheng (Zhang Aiping's son-in-law, Mayor of Yantai)
23 Xi Zhengping (Xi Zhongxun's son, Secretary, Ningde District, Fujian)

24 Xi Zhengning (Xi Zhongxun's son, Deputy Director, Organization Department, Shaanxi Provincial Committee)
25 Li Tieying (Li Weihan's son, member of Politburo)
26 Li Peng (adopted son of Zhou Enlai)
27 Deng Nan (Deng Xiaoping's daughter, Section Head in State Science and Technology Commission)
28 Zhao Liang (Zhao Ziyang's son, Deputy Manager, Changcheng Hotel, Beijing)
29 Zhao Baojiang (Deng Xiaoping's son-in-law, Mayor of Wuhan)
30 Wu Jianchang (Deng Xiaoping's son-in-law, Deputy Director, China Non-ferrous Metals Company)
31 Li Yang (Li Peng's son, Deputy General Manager, Kaifa Company, Hainan)
32 Zhu Lin (Li Peng's wife, Deputy Manager, 'a large firm in the south of China')
33 Liu Zhen (Liu Shaoqi's son, Vice Mayor, Qingdao)
34 Wan Runnan (son of Wan Li [?])
35 Wang Zhi (Wang Zhen's son, General Manager, Changcheng Computor Company)
36 Bo Quan (Bo Yibo's son, Manager, White Peacock World Company)
37 Zhang Haoruo (Zhang Aiping's son, Section Head in the State Council)
38 Zou Jingmeng (Zou Jiahua's brother, Director, China Meteorological Bureau)
39 Jia Chunwang (Jia Tingsan's son, Minister of State Security)
40 Chen Guangyi (Xi Zhongxun's son-in-law, Party Secretary, Fujian Province)
41 Peng Peiyun (Peng Zhen's daughter, Director, Family Planning Commission)
42 Song Ruixiang (Song Renqiong's son, Governor, Qinghai Province)
43 Li Chang'an (Li Fuchun's son, Deputy Secretary General, State Council)
44 He Quan (He Changgong's son, Vice-Minister in the PLA General Staff)
45 He Pengfei (He Long's son, Minister of Logistic Support, PLA)
46 Hu Qiheng (Hu Qili's sister, Deputy President, Chinese Academy of Sciences)
47 Tian Jizhen (Tian Jiyun's brother, Mayor, Xinbang City, Henan)
48 Xiao Congci (Xiao Jingguang's son, Secretary, Datong Municipal Committee, Shanxi).

This list dates from 1989, and some of the positions may no longer be correct. As far as I know, Wan Runnan was not the son of Wan Li, but he was the ex son-in-law of Liu Shaoqi.

Source: *Zhongguo zhi chun* 1989, 'Zhonggong gaogan zinü guanzhi da baoguang' (Exposure of sons and daughters of high level cadres in the CCP occupying official positions), *Zhongguo zhi chun*, no. 6, pp. 37–8.

Index